CONTENTS

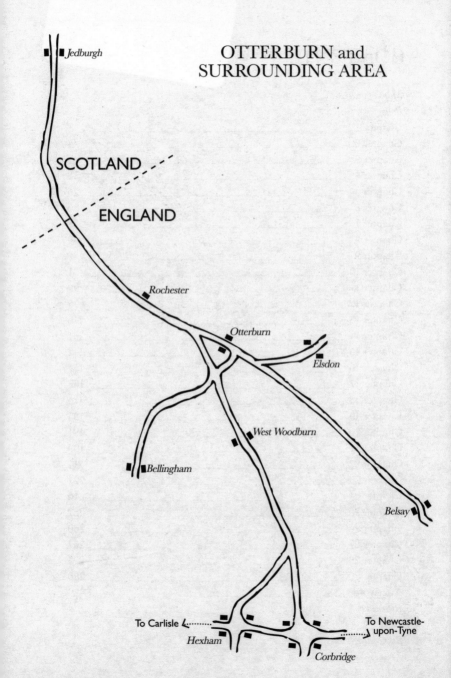

OTTERBURN and
SURROUNDING AREA

Jedburgh

SCOTLAND

ENGLAND

Rochester

Otterburn

Elsdon

West Woodburn

Bellingham

Belsay

To Carlisle

To Newcastle-upon-Tyne

Hexham

Corbridge

Please note: maps are not to scale

THE ROAD NORTH

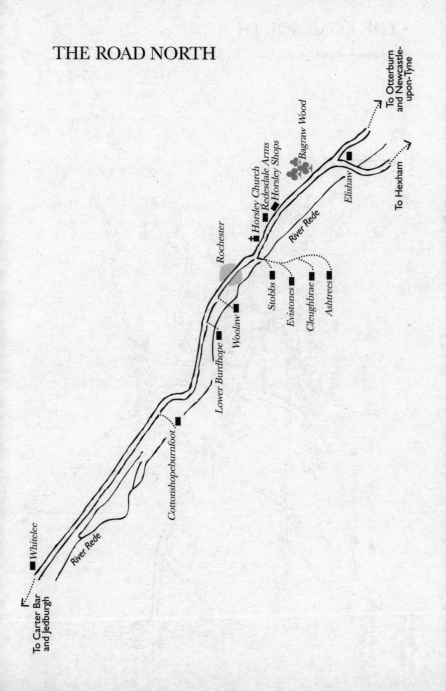

To Otterburn and Newcastle-upon-Tyne

To Hexham

Bagraw Wood

Horsley Church
Redesdale Arms
Horsley Shops

River Rede

Elishaw

Rochester

Stobbs

Evistones

Cleughbrae

Ashtrees

Woolaw

Lower Burdhope

Cottonshopeburnfoot

River Rede

Whitelee

To Carter Bar and Jedburgh

THE ROAD SOUTH

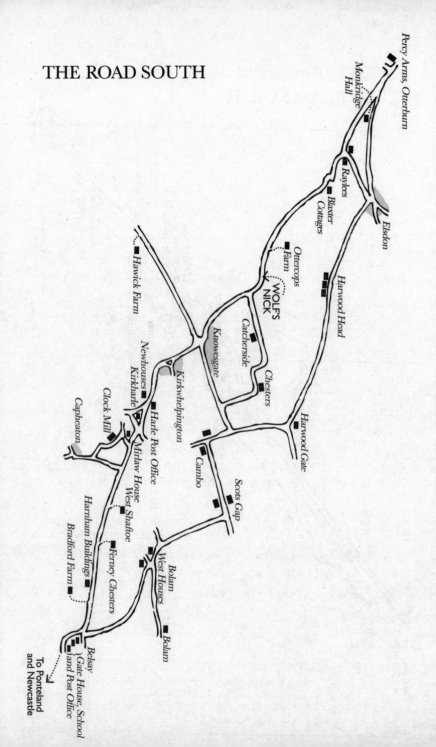

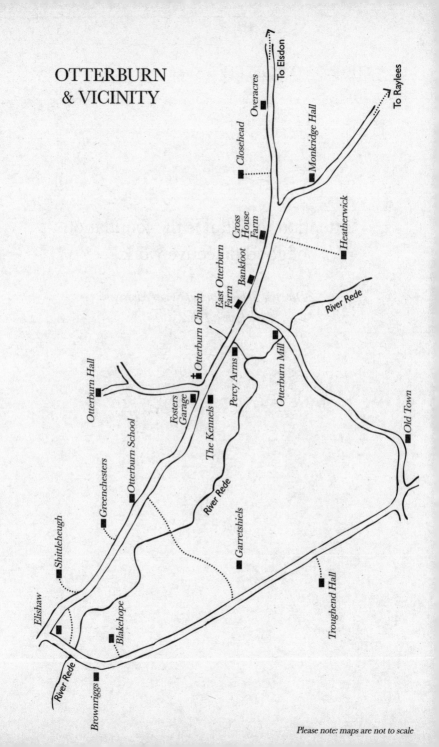

OTTERBURN & VICINITY

To Elsdon

To Raylees

Overacres

Monkridge Hall

Closehead

Heatherwick

Cross House Farm

Bankfoot

East Otterburn Farm

River Rede

Otterburn Church

Otterburn Mill

Otterburn Hall

† Otterburn Church

Percy Arms

Old Town

Fosters Garage

The Kennels

Otterburn School

River Rede

Greenchesters

Garretshiels

Shittleheugh

Troughend Hall

Elishaw

Blakehope

River Rede

Browniggs

Please note: maps are not to scale

'Attention to detail is the foundation of good detective work.'

Detective Superintendent Stuart Morrison,
Lincolnshire Police, 2015

Prologue

It was a crime that was as baffling as it was brutal: in 1931, a young woman was found dying on the Northumberland moors next to her smouldering car, covered in horrific burns. She alleged that she had been attacked, doused in petrol and set alight by a bowler-hatted stranger.

Of all the so-called 'classic' British crimes, the Evelyn Foster mystery has always held a particular fascination for me: perhaps it was the strangeness of the story, with its phantom killer, who seemingly vanished into thin air. Had there even been a crime at all? Right from the very beginning there were those who thought that the alleged crime was an elaborate lie.

Back in 2012, I was granted access to the original police files on the case, files that had remained closed for almost 80 years, and as I read them I came to appreciate just how many victims there had been. There was Evelyn herself, of course, but far too many others had also become caught in the net of injustice and untruths, both as a result of the original investigation and also thanks to things that were said and written in the intervening years, often based on second-hand gossip or a partial grasp of the facts. Evelyn's family, some of her neighbours, witnesses, even some of the policemen who assisted in the investigation of the crime, have been poorly served by what was written at the time and later. Worse still, there could be no doubting the fact that, in the aftermath of her death, Evelyn had been the victim of prejudice against her sex and her class.

After devoting many hours to the reports, witness statements and various other evidence contained in the police files and elsewhere, it is now my privilege to be able to tell the true story of what happened on that fateful night, and to set the record straight at last.

Diane Janes
April 2017

CHAPTER 1

Tuesday, 6 January 1931, had been a bitterly cold day in the Northumberland village of Otterburn.[1] By 6.30 in the evening, the regular bus service bringing farmers and shoppers back from Hexham market was due to arrive. The journey terminated at Foster's Garage, where the driver would turn the vehicle in readiness for the last southbound journey of the day back to Newcastle. A handful of passengers were already waiting at the bus stops serving either end of the village street, all of them well muffled against the bitter weather. The temperature had not risen above freezing all day and two of the waiting women were so cold that they asked a passer-by if she would watch their luggage for them while they walked up and down for a few minutes to try and get warm.[2]

As well as those awaiting the bus, there were plenty of other people out and about. Villagers were walking home from work, running errands and popping into the shops, which in 1931 mostly remained open until at least 7 p.m. Some overnight guests had just driven up to the Percy Arms Hotel, Otterburn's only licensed hostelry, where early evening drinkers were already starting to gather in the bar.

Many others continued working into the early evening, including the mechanics at Foster's Garage who were still hard at it, working on the broken-down Bean bus that was defying all attempts to fix it. Joseph Foster and Son was one of the principal employers in Otterburn; as well as running a small fleet of buses and lorries, they provided car and taxi hire, a vehicle maintenance and repair service, and the sale of petrol. Foster's main garage was on the north side of the village street, but they also had a complex of sheds and workshops on the opposite side of the road, adjacent to the Foster family home, a house called The Kennels.

In spite of employing more than 20 other people, Foster's was still very much a family affair, with Joseph and Margaret's four grown-up children pitching in to assist with everything from driving to bookkeeping. On this particular evening, Joseph was in the house, sorting out some accounts, his son, 30-year-old Gordon, was among those trying to repair the Bean bus, while the Fosters' youngest, 19-year-old Margaret, was out working a shift as a conductress on the Otterburn to Bellingham run. Their other daughters, Dorothy and Evelyn, had both been at The Kennels all day, helping with clerical work and various domestic jobs.

Twenty-eight-year-old Evelyn had long since graduated from serving as a bus conductress to becoming the regular, trusted driver of her own hire car, which she ran as a successful concern under the Foster umbrella. Though there had been no call for her services so far that day, one of

Evelyn's usual runs was associated with the arrival of the Hexham bus, when passengers who required transport further north than Otterburn shared Evelyn's taxi. In addition to the human passengers, there were sometimes goods and parcels, too: items put onto the bus in Hexham to be dropped off with someone waiting further north along the main road. Market day generally brought requests of this nature, but until the bus arrived no one could be absolutely sure whether or not the taxi would be needed, so Evelyn had left her Hudson Super Six motor car in the garage and was waiting by the kitchen fire.

Outside, the night sky was already glittering with stars and a full moon was rising. If Evelyn had entertained any hopes that she wouldn't be required on such a cold night, she was destined to be disappointed, for when the bus arrived there were three passengers for her taxi, to say nothing of some bales of straw and some firebricks to be left at various drops. So Evelyn donned her coat, scarf and hat, and crossed the road to retrieve the car from the garage, in readiness for what would turn into the most terrible night of her short life.

CHAPTER 2

Otterburn was smaller in 1931 than it is today, and despite its position on one of the two main roads from Newcastle-upon-Tyne into Scotland, it was a peaceful place, surrounded by wild but beautiful countryside. The majority of its inhabitants worked on the land, or else at Otterburn Mill, famed for its fine tweeds and blankets, and happy to boast royal connections, such as the provision of a pram rug for Princess Elizabeth in 1926. The remainder of the population worked at one of the village shops or garages, plied a specialist trade such as blacksmith or cobbler, or were in service at one of the larger houses nearby.

It was no more than two minutes' walk from the Percy Arms Hotel at one end of the village street to Foster's Garage at the other (three or four minutes if the walk was extended south of the Percy Arms to East Otterburn); nevertheless, Otterburn in those days boasted half a dozen shops and not one, but two, garages: Foster's and Reed's. (Today there is no filling station within 20 miles.) The village enjoyed a lively social life, with regular Saturday night dances held in the Memorial Hall (usually known as 'The Institute'), where a mixture of modern foxtrots and waltzes interspersed with traditional reels were well attended by the villagers and people who travelled in from outlying farms and beyond. On other nights the Memorial Hall was a popular meeting place for card games, dominoes and billiards.[1] The little church, presided over by Reverend Joseph Brierley, provided another focal point. Everyone knew everyone else.

Joseph Foster had come to live in Otterburn some time after 1901 and built a business from the ground up.[2] It has been suggested elsewhere that the Fosters were hard taskmasters, but I found no particular evidence of this in the documents relating to the Evelyn Foster case. The interwar years were tough, particularly in the north of England where unemployment was high and employers routinely demanded long hours for low wages. Police witness statements tend to suggest that while Foster's employees worked long hours, they also had respect and even affection for the family. Joseph Foster may have expected his men to work well into the evening on a broken-down bus, but his son Gordon worked alongside them. Tellingly, the men addressed Gordon by his first name and likewise referred to his sister as Evvy, or Evie, rather than Miss Foster.

The working day started much earlier and finished much later for most people at that time – and this was particularly true of transport providers. To complement their regular buses from Otterburn to Newcastle, the Fosters organised an early morning pick-up service linking people who lived off the bus route to its stopping places on the main road. This entailed Gordon Foster setting off from the garage in Evelyn's Hudson car at 7.50 a.m. to collect anyone waiting for him on a triangular route between Otterburn and Raylees, via Elsdon. On 6 January there had been just one woman waiting at Elsdon Gate, and once Gordon had driven her to meet the southbound bus he drove back to Otterburn, calling in at his parents' house, where he found everything just as usual, before returning to his own house a few yards further down the street for his breakfast.[3]

Though Gordon was married and living in a separate house with his wife and young son, his sisters, Evelyn, Dorothy and Margaret, were still living at home with their parents. Evelyn had been up since 7 a.m. and, as usual, had cooked breakfast for the rest of the family. After that, she had helped with the housework and carried out some clerical duties before lunch, not venturing outside until around 2 p.m., when she was spotted by Gordon's little son John, who remarked: 'There's Aunty Evelyn, away to feed the hens.' On her way back from dealing with the poultry, Evelyn had popped into Gordon's house for a few minutes to chat with her brother, who had come home from the garage for his lunch. It was just chit chat, Gordon remembered afterwards, an inconsequential sort of conversation.

Evelyn's afternoon was spent much as the morning had been, and only with the arrival of the Hexham bus at around 6.30 p.m. did the pace of activity step up. Her passengers were two local farmers, Robert Wilson of Woolaw and William Glendinning of Ashtrees, and a farmer's wife, Mary Murray, who lived much further north at Cottonshopeburnfoot. The first intimation that the car was needed came when Mr Wilson and Mr Glendinning entered the house to see Joseph Foster, as both men needed to settle accounts for the carriage of livestock to and from the market. Evelyn had at once begun to get ready, but before she had got into her outdoor things, her brother Gordon put his head round the door and told her there were some passengers for Rochester. 'Yes, I know. There are some of them in the house and I am getting ready to go out.' Then, knowing that Gordon had used the car that morning, she asked him whether there was enough petrol in the tank to get to the village of Rochester and back, and he confirmed that there was.

Once Evelyn had brought the car out from the big garage, William Glendinning took the front seat, while Mary Murray and Robert Wilson sat in the back, with Mrs Murray's shopping alongside them and three bags of straw across their knees[4] (this was a time when relatively few households had their own car, so no one in the farming community was likely to quibble about nursing a bag or two of straw when all were equally reliant on mutual co-operation between neighbours to get themselves and the necessities of their lives back and forth in whatever transport was available).

People and packages on board, the Hudson set off north, leaving the lights of Otterburn behind. A moment or two later they would have passed the village school, which stood some distance north of the village itself, and in a very few minutes they would have passed the junction with Dere Street, now designated the A68, where the main road from the Scottish border branches south-west towards Hexham and Darlington, a junction known locally as Elishaw Road Ends.

Evelyn's first stop was at Horsley, a small row of cottages some three miles north of Otterburn and just south of the Redesdale Arms, whose sign then, as now, advertised it as the Last Hotel in England or the First Hotel in England, depending on the direction of travel. At Horsley, Mr Glendinning got out and offloaded the firebricks Evelyn had been asked to deliver. They were received by Hedley Anderson, the Horsley blacksmith.

Glendinning was expecting one of his sons to bring their horse-drawn wagon across from the farm, in order to collect some calves he had bought in Hexham,[5] and as he got out of the car, he asked Mr Anderson if his boys had arrived. Anderson said they had not, but pointed out a light across the fields, close to the ford across the River Rede, saying it would 'likely be them coming now'. Later William Glendinning would recall that while they were having this conversation, he thought he noticed the headlights of a car standing on the forecourt of the Redesdale Arms.

Meanwhile, still inside the car, Mrs Murray was sure that she saw some headlights pass them, going south. Robert Wilson didn't recall any car headlights, but he did notice Douglas Nelson from Rochester, cycling south towards Elishaw Road Ends on his nightly newspaper round.

With the firebricks delivered, the party of four continued

north towards Rochester, the last village before the Scottish border. Before they reached the village, however, Evelyn stopped the car again at a point known as Stobbsgate, where William Glendinning got out and began his walk home along the rough track which led to several farms, including Ashtrees. The Hudson and its occupants continued the run north. As they reached the village school on the southern outskirts of Rochester, they met a car coming the other way, which Evelyn slowed down to pass. Neither of her passengers got a very good look at the car, whose bright headlights dazzled them both.

In Rochester they made another stop to leave the bags of straw with a couple of men who had come down from Bellsheil Colliery to collect it. Evelyn herself passed out the sacks and then drove on again beyond the village, until she reached the track which led to Woolaw, where Robert Wilson got out of the car. As he began to walk towards his farm he was able to see the lights of the Hudson for a short distance as it continued north with its one remaining passenger, and a few minutes later he saw the lights of the car again as it returned in the direction of Otterburn.

Mary Murray was the last passenger to leave the car. She got out at Birdhopecraig Farm and then walked the remaining three miles home. This appears to have been the normal arrangement, presumably because Mrs Murray could not afford sole occupancy of a private taxi for the full distance. (In 1931 a walk of three or four miles was not regarded as an excessive distance for a child to walk to school each day and was 'nobbut a step' to a fully fit adult.)

After dropping Mrs Murray, Evelyn turned the car around and drove back in the direction she had come. What happened next has become the source of multiple conjectures and theories.

CHAPTER 3

Mrs Foster and her daughter Dorothy were in the kitchen of The Kennels and Joseph Foster was in the next room, still attending to his bookkeeping when Evelyn returned from her trip at just after 7 p.m., using the kitchen door as the family invariably did. To her mother's surprise, Evelyn announced that she was going straight out again as she had picked up another fare. Her mother recalled her words as: 'I have brought a man down from Elishaw and he wants to get to Ponteland to catch a bus.'[1]

Mrs Foster wanted more details, as well she might, because Elishaw Road Ends – often shortened to Elishaw – was no more than a junction. There was nothing there apart from an AA call box and a farmhouse a few yards off the main road, which made it an unlikely place to pick up a fare, particularly on a cold winter's night. However, Evelyn quickly made sense of the encounter for her mother, explaining that as she was driving back towards Otterburn after dropping Mrs Murray, she had been hailed or waved down by the occupants of a car standing at the Elishaw junction. When she pulled up, a man had approached the car and told her that he was heading for Newcastle, but had missed the last southbound bus at Jedburgh. Someone in Jedburgh had told him he would be able to get a Newcastle bus if he could get to Otterburn, and the people in the car had offered him a lift. They had all had tea together in Jedburgh first and then driven south, but as these good Samaritans were bound for Hexham, they had stopped at the junction, thinking they might be overtaken by a Newcastle-bound car, or else could phone from the AA box to arrange a lift on to Otterburn. Having spotted Evelyn's approaching car, they had flagged it down.

One immediate oddity at this point in the story is the travellers' decision to stop and telephone from Elishaw Road Ends, rather than simply driving two miles further down the road, dropping their passenger in Otterburn, then taking a right turn which would have brought them back onto the Hexham Road. The extra distance involved was negligible, with this minor diversion arguably less time-consuming than stopping to make a telephone call. On the other hand, in an era when many people navigated by using signposts rather than a detailed road map, if the occupants of the car were not local, it is possible that they may have thought a detour into Otterburn would take them well out of their way.

Whatever the reason for stopping at Elishaw, Evelyn immediately dashed the man's hopes of catching a bus from Otterburn, telling him that the last service for Newcastle had already gone, and explaining that the next place where he would be able to catch a bus to Newcastle at that time of night was Ponteland, where she could drive him if he wished. In the twenties and thirties, it was not at all unusual for a stranded traveller to receive assistance from a passing motorist, and the man had probably entertained hopes that the car he flagged down at Elishaw was going as far as Newcastle. He had no way of knowing that the Hudson was actually a private hire vehicle, and that while Evelyn was willing to give him free passage as far as Otterburn, any further journey would be as a fare-paying passenger.

According to Evelyn, the man accepted her offer of a lift to Otterburn and before he got into the car with her she overheard him thanking the person, or people, who had brought him thus far. On the short drive from Elishaw to the village, he had asked her how much the fare would be to Ponteland and she had replied that she thought it was about £2, but would have to check when she got back to the garage. In 1931, when a labourer scarcely earned £3 per week, £2 was a considerable sum, so it would have come as no surprise to her mother and sister when Evelyn told them that rather than wait in the house or at the garage while she refuelled the car in readiness for the journey, the man had elected to walk down to the Percy Arms and see whether anyone there happened to be going towards Ponteland and could give him a lift. However, he had agreed with Evelyn that if he was unable to get a lift from someone else, she would pick him up on the bridge outside the hotel. And if he was not waiting for her there, she would check inside, where he would leave word if he had already left with someone else.

It would subsequently be suggested that this was an odd arrangement. If a lift to Ponteland was not available, why couldn't the man simply walk the matter of a few yards back along the village street to where the car was parked alongside the petrol pumps outside The Kennels? It would perhaps have made more sense for the man to come back and knock at The Kennels if he needed a lift, but against this is the fact that Evelyn would have known the man's chances of picking up a lift to Ponteland at that time in the evening were remote. She may well have thought that it would take him as long to make enquiries at the Percy Arms as it took her to fill up the petrol tank, and that driving to the south end of the village to pick him up would save time in the long run.

Evidently a cautious mother, Mrs Foster then asked her daughter what kind of man this prospective customer seemed to be, and Evelyn said he looked 'very respectable and gentlemanly ... a bit of a knut', meaning fashion conscious or a dandy. Mrs Foster also commented that she thought the £2 Evelyn had quoted sounded a bit on the high side, and her daughter replied that she was going to ask her father to work it out for her while she went back outside to fill up the car. (Fares were worked out by a formula which factored in both the distance and time of day.)

At this stage certain things became a little confused in people's memories. According to one version of events, it was Mrs Margaret Foster who popped into the next room and enquired with her husband about the fare, which is supported by a statement in which Joseph Foster said he did not see Evelyn himself. He calculated the fare at £1 16s, which Mrs Foster conveyed to Evelyn when she returned to the kitchen. However, in a separate statement, Evelyn's father reports the enquiry about the fare and the conversation about picking up the man at Elishaw as if he had spoken with Evelyn personally. There is nothing suspicious or sinister in a discrepancy of this nature. In the days and weeks after the tragedy, the Foster family must have relived those events together time and again, going over and over these final conversations in the hope of divining some further clue that might help shine some light on what happened next. In the course of such discussions, it is not unusual for people to establish such a vivid picture of an incident or conversation that they believe themselves to have been a party to it when in reality they were not.

We do know that, having filled up with petrol, Evelyn briefly popped back into the kitchen where she received confirmation of the fare. At this point, her sister Dorothy piped up and suggested that Evelyn take George Phillipson on the journey with her, to which Mrs Foster said: 'Oh yes. You can call and get him as you go through the village.'

'All right, Mother,' Evelyn replied.

Whether Dorothy's suggestion was in the spirit of mischief or matchmaking, Mrs Foster no doubt had an eye to Evelyn's safety when she seized on the idea of taking a trustworthy chaperone along. In Evelyn's response, however, it is easy to detect the resignation of the grown-up daughter who feels that she can look after herself. In spite of appearing to agree to her mother's suggestion, Evelyn had no intention of soliciting George Phillipson's company for the trip, as would become evident from subsequent events.

George Lancelot Phillipson, a joiner, had only been working for Foster's Garage a matter of weeks: he started with them in December 1930 and had taken lodgings in the village with a Mrs Scott. There is no doubt that he had become friendly with Evelyn, but it is difficult to determine how far any attraction went on either side. According to Jonathan Goodman, who wrote about the case in his book The Burning of Evelyn Foster,[2] wedding bells were expected by the entire village by January 1931, but although this may have become part of the subsequent myth surrounding the case, Goodman's description of this blossoming romance is completely disproved by police statements and other supporting evidence from the time.[3] It is therefore entirely possible that Evelyn was not nearly so keen on Mr Phillipson as her sister Dorothy may have thought, or perhaps she felt that to seek out his company in so obvious a fashion looked horribly like throwing herself at him. Whatever her reasons, Evelyn made no attempt to locate this potential companion.

As she left via the kitchen door she turned back to collect a torch from the table, saying, 'I'll take your flash-light, Mother.' [4] A moment or two later, having finished his bookkeeping for the night, Joseph Foster decided to cross the road to the garage and see how his men were getting on with the bus repair. He opened the front door just in time to see Evelyn's car move off. The next time he saw the car it would be a burned-out wreck and his daughter would already be dead.

CHAPTER 4

With Evelyn gone the family continued the usual business of the evening. Over in the garage, where Gordon and a couple of other men were still trying to coax the bus back to life, Joseph Foster mentioned in passing that Evelyn had taken a fare down to Ponteland. It was a 40-mile round trip and the state of the roads required a careful passage, so no one was expecting her back in much under an hour-and-a-half to two hours. All the same, a faintly worrying note was struck at around 8.45, when Margaret Foster returned home from her shift on the Bellingham bus and mentioned that she had just spoken to George Phillipson out in the village street.[1]

No doubt Mrs Foster was a little irritated that her elder daughter had ignored her advice about calling for Phillipson, and in her statement to the police she said that, when she realised that Phillipson had not gone with her daughter, she 'began to feel uneasy, as the man was a stranger'. But in spite of this, there was no real reason for anyone to have become unduly concerned at this stage. It was not the first occasion when Evelyn had taken a stranger on a long trip at night, and not particularly unusual for a fare to take longer than anticipated: after all, there was always the possibility that the man would change his mind when he got to Ponteland and decide to have Evelyn drive him all the way to Newcastle. If he decided not to exchange the relative warmth of the car for a freezing wait at a bus stop, the round trip would have extended to almost 60 miles, with Evelyn hardly likely to return to Otterburn much before 9.30 at the earliest. As time went on, however, Evelyn's parents definitely began to worry and Mrs Foster commented to Margaret that she would 'wait until the bus from Newcastle came in' – presumably before suggesting to her son or husband that some sort of search be organised. This made perfect sense, because the northbound bus would be following exactly the same route as Evelyn would have taken, so if the car had broken down or met with some accident en route, the last Foster's service of the evening would inevitably have encountered it.

At about 10 p.m., one of the Fosters' mechanics, Tommy Vasey, was walking home from the Memorial Hall and noticed a light burning in the big garage. He popped in to check that all was well and found Joseph Foster inside. The boss reassured him that all was as it should be in the workshop and Vasey returned home, but not before Mr Foster had commented a little anxiously on Evelyn's failure to return.

At around 10.30, Mrs Foster finally heard the bus draw up outside the house and from then on events unfolded quickly. Outside, the driver of the bus, Cecil Johnstone, immediately leaped down and raced to summon Gordon, telling him that the Hudson had been burned 'and Evvy too'.

The minutes that followed are not easy to piece together. Each of those involved later made several separate statements to police, during which the precise sequence of events inevitably became confused. Gordon Foster was the first to be alerted and he ran almost at once to the nearby home of Tommy Vasey, who also rushed to help. Bus driver Cecil Johnstone and his conductor Tommy Rutherford were also on the scene. Gordon got into the bus where he found his sister on one of the passenger seats. Even in the poor light, he could see that she was badly burned, although the full extent of her injuries was not apparent as she was covered by Cecil Johnstone's overcoat.

Gordon remembered asking her, 'Who's done this?' and his sister replied, 'That awful man's done it. Gordon, do bring us a drink.'

Evelyn's terrible thirst – a constant theme of her conversations with everyone from now on – was a symptom of the dehydration that inevitably follows severe burns.

Gordon ran to fetch his sister a drink and also obtained some rugs to wrap her in, while Tommy Vasey stayed with her and tried to help her sit up. While Evelyn was still in the bus, various other family members came out to see what was happening, including her sisters Dorothy and Margaret. When Mrs Foster realised that her daughter was badly hurt she hurried back inside to get a bed ready, instructing others to send for a doctor and the district nurse, and also to fetch their next-door neighbour, Adeline Jennings. It was an era before the existence of the emergency services as we know them today. In rural areas, even serious illness and injury was usually dealt with at home and most mature women had some experience of home nursing – seeking assistance from a female neighbour would therefore have been the automatic response in most households.

Joseph Foster also went out to the bus, and he, too, was urged by Evelyn to bring her a drink. He hurried back to the house and grabbed his own recently poured cup of coffee, which he took out and helped her to drink. When she had finished it, he asked her who had done this terrible thing, but she merely looked up at him and held up her burned hands. It was the last interaction father and daughter would ever have.

Gordon returned with another drink and then, with the assistance of Tommy Vasey, carried his sister into the house and up the stairs. As they carried her inside, Vasey also asked what had happened and Evelyn said: 'He threw something on us and I went up in flames and the car, too.' A point on which all witnesses agreed is that, though in great pain, Evelyn was completely lucid and fully aware of her surroundings.

By now the story of how Evelyn came to be in the bus was unfolding. Cecil Johnstone and Tommy Rutherford explained that they had left Newcastle on time at 9 p.m. and reached Ponteland at 9.20. This final run of the day was always a quiet one and the last of their passengers had alighted at Kirkwhelpington. The bus then trundled on, seeing very few signs of life at all until it crested the rise at Wolf's Nick, a lonely spot where the northbound road ascends to a gap in the ridge of low hills known as the Ottercops, then swings left, opening up a broad vista of deserted moorland to the north east. That night, as their bus breached the gap at the top of the rise and began the descent, driver and conductor were surprised to see that a short distance to the east of the road, there was something on fire. Cecil Johnstone stopped the bus and both men got down onto the deserted road. In the moonlight they could just discern the outline of a saloon car, whose wheels were still smouldering, though the rest of the fire was out.

The men decided that they ought to investigate and walked across the rough ground towards the car. Johnstone noticed that both offside doors were open, but there appeared to be no one about. At this stage neither of them had recognised the vehicle and it had not occurred to them that anyone they knew was involved, but as they circled the car they caught sight of a shape on the ground, about eight or nine yards from the burned-out vehicle, and on drawing nearer they realised that it was a woman. Only when Cecil Johnstone knelt down beside her did he discover that it was his employer's daughter. As Evelyn saw him she said, 'Oh that awful man.'

Even in the moonlight the men could see that there were no clothes left on the lower part of her body, so Johnstone took off his overcoat and did his best to wrap it around her. Evelyn said she would try to walk to the bus, but seeing the distressed state she was in, the driver and his mate carried her. She was clearly in pain and continued to repeat the words, 'Oh that awful man', and asked for a drink.

Johnstone drove back to Otterburn as fast as he could, while Tommy Rutherford sat alongside Evelyn, offering what comfort he could. Afterwards, Rutherford, who seems to have been in a state of shock himself, remembered her saying nothing on the journey home apart from 'That awful man', and repeatedly asking for a drink. At Blaxter Cottages, a few miles south of Otterburn, they stopped the bus and knocked on a door to obtain a drink of water for Evelyn, before continuing to The Kennels.

Once Evelyn had been carried upstairs and laid on the bed, Tommy Vasey and Gordon Foster withdrew. Mrs Foster surrounded her daughter with hot water bottles, provided her with another drink and set about removing what was left of her clothing.

Evelyn's hands were badly burned and her face had suffered sufficiently that she had lost some skin from her nose, chin and mouth. Her eyelids were burned and swollen, her eyelashes and eyebrows charred. While distressing enough, only when she removed the rugs and overcoat, in which her daughter had been carried upstairs, did Mrs Foster truly appreciate the severity of Evelyn's injuries.

The clothing previously covering the lower part of Evelyn's body and the upper part of her legs had been completely destroyed. There were severe burns on both her inner thighs, where the outer tissue had burst in the intense heat, creating deep fissures several inches long, which exposed the damaged muscle and bone beneath them. These burns extended around her outer thighs and on to the lower part of her abdomen and buttocks. Burns of a marginally less serious nature extended upwards and downwards from this area. Superficial layers of skin had been burned away down to the middle of Evelyn's legs and there was blistering to her right ankle and foot. (The left ankle and foot were almost free of burns.)

The damage on and above her breasts consisted of small patches of burning, the size of coins, interspersed with areas of virtually undamaged skin. The upper part of her chest and her chin were completely free of burns. Her right arm and hand and been badly burned from shoulder to finger tips, while the left arm and shoulder had suffered only superficial burns in comparison, though her left hand was as badly damaged as her right.[2] It was a terrible sight and one that Evelyn's mother and sisters were unlikely ever to forget: a situation for which their normal experience of home nursing would have left them ill-equipped.

Their next-door neighbour, Adeline Jennings, was equally shocked. Having been summoned from her bed by one of the Fosters, she had hurried next door, where she found Evelyn already in bed and covered by the bedclothes. She could see at once that Evelyn's hands and face were burned and described her face as 'puffed up and blue', with her left eye closed. It was Mrs Jennings who helped Evelyn to sit up while Mrs Foster cut away what was left of her jumper and drew Cecil Johnstone's coat from under her. The bedclothes were drawn back so that

Mrs Jennings also saw the dreadful injuries to the lower part of Evelyn's body.[3]

Trained medical help initially arrived in the shape of Wilhelmina Lawson, the district nurse, who asked for olive oil and lime water – fortunately Mrs Jennings had both and went next door to fetch them. Nurse Lawson was applying these preparations (they were standard treatments of the period) when Dr Duncan McEachran arrived and took charge. He applied picric acid, which reduced pain in burns, and began dressing the various damaged areas, starting with Evelyn's hands and face. Mrs Jennings was asked to tear bed sheets into strips to improvise more bandages, which she did. While they were working on Evelyn's legs, a second practitioner, Dr Miller, arrived to help.

When all the dressings were finished and Evelyn had been made as comfortable as possible, Dr McEachran went downstairs to talk privately with Joseph and Margaret Foster. He sat down with them in the kitchen and explained that their daughter's injuries were too severe for her to have any hope of survival.

CHAPTER 5

Until now, the definitive account of the Evelyn Foster case was provided by Jonathan Goodman in his 1977 book The Burning of Evelyn Foster.[1] Though Goodman managed to speak to a few of the people directly involved, he was forced to rely heavily on a handful of statements made at the coroner's inquest and a variety of reports in local and national newspapers. This resulted in the emergence of an incomplete and often misleading picture of the events of 6 January 1931 and the conduct of the police investigation that followed.

Goodman was particularly critical of the police on the night of Evelyn's fatal journey, claiming that they wasted vital time in failing to interview her and generally ridiculing their every action. But it becomes plain on reading the witness statements of all those involved that, while the police undoubtedly made a number of mistakes during the course of a complex investigation that was without precedent in the experience of the Northumberland force, they cannot be criticised for any tardiness in attempting to extract a statement from the victim. On the contrary, the local police were prevented from doing this by the doctor in charge of the sick room, and the fact that the police eventually had to work without a complete, coherent statement from Evelyn Foster is directly attributable to the decisions and actions of Dr Duncan McEachran that night. It is somewhat ironic, therefore, that in Goodman's account of the case, he suggests that it was only at the prompting of Dr McEachran that the police troubled to ask the victim any questions at all.[2]

News of the attack on Evelyn Foster had reached Police Constable Andrew Ferguson, the officer based in Otterburn, at 10.45 that night, a short time after the bus had drawn up. The original telephone message still survives in Northumbria police files and, although scrawled hastily in pencil, it is surprisingly detailed. It reveals that the caller was Joseph Foster, who explained that his daughter Evelyn had been brought home by one of Foster's bus crews, badly burned. It goes on to explain how Evelyn had picked up a man at about 6.30, brought him to the village and then taken him south. The attack on Evelyn is described as follows: 'When about six miles south of Otterburn and three miles north of Kirkwhelpington, he pulled her out of the driving seat and hit her over the head, then threw something over her, he then started to drive the car, the car took fire while they were in it. Just then another car came up, picked the man up and took him off, but cannot say in what direction.'[3]

Realising at once that he was dealing with a serious situation, PC Ferguson immediately telephoned his superior officer, Sergeant Robert Shanks, who was stationed in Bellingham. Shanks said he would get there as soon as he could, but that this was dependent on obtaining transport (at the time, the majority of police officers in Northumberland were not provided with vehicles).[4]

After speaking with Shanks, Ferguson got dressed and walked the length of the village street which separated the police office where he lived from The Kennels. Here, he spoke to Cecil Johnstone, Joseph and Gordon Foster, who were all standing out in the main garage; but he was unable to see Evelyn herself as she was upstairs being tended by her mother, sisters and Mrs Jennings.

It must have been immediately obvious to Ferguson that, for any kind of effective investigation to be launched, more information would need to be sought from Evelyn herself, and no doubt he assumed that he or his superior officer would be allowed to question her once she had received suitable medical attention. No policeman, then or today, expects to jackboot into the sick room and interrogate an injured witness until given the all-clear to do so by a nurse or a doctor. In addition, according to the information Ferguson had received, there would have been no point in hotfooting it to the scene of the crime, since the attacker was already long gone, having apparently made his getaway by car some considerable time previously. Significantly, no one had suggested to Ferguson at this point that Evelyn's injuries were life threatening. The policeman was aware that she had been burned – no more than that. The men in the garage knew only of the damage to Evelyn's face and hands, which were not the worst of her injuries. At that stage, Ferguson had no way of knowing that time was running out.

There was no doctor in Otterburn, but the village did enjoy the services of a district nurse, Wilhelmina Lawson. On learning that Nurse Lawson was out attending a case in Elsdon, Joseph Foster had dispatched Cecil Johnstone and Tommy Rutherford in their bus to collect her, having previously telephoned the police and his GP, Dr Kirk, who lived in Bellingham. Unfortunately Dr Kirk was unwell, so he sent his temporary assistant, Dr McEachran, in his place.[5] The initial message McEachran got from Mrs Kirk was that someone had been injured in a car accident, but then someone from The Kennels rang again and McEachran learned that burning was involved and that the Fosters wanted two doctors to attend. While McEachran was getting ready, Sergeant Shanks arrived on his doorstep, hoping for a lift, and together the two men travelled the half-hour journey to Otterburn.

In the meantime, having been unable to reach another GP, Joseph Foster turned instead to Dr James Miller, who had been the Foster family doctor until his retirement. Retired or not, Dr Miller answered the call at once. As he readied himself and his motor car for the trip from his home in Bellingham, the local constable, PC Henry Proud, passed by on his nightly patrol and, seeing a light in Dr Miller's garage, popped in to see if all was well. When the doctor explained that Evelyn Foster had been badly burned in an accident, and that he was attending in spite of having some difficulty in driving due to an injured foot, Proud offered to accompany him and the offer was accepted, thereby coincidentally introducing a third police officer onto the scene.

Sergeant Shanks and Dr McEachran were the first arrivals from Bellingham. McEachran was taken upstairs where, along with Evelyn, he found Mrs Foster, her daughter Dorothy, neighbour Mrs Jennings and Nurse Lawson. Evelyn's sister Margaret was also in and out of the room, running errands to and from the kitchen.[6] Sergeant Shanks had helped carry the doctor's bags up to the bedroom, but of all the would-be helpers, only he retired from the scene.

While McEachran was applying dressings, Dr Miller arrived, adding a sixth person to the ever-growing number around the bed. Although Evelyn's eyes were by now covered with bandages, she recognised Dr Miller's voice and told him she was sorry to have brought him out on such a cold night.

From the point of view of the investigation, little could be done until the police had at least obtained some sort of description of the attacker. By the time Dr Miller arrived, Sgt Shanks and PC Ferguson had been invited into the kitchen, where they attempted to question the Foster menfolk, who could tell them relatively little, and all of it second hand. Meanwhile up in the bedroom, Mrs Foster had been attempting to get to the bottom of things with Evelyn. One of the first questions Mrs Foster appears to have asked Evelyn as she was laid on the bed, was, 'Why did you not take Phillipson?'

Evelyn replied, 'I did not see him, going down the road.'

'Why did you not call at his lodgings?'

'I thought I would not be long in getting back.'

It was an unfortunate beginning. In focusing on Evelyn's failure to heed her advice and include George Phillipson in the excursion, Mrs Foster was already (either subtly or bluntly) suggesting that Evelyn's own foolishness had in some way contributed to the situation. As well as potentially adding to her daughter's distress, Mrs Foster was not creating a good climate for a young woman to provide evidence of any form of sexual assault. From the statements made by the other female witnesses, it is clear that in the period before the first doctor's arrival, Mrs Foster had continuously plied her daughter with questions, some of which seemed to imply a lack of trust in Evelyn on Mrs Foster's part. For example, she asked Evelyn whether the man who had assaulted her was, in fact, her ex-fiancé, Ernest Primrose – a question which clearly implied that she suspected Evelyn's story of picking up a stranger might be false. This interrogation was only halted when, according to Mrs Foster, Dr McEachran said, 'Don't trouble her too much just now.'

The differing approaches of Mrs Foster and Dr McEachran underline the dilemma between the need to extract information from a victim of crime and the desire not to add to their distress in what were to be the last hours of their life. Unfortunately, each of them seems to have erred too far towards either extreme. Mrs Foster, who must have been understandably distraught, peppered

Evelyn with questions then reacted emotionally to the answers, whereas Dr McEachran's sole concern was to lessen the stress of his patient.

Having put a stop to Mrs Foster's cross-examination, McEachran and his team did their best to make Evelyn as comfortable as possible. Although Dr Miller was by far the more experienced, McEachran had arrived first and was deputising for the family GP, Dr Kirk. Miller, therefore, appears to have deferred to his younger colleague and taken a subsidiary role. However, when the period of active treatment was over and Dr McEachran instructed Nurse Lawson and Mrs Jennings to keep Evelyn warm and not to bother her with further questions, Dr Miller appears to have suggested privately to McEachran that as Evelyn had not long to live, she should 'make a deposition'. In Duncan McEachran's statement at the inquest, it is implied that it was he who suggested the police should question Evelyn at this point, but the statements of other witnesses suggest otherwise.

With Evelyn's active treatment at an end, she was left in the care of Nurse Lawson and Mrs Jennings while Dr McEachran went downstairs to the kitchen to break the news to Evelyn's parents that there was no hope of their daughter's recovery. While this conversation was taking place, the two policemen, Shanks and Ferguson, were asked to withdraw to the hall. At the inquest, Dr McEachran would claim that he also conveyed this prognosis to the officers before they went upstairs to question Evelyn, but by that time, the police were being criticised for their failure to obtain a proper statement from the dying girl, and it is therefore necessary to question Dr McEachran's testimony, which conveniently places him on the side of those who perceived the importance of obtaining an immediate statement. Shanks and Ferguson individually made statements and filed reports from which it is clear that it had not been suggested to either of them that Evelyn's death was imminent.

It was ten minutes past midnight when the two policemen were finally admitted to the sickroom, and the circumstances confronting them were hardly ideal for the conduct of an interview. The forceful Mrs Foster had taken up position in a chair beside her daughter's head and, given that Mrs Jennings, Nurse Lawson, Dorothy Foster, doctors McEachran and Miller were also in the room, it is hard to imagine how Ferguson and Shanks managed to squeeze in and harder still to see how they could have tactfully dislodged Mrs Foster from her position as primary interrogator. Shanks and Ferguson had considerably less clout in the sickroom than did McEachran, but though it is easy with hindsight to suggest that the doctor should have taken charge and removed all extraneous persons while the police asked their questions, in practice he, too, faced the difficulty that Mrs Foster was in her own home and obviously did not wish to leave the bedside of her dying daughter. However, Evelyn clearly did not require the ministrations of two doctors, a nurse, her mother, sister, and next-door neighbour at this point, and their presence undoubtedly made it extremely difficult for the two policemen.

At the inquest, the police were asked how it came about that Mrs Foster, rather than themselves, had ended up putting questions to Evelyn. PC Ferguson replied that it had been difficult to hear Evelyn's responses, an explanation ridiculed by Jonathan Goodman when he wrote about the case. However, it is clear from the statements made by Nurse Lawson, Mrs Jennings and Dr Miller that they, too, had difficulty in hearing some of Evelyn's answers, which were presumably audible to those on the side of the bed where her mother was sitting and Evelyn was facing, but were not always clear to those crammed in on the opposite side of the room. It might be argued that the police themselves, in particular Shanks, the senior officer, ought to have insisted on creating better circumstances in which to obtain a statement, but the police reports strongly imply that they made the best of a bad job because they believed that this would be a preliminary interview, and that Evelyn Foster would be able to make a proper, coherent statement when questioned the following day.

Ferguson and Shanks were allowed just 20 minutes in the sickroom. Not long after their departure, Evelyn realised that she had lost her sight. Soon after this, while her mother was temporarily out of the room, she said, 'I don't think I will get better this time, nurse,' to which Nurse Lawson attempted to make a comforting reply. Within about an hour of this exchange Evelyn lost consciousness.

Dr Miller left for Bellingham some time between 4.30 a.m. and 5 a.m., and Dr McEachran left about an hour later, leaving Nurse Lawson in charge of the patient and saying that he expected death to take place very shortly, and that in his opinion the patient would not regain consciousness.[7] It was possible for him to anticipate death with some certainty, since it was customary then (and considered perfectly proper and legal) for GPs to cut short the suffering of terminally ill patients by administering a very large dose of painkilling drugs, such as morphine.[8] McEachran must have known that once he had given the final dose of medication, his patient's loss of consciousness, then death, was inevitable, and therefore that the opportunity for obtaining a further statement never existed – that he appears not to have made the attending police officers aware of this is inexcusable.

CHAPTER 6

Though Dr Miller had spoken of a 'deposition' and others have referred to Evelyn's story as a 'dying statement', the fact is that Evelyn Foster never made a statement in the strictest sense. In 1931, the normal method of obtaining a witness statement was for a policeman to ask a series of questions, noting the answers, then reading this back and requiring the witness to sign it. In itself, this method left much to be desired: responses were reported as if they formed a continuous narrative, but as the questions that prompted them were not recorded, these responses could be (and often were) taken out of context, with their original meaning distorted or lost. However, the reading back of the statement did at least offer the possibility for the witness to clarify, add or refute items that were misleading or inaccurate. It is true that Evelyn, with her injured hands and bandaged eyes, would not have been able to sign a statement, but the 'statement' recorded that night, such as it was, was not even read back to her, presumably because the police officers were working to the premise that a proper statement would be obtained the following day.

PC Ferguson took some notes of Evelyn's responses, but he had difficulty in hearing what she said. (The consensus among the witnesses was that Evelyn spoke quietly throughout and that her voice was very low by the time the interview concluded.) As well as PC Ferguson there were six other witnesses hanging on every word, and all agreed that Evelyn appeared to understand the questions and was perfectly lucid, but a similar level of agreement was not always achieved when it came to interpreting her responses. In the days that followed, all of those present would be asked what they recalled of Evelyn's answers, and out of this would emerge the somewhat confused account on which the police would be forced to rely. [1]

The witness upon whom greatest reliance was eventually placed was Mrs Margaret Foster. Mrs Foster put all the questions to Evelyn and sitting at the head of the bed she was in the best possible position to hear the answers. However, whether Mrs Foster accurately remembered her daughter's answers, or subsequently placed her own interpretation upon them, is another matter entirely. At the inquest, Mrs Foster described this process as her having 'a conversation' with Evelyn while the police 'were there'. Everything appears to indicate that Mrs Foster directed the course of the conversation, with the police only managing to interject occasionally, and there is little to suggest that the police were encouraged to take a particularly active lead in the process. It is perhaps also significant that although Mrs Foster claimed to have perfect recall of a whole variety of things her daughter said, her recollections did not always accord with those of other witnesses to the conversation and by the time of the inquest she was, for example, unable to confirm the identity or rank of the policeman who had accompanied the village constable to her daughter's bedside that night.

The only other non-police witness whose testimony was taken at the inquest was Dr McEachran, whose presence before the coroner was primarily required as the doctor who had attended the dying woman, rather than as a source for Evelyn's own account of the evening. McEachran was a particularly vague and unreliable witness when it came to recalling what Evelyn had said, so the fact that his version of this 'conversation' was among the few that entered the public domain is particularly unfortunate; indeed, he admitted in his witness statement that his recollection of the question and answer session 'is very hazy'.

Although Evelyn was never taken through events in any particular order, in attempting to summarise what emerged it is best to adopt a chronological approach, beginning with what Evelyn had to say regarding the initial encounter with the alleged attacker at Elishaw Road Ends.

Mrs Foster remembered that her daughter said the man had got out of the car in order to shout or hail her, though others in the room were unsure whether Evelyn said that he had attracted her attention from the roadside or from within the other car. Tracing the car in which the man had travelled to Elishaw was liable to be extremely important in the subsequent investigation, so it is quite astonishing that in spite of the star witness being an experienced driver who was passionately interested in cars, there is nothing to suggest that anyone thought to ask Evelyn whether she had noticed the make, colour or model of this mysterious vehicle.

Mrs Foster and the others took a similar lack of interest in the occupants of the car, and again there is no evidence that Evelyn was asked if she could describe them. Even the exact number of people travelling in the car was open to doubt, though there must have been at least two of them in addition to Evelyn's alleged attacker, because Nurse Lawson remembered that Evelyn said she heard the man thanking 'the people' for the lift, and her mother says, 'she saw him speak to them', again indicating that more than one person remained in the car after the man had got out of it. Similarly there is universal agreement among the witnesses that one of them was a woman, and though not everyone could recall Evelyn specifying that the woman was driving, the majority felt able to confirm this point. However, in spite of this clear evidence that, so far as Evelyn knew, the attacker had previously travelled with a minimum of one other passenger and a woman driver, confusion quickly arose on the question of how many people had come down with the man from Scotland, and this same confusion has surrounded the question ever since.

It was agreed by the witnesses to Evelyn's statements that, during the brief initial conversation before the man got into Evelyn's car, he had asked about getting a bus to Newcastle. Either during this same initial conversation, or on the drive between Elishaw and Otterburn, he had explained about missing his bus and having tea in Jedburgh with the people who had offered him a lift. The veracity or otherwise of this tea party would be significant when it came to tracing the man and the occupants of the mystery car. Had they really taken tea in Jedburgh, or was this simply part of a story the man had provided for Evelyn's benefit? At the inquest, Mrs Foster clearly believed that the fact of the man's having had tea with these people was confirmed by Evelyn saying that she had overheard him thanking them for tea before he got into her car. Nurse Lawson, however, thought that Evelyn said she had heard him thanking them for the lift. To confuse matters further, in an earlier police statement Mrs Foster had said that Evelyn told her she had not been able to hear the man's parting conversation with the people in the car, and this is supported by the recollections of Sgt Shanks.

At least Evelyn was asked to describe the man who had attacked her. She said that she had not initially taken much notice of him. He had been very respectable looking, wearing a dark-coloured overcoat of black or blue, and a bowler hat. He was dark haired, clean shaven and between 5ft 6in to 5ft 8in tall. She had not seen the colour of his eyes. Her description of his speech is remembered differently by different witnesses. Dr McEachran claims that Evelyn said he was neither Scotch nor Tyneside, 'but was a plausible spoken man'. Mrs Foster thought Evelyn had said that the man had a north country accent, but not as broad as Tyneside.

When they arrived outside The Kennels, Evelyn said the man had got out of the car and walked down the street in the direction of the inn. She had briefly gone into the house, then gone out and refuelled the car, popped back inside to check the fare, then driven through the village and found the man waiting for her at the bridge. He had got into the car and she had driven south, getting as far as Belsay.

This initial stage of the journey appears to have been uneventful. The man sat alongside her in the front of the car and Evelyn was adamant that he had done nothing at all to make her uneasy or suspicious. When asked whether he was drunk, Evelyn responded that he was not drunk, but he had smelled of drink. (It is possible that she did not notice the smell of drink until the man forced himself into much closer proximity, as an initial smell of drink might well have made her more suspicious of him, and less inclined to describe him as 'very respectable and gentlemanly' when her mother first asked about him.) While she drove south he had smoked several cigarettes and there had been some limited conversation. Mrs Foster asked what they had talked about and Evelyn said 'nothing much'. They had talked a little about cars and driving. According to some of the witnesses, the man had said that he did not know the surrounding countryside, but he knew the Midlands. In Mrs Foster's version, the man said he did not know Newcastle, as he came from the Midlands – this was an important difference, but it is impossible to decide which witnesses were correct on the point.

Evelyn was adamant that it was only when the car reached Belsay that events had taken a worrying turn. Again, it is unclear from the various witnesses whether Evelyn suggested that the trouble began during some preliminary conversation, in which the man said that he wanted to drive the car himself, or whether problems began with him abruptly announcing that he wanted to turn back. When Evelyn asked why he wanted to turn back, he responded that it had nothing to do with her. (Nurse Lawson recalled the words as, 'It is no business of yours.') The man also said something about there being no bus there, at which Evelyn had attempted to explain that the bus would not be at Belsay but at Ponteland. Shanks recalled that Evelyn said she had asked why he wanted to turn back when they had come so far, and protested that in taking the road back towards Otterburn they would be going on 'the road to no place'.

While it is evident from all this that a disagreement had broken out between passenger and driver in or near to Belsay, it is far from clear at precisely what point the car actually turned around, or even who was at the wheel at the time. Some of the witnesses appeared to understand that Evelyn had already gone through the village, others that this occurred in the village itself. Similarly, some of their accounts read as if Evelyn was in the process of turning the car when her passenger grabbed the wheel, others that he grabbed the wheel in order to turn the car himself.

Confronted with this alarming turn of events, Evelyn said she had protested, saying, 'Oh no, I will do the driving,' but the man slid across the seat, took control of the car, and he drove from then onwards. There is a suggestion from some witnesses that Evelyn claimed that the man had struck her in the face prior to seizing control of the car, but thanks to the random order of Mrs Foster's questions, this is far from certain. By the inquest, Mrs Foster certainly believed that the man had hit her daughter in the eye just before grabbing the wheel, and that as a result Evelyn's eye was painful and 'felt as if it had some sand in it'. During the earlier part of their journey, the man had mentioned to Evelyn that he had a car of his own, and now, as they headed back north, he commented, 'I think I will go and get my own car.'

Mrs Foster asked her daughter why she had not got out of the car in Belsay and solicited help, or telephoned her father from the call box in the village. Evelyn, who was probably fed up with questions implying criticism of the way she had handled – or failed to handle – the situation, replied, 'Well, Mother, I couldn't,' with several witnesses noting that she spoke sharply and with emphasis, as if her mother didn't understand the position she had found herself in.

Later in the conversation, Evelyn explained that she had become afraid of the man and had feared that if she attempted to take back control of the car, there could be an accident. Logical as this may have seemed, Mrs Foster was evidently not satisfied with Evelyn's contention that she could not simply stop the car and obtain assistance in Belsay and she continued to press her daughter as to why she had not attempted to get some help. Evelyn responded that she had not seen anyone to whom she could have shouted or signalled, or any cars from whom she could have solicited help.

At some point, Evelyn was asked whether she was sure she had gone as far as Belsay. There is no evidence as to who initiated this particular query, but to ask this of someone who knew the road as well as Evelyn was little more than a thinly veiled suggestion that she was being less than truthful, and again you might wonder at the thinking behind this process. Evelyn replied firmly that she had definitely gone that far. There appears to have been a similar reluctance to accept that she did not know her attacker. Nurse Lawson recalled her being asked this same question several times, with Evelyn at one point responding emphatically that she 'did not know him from Adam'. When the two policemen had left the room, Dorothy, whispering low so that she thought no one else could hear, again asked her sister if she knew the man, to which Evelyn replied, 'No, Dot. Do you think I would lie here and suffer if I did?'

When asked if she had seen any cars she recognised on the road, Evelyn replied that she had seen none on the drive north from Belsay to Wolf's Nick, but while driving south she had passed two cars she thought she knew, one of which belonged to Mr Kirsopp-Reed, a local farmer.

Strangely, no one appears to have thought to ask her to whom she thought the other car belonged.

According to Evelyn, the man had eventually brought the car to a standstill on the top of the hill at Wolf's Nick. There is nothing in anyone's statement that helps us to understand how Evelyn's assailant managed to drive the car a distance of almost 11 miles with her presumably crushed against the driver's door. No one appears to have asked her who was operating the pedals, or interrogated her in any way about the practicalities of this arrangement, though she was asked whether she believed the man could drive, to which she responded, 'He could drive all right, though he was not as fast as me,' which tends to suggest that the man had control of the pedals as well as the steering.

Once they were stationary the man had offered her a cigarette, but Evelyn declined – she was a non-smoker. (Mrs Foster would say at the inquest that he 'ordered' Evelyn to have a cigarette, but this is not the way any of the other witnesses originally perceived it.) He then said, 'Well you are an independent young woman,' and began pinching (or nipping as it was known in the north) her arms. At this point there is a further element of confusion. In all the witness accounts bar one, this initial activity appears to have been followed by a sustained attack, which culminated in the man hitting Evelyn, and 'knocking her into the back of the car'. This particular element in the story is among those that have helped to cast doubt as to what actually happened. At 5ft tall, Evelyn was not a large woman, but even so it is difficult to imagine how anyone could hit her in such a way that she was knocked from a sitting position in the front seat and ended up in the rear passenger compartment.

In focusing on the problems presented by this acrobatic feat, investigators then and later have sometimes failed to apply common sense. As has already been pointed out, a chronological account of Evelyn's ordeal had to be pieced together from the answers Evelyn gave to questions asked in a random order. No attempt was made to clarify a whole variety of unsatisfactory issues arising from these answers, and this resulted in queries and doubts arising over matters that Evelyn could probably have clarified in a sentence had she only been given the opportunity.

In order to make sense of how Evelyn finished up in the back seat of the car, it is worth considering the situation as she herself presented it. She was in a stationary car, being assaulted by a strange man, who had already hit her at least once and of whom she had good reason to be afraid. The natural instinct of most women in such a situation would be to get out of the car, thereby putting as much distance as possible between themselves and their assailant. At this point, it is vital to refer to the testimony of Mrs Adeline Jennings. Having said that Evelyn was frightened, Mrs Jennings' statement reads: 'She thought she would get out of the car and he struck her again and bundled her into the back of the car.'

The stop at Wolf's Nick afforded Evelyn her first real opportunity to get out of the car, but on following this instinct, she would probably then have hesitated alongside the vehicle, realising that there was nowhere for her to get help and that if she attempted to run, the man would soon outpace her.

The most obvious scenario is that the man followed her out of the car, resumed his attack, opened the offside rear door, then bundled her into the back seat, and Mrs Jennings' choice of words implied that this is how she saw the situation unfolding. When questioned at the inquest, Mrs Foster admitted that no one had asked Evelyn exactly how she got into the back of the car, but Mrs Jennings' interpretation is surely the most logical and it is not hard to believe that it is the correct one.

For several generations of parents in the twentieth century, the information that their daughter had been alone with a man in the back of a car conjured an instant suggestion of inappropriate sexual activity. Mrs Foster was no exception. When Evelyn said that she had been knocked into the back of a car, rather than asking precisely how this had happened, Mrs Foster immediately asked what had happened next, and when Evelyn hesitated she pressed the point, asking: 'Did he interfere with you?'

Evelyn replied, 'Yes, Mother,' at which Mrs Foster, on her own admission, cried out, 'Oh my God.' Dr Miller reported that Mrs Foster was 'very upset and pulled her own hair'. Whatever the precise details of Mrs Foster's anguished reaction, poor Evelyn seems to have felt obliged to defend herself and immediately added, 'Oh Mother, I couldn't help it. I fought for my life.'

Mrs Foster's euphemism for sexual assault, coupled

with her hysterical reaction to her daughter's response were to prove disastrous for the enquiry. Presumably realising the importance of clarifying this aspect of the attack, Sgt Shanks said he was not quite sure what Evelyn meant and asked Mrs Foster to try to get more information. Unfortunately Mrs Foster's next question was even more ambiguous than the first, for she asked Evelyn, 'Did he do anything to you?'

Evelyn's response to this again suggests that the need to defend herself against her mother's accusatory tone was overriding the need to establish precisely what had taken place. Instead of explaining what the man had done to her, Evelyn merely said, 'Yes he did, but you see I could not stop him. I did my best.'

It is possible that Shanks was aware of how inappropriate it was to question a potential rape victim in front of an assortment of relatives and neighbours, and perhaps also that Mrs Foster's involvement in this process was achieving nothing but distress for the witness. Perhaps he hoped that by the next day the police would be able to gain some control over the interviewing process and keep the young woman's mother out of it. Whatever his thinking, Shanks pursued the matter no further, and nothing was done to clarify in what way the man had 'interfered' with Evelyn. With hindsight we can see that this was a key moment at which someone – Shanks or McEachran – needed to tackle the Mrs Foster problem. Evelyn's reluctance to answer some of her mother's questions, and her particular hesitation when asked what had taken place in the back of the car, were mentioned by most of the other witnesses, but unfortunately neither the doctors, nor the policemen, were prepared to tackle the girl's mother or find a way of removing her from the room.

After the attack in the rear of the car, the exact nature of which was uncertain, the story reached another critical, but hopelessly confused period: the point at which the car and Evelyn herself came to be on fire. According to everyone present, Evelyn said that the man had taken something from his pocket – either a bottle or a tin – and thrown it over her. She thought he had then set her alight, although she did not know how, because she remembered nothing more until she felt the car 'bump bumping'. When Mrs Foster asked what she meant by that, Evelyn told her it was as if the car was bumping over rough ground, and that this had roused her. She had found herself alight, somehow managed to get out of the car, tossed off her burning coat, then attempted to put out the flames engulfing the remainder of her clothing.

Mrs Jennings added the information that when she found herself alight in the car, Evelyn felt as if she was choking. PC Ferguson also recalled that Evelyn said she was 'choking with fumes' as she got out. Dorothy remembered that Evelyn said she had had an awful job getting the door open and nearly suffocated.

Evelyn told them that after she had completely extinguished her burning clothes, she had lain alongside the car for a long time, becoming so thirsty that she had sucked the frozen grass. While she was lying on the ground and the car was still burning, she heard what she thought was the petrol tank exploding. At some point (witnesses were divided as to whether this was soon after she escaped from the car, or some time afterwards) she had heard whistling and screeching as a car pulled up, but though Evelyn had tried to call out and attempted to crawl towards the road, no one came to help her. She then heard the car drive away but she could not tell in which direction it came or went.

Eventually after 'a very long time' she had seen the bus on the road and tried to creep across the moor towards it, and this was when she had been found and brought home by Johnstone and Rutherford.

CHAPTER 7

The formation of modern police forces in England and Wales had been a piecemeal affair that began several years before Victoria arrived on the throne and continued on an ad hoc basis for the next 40 years. By the mid-1850s, a government survey established that one third of counties in England and Wales were still without a police force, and set out to remedy this by passing the 1856 County and Borough Police Act, which made the provision of a police force compulsory. Northumberland, one of the largest, least populated regions, was among the last to acquire a county police force, setting one up at the last possible moment in 1857. (Newcastle-upon-Tyne had by that time been enjoying the benefits of its own city police force for more than 20 years and this continued to operate as a separate entity.)

Victorian police forces were a very different proposition to their twentieth-century counterparts. County forces were predominantly made up of isolated police constables, whose job it was to patrol their local beat (usually the village where they were stationed), keeping a friendly eye on their 'patch'. Their function was primarily preventative and the majority had no resources for undertaking the pursuit or detection of criminals and no trained detectives on whom to call for assistance.

Initially, the British police force was such a new idea that there was no recruiting ground from which to draw officers who could combine experience of policing with organisational skills, so senior officers, in particular chief constables, were drawn from among retired army officers. By the end of the Edwardian era, many forces had begun to modernise, improving their training programmes, initiating detective branches and acquiring cars and telephones, with some even appointing experienced policemen to head their operation rather than upper-class figureheads, but the pace of modernisation varied greatly from one area to another.

Northumberland lagged well behind. In 1899 Captain M.L. Sant, ex-Northumberland Fusiliers, left his position as chief constable of Northumberland to become chief constable of Surrey, and he was replaced by Captain Fullarton James, another retired army officer from an aristocratic background. Sant was a mere stripling of 36 when he went to Surrey and the county decided to put its trust in another comparatively young officer. Like many flawed initiatives, it must have seemed like a good idea at the time.

Fullarton James was 35 in 1899 and had previously spent three years as chief constable of Radnorshire. He combined experience of running a rural police force with service as an officer in the British army. The worthies of Northumberland may have imagined that in Captain James they were getting a bright young man with an excellent pedigree to take their law-enforcement service into the new century. If so, they could hardly have been further from the mark. Under the command of Fullarton James – unusually for the period, he tended to be known by his full name, using it as if it was a double-barrelled surname – the Northumberland County Police stagnated, remaining one of the most backward and least fit for purpose in the country. By the time Captain James retired from the position of chief constable at the age of 70, he had been occupying the role for more than half his life, during which time he had made next to no changes.

In 1931, the only Northumberland police officer who had regular access to a motor car was the chief constable himself. A handful of officers had motorbikes, while the remainder made do with pushbikes or coped with their duties on foot. PC Proud only reached Otterburn on the night of the attack on Evelyn Foster because he was able to beg a ride from Bellingham in Dr Miller's car, while Inspector Russell noted in his report[1] that he had to knock up a local hire car driver in order to reach Otterburn early the next morning. It was fortunate that PC Ferguson's office at Otterburn was equipped with a telephone, because even this was not standard.

To make matters worse, Northumberland had no specialist detectives within its ranks. Serious cases were directly overseen by the chief constable himself, a task for which his aptitude was debatable. The Evelyn Foster files suggest that many of the officers under Fullarton James's command were diligent and hardworking, but they lacked the proper resources to respond to any major emergency and moreover it is clear from the progress of the enquiry that any officer attempting to demonstrate intelligence or initiative was likely to be stifled under the autocratic approach adopted by the man in command. By January 1931 Captain James had been awarded the OBE, CBE and King's Police Medal, apparently for no better reason than that he had been in his post for an exceptionally long period. He was in line to inherit his brother's baronetcy, and appears to have been possessed of considerable belief in his own infallibility. He was by then approaching his sixty-seventh birthday and in the context of 1930s policing was a dinosaur. It would therefore be a considerable understatement to say that the officers charged with investigating the attack on Evelyn Foster were working under a number of significant disadvantages.

As we've seen, the creaking structure that was then the Northumberland Constabulary swung into action as soon as Mr Foster made his initial call to the village police office. Having taken the call, PC Ferguson telephoned his immediate superior Sergeant Shanks in Bellingham. Ferguson then got dressed, walked down to Fosters' premises and obtained as much information as he could from the various people there, including the Foster menfolk, after which he returned to his police office and reported to Superintendent Thomas Shell at around 11.45 p.m. Joseph Foster appears to have become exasperated by the fact that Ferguson returned home to make this call on his own phone when there was one available at The Kennels, but Ferguson had perfectly good reason for following procedure and undertaking his calls where witnesses and onlookers could not overhear. In addition, it is difficult to accuse Ferguson of wasting time, since the biggest hold-up was the police's inability to follow up the most urgent avenue of enquiry – interviewing the victim – because she was still undergoing the attentions of the doctors.

Superintendent Shell ordered Ferguson to obtain a statement from Evelyn as soon as possible and then to proceed to Wolf's Nick with as many officers as were available to instigate a search for the man.[2] In the meantime, Shell also began to spread word of the attack, telephoning not only Northumberland Police Headquarters in Morpeth, but also those in Carlisle, Gosforth and Jedburgh, notifying neighbouring forces that a serious incident had occurred and passing on what little information he then had available. The chief constable himself was made aware at 1.20 a.m. that a serious situation was unfolding.

At 1.45 that morning, motorcycle patrols were sent out from Morpeth and Gosforth to cover the main roads and enquire at all garages, and officers were sent to investigate in Ponteland. It is easy to criticise Shell for not undertaking a large-scale search sooner, but we need to bear in mind that he would have been awaiting some more definite information regarding the attacker before sending officers out. In pre-radio days, once officers were sent out, contact with them would be lost and any potentially important information would not then be available to them for several more hours. Once Shell had the best information he was likely to get that night, he began to spread the net. By 2.15, the police forces covering North Yorkshire and County Durham had also been informed of the ongoing manhunt.[3]

Even as Constable Ferguson and Sergeant Shanks were waiting to question Evelyn, Gordon Foster began preparing one of the firm's cars to drive up to Wolf's Nick. This activity was observed by PC Proud, who seems to have persuaded Gordon to wait for the officers who were still in the house, explaining that the police would need to beg a lift as they had no transport of their own. While they were waiting to leave, Proud kept watch on the road and noted that no vehicles passed by in either direction.[4]

When Shanks and Ferguson emerged from the house they joined PC Proud and two of Joseph Foster's employees, Cecil Johnstone and Tommy Vasey, for the journey to Wolf's Nick. On arrival, Johnstone pointed out the car and showed the others the route that he and Tommy Rutherford had taken to get to it from the road. The five men then followed this same line in order to avoid creating any tracks. Today, anyone familiar with twenty-first century crime scene procedures will perhaps be astonished that the men made any approach to the car at all, but forensics were still in their infancy in 1931 and even this degree of awareness was not always displayed by police constables of the era.[5]

Once the men reached the car it seems that any crime-scene protocols were temporarily forgotten. According to Proud's subsequent report and statement, he and the other men walked around the car, and he himself picked up and replaced a piece of charred cloth he had noticed lying about 18 inches from the nearside wheels. However, on seeing one of the other men repeat this action, he advised everyone to leave things as they were and would later claim that he did not notice any of the men actually touching the car itself. While looking around the outside of the vehicle, Proud noted that the luggage box previously at the back of the car had been completely destroyed by the fire. However, the metal shelf that supported the box was still in place and on this shelf was a petrol tin. Proud said that when he first noticed the tin, it was lying on its side and that he did not see the cap, which he assumed was missing.

PC Ferguson discovered an empty glass bottle not far from the rear of the car, which smelled of lime juice. Mindful that Evelyn had said the assailant had thrown something over her from a bottle, Ferguson immediately took charge of the object. Proud discovered a woman's purse lying about a yard from the rear wheel, burned in such a way that a ten shilling note was now protruding from it and he handed it over to PC Ferguson. The purse was later found to contain £1 9s 6d.

Vasey drove back to Otterburn, pausing en route to allow the policemen to check at roadside farmhouses, rousing occupants to ascertain whether they had seen or heard anything unusual, as well as checking barns and outbuildings for anyone hiding inside, but this provided nothing immediately helpful. They saw no cars or pedestrians at all during their excursion.

When subsequently questioned, the men involved in this initial visit to the crime scene did not always agree about which of them had seen and touched what, and it is unclear whether anyone made any notes at the time. Proud later recorded that when they first reached the scene, both the offside doors of the car were open and both the nearside doors were closed. Ferguson and Shanks agreed with him. Ferguson also recollected the need to caution his companions regarding the potential contamination of evidence, recording that when he heard Tommy Vasey commenting that the car was in gear, he at once warned him not to touch anything. In spite of this, Vasey's statement includes the information that he lifted the bonnet and found that the engine had been virtually undamaged by the fire.

Cecil Johnstone was always absolutely clear that when he and Rutherford initially reached the car, both offside doors were open, and that this was still the situation when he returned after midnight with the police officers and Vasey, but by the time they came to leave the scene, someone – he said he did not know who – had opened the front nearside door. It is quite possible that the culprit was Vasey, given that he clearly took a particularly close interest in the car – and equally possible that Ferguson and Johnstone, both fellow residents of Otterburn, maintained a discreet silence on the matter. Though much has subsequently been made of the way in which the four car doors were variously seen to be open and closed at different points in the hours that followed, the position of the doors in the immediate aftermath of the attack – offside doors both open, nearside both closed – was never really in dispute.[6]

Among the various criticisms levelled at the police was their failure to secure the crime scene at this point. Nothing in the surviving documents suggests that keeping guard over the car was discussed during this first visit in the early hours of Wednesday morning, but even if the matter had come under consideration, there were practical difficulties, since any officer appointed to the task would have been effectively stranded out on the moor, with no means of communication available to him.

Essentially, a chronic lack of resources and training were already compromising the enquiry. In those crucial first six hours, the only policemen on the scene were a sergeant from the nearest small town and two village constables, one of whom had arrived there almost by accident. But all this was about to change.

CHAPTER 8

It seems to have taken some time to occur to the man commanding operations from afar that reinforcements would be needed on the ground. It wasn't until some time between 3 and 4 a.m. that Inspector Edward Russell, who was stationed at Prudhoe, was notified of the attack by telephone and instructed to take charge of the enquiry. Russell's first priorities were to secure the crime scene and procure a proper statement from Evelyn Foster.[1]

On his way to Otterburn, Russell made a minor diversion to call on PC William Turnbull, who was based at Ridsdale, requesting that he go and take charge of the crime scene. Turnbull rode to Wolf's Nick on his motorbike, arriving at around 6.30. It was still dark and there was no one about. Turnbull did not approach the car, reasoning that he did not want to contaminate the site by leaving any footprints. He remained out on the moor until relieved of his duty some seven-and-a-half hours later, allowing no one other than his fellow officers to approach the burned-out car.[2]

Unfortunately, Turnbull's conscientious guard duties began too late to prevent at least one further party gaining access to the site. On 9 January the police received a phone call at their Hexham office from Jack Jerome, a reporter from the North Mail. Jerome had driven out to Wolf's Nick, arriving there a good hour before PC Turnbull. Mr Jerome had no scruples about mooching around and handling anything that caught his attention, including Evelyn Foster's scarf, which he found on the ground, picked up and handed to his driver to have a look at before the latter left it draped across one of the headlamps. Mr Jerome disingenuously excused the fact that he had been tampering with evidence and might have left his footprints at the crime scene by saying that he 'did not know there had been a murder'.[3] At that point there had not technically been a murder, because Evelyn Foster was still alive. There had, however, been a serious assault and there can be little doubt that the reporter had driven out to the spot in full knowledge of this, hoping to obtain a scoop. Mr Jerome had received his information direct from police headquarters who noted in their log that they notified the Newcastle newspapers of the crime at around 4.30 a.m. Presumably it never occurred to the officer responsible that the crime scene had been left unguarded, or that a newspaperman had the means to get there faster than the police themselves.

[4] Inspector Russell arrived at Foster's Garage at a few minutes after 6 a.m., intending to take a statement from Evelyn immediately, but when he asked to see her he was told that she was unconscious. He telephoned this information back to Supt Shell at Hexham, explaining that the Fosters were expecting the doctor to return at around nine and that in the meantime he would go up to the

Redesdale Arms to make some enquiries. After visiting the inn, he returned to Foster's Garage at about 8.45 and Joseph Foster informed him that Evelyn had died without regaining consciousness.

Russell immediately phoned this information through to his superior, coupling it with the news that several more of the witnesses he wished to interview urgently, including Johnstone, Rutherford and another Foster's driver, John Robson, who was said to have seen Evelyn's car on the road the night before, had been sent out on their usual shifts and were not due back for several hours.[5] To say that things were not going well for Russell is something of an understatement, and the situation was about to worsen because, as the series of telephone messages in the police files make clear, Russell quickly found himself reporting direct to the chief constable, who had taken personal charge of the investigation. Captain Fullarton James's first directive to Russell was that he should travel down to Wolf's Nick in order to view the crime scene, but it would be another couple of hours before he thought to issue another order that one sergeant and four constables from any division that could spare them should be sent to assist Russell in Otterburn. The number of officers dispatched would prove wholly insufficient for the task.[6]

By six that morning, sightings of strange cars and men in bowler hats were already starting to come in and it was this that had initially directed Russell's attention north to the Redesdale Arms. It transpired that Alfred Anderson, who kept the garage in Rochester, had been outside getting a pail of water at around six the previous evening, when what he described as an Essex car with a TN registration number had pulled up to ask if there was an inn nearby. (TN was the registration number for Tyneside, so the overwhelming majority of cars in the area shared this combination.) Anderson told the driver there was one in about a mile, very noticeable because of the sign 'the first hotel in England'. The driver, who spoke in Northumbrian dialect according to Anderson, but had a Scottish accent according to other witnesses, said 'that's a good job' and drove away. Anderson had noticed that the motorist had two other men in the car with him.[7]

Benjamin Prior, the licensee of the Redesdale Arms, recalled these travellers clearly. On arrival, the driver had ordered whiskies for himself and his passengers, but there had been little conversation, Prior said, except that they had all expressed pleasure at having found an inn. They had appeared in reasonable spirits and the shortest of the three men had sung a song. The landlord evidently had not liked the look of the two passengers, however, and when the party was leaving, he had taken the driver to one side and asked if he had picked them up on the road. On hearing that he had, Prior had cautioned the stranger to 'be careful in these times, as this is a very quiet road'. The man had seemed unperturbed and replied that he would soon kick them out if they gave any trouble, at which point Prior formed the impression.[8]

Prior and some of his customers from the previous evening gave the police detailed descriptions of the three men, none of whom it has to be said was wearing a bowler hat, or appeared to be a 'bit of a knut'. More significantly, the party appeared to have left the Redesdale Arms at roughly the correct time to have been passing Elishaw when the man who hailed Evelyn was dropped off, which made them potentially important witnesses, but hardly placed them well up the list of suspects. In spite of this, the trio of whisky drinkers received disproportionate amounts of interest during the initial hours of the enquiry. As well as Inspector Russell's early morning visit, Prior would receive several more visits from the police, including an interview with the chief constable himself.

It was thanks to information received at the inn that the investigation latched on to 19-year-old Cuthbert Stappard as a possible suspect. Prior told the police that he believed Stappard had slept rough somewhere on the Ottercops the night before. Inspector Russell apprehended Stappard at around midday, while he was still walking along the road near Rochester.[9]

Cuthbert Stappard appears to have been a rather tragic character. Unemployment was rife in 1931 and Stappard, who was among the many hundreds of young men seeking work, had managed to obtain a few days' employment with the rector of Elsdon, Reverend Charles Winter. The fact that Stappard describes this work as gardening, and that the dates of his employment were 22 December to 3 January, suggest that the kindly rector was more concerned with ensuring that Stappard passed a reasonably comfortable Christmas than with getting his weeding done. Though this employment had finished on 3 January, Stappard told the inspector that he had continued to stay at the rectory until that morning, 7 January, not leaving until eight o'clock. Russell took Stappard back to Elsdon, where Rev. Winter confirmed his statements.[10]

Stappard's story ended in tragedy. Six months later he was found suspended from a tree in a plantation near Acklington, where he had hanged himself. The newspapers reported that Stappard had been grieving over the loss of his sweetheart, Jessie Crisp, who was at one time in service at Belsay Hall and had died of tuberculosis, but the police took a somewhat different view, dismissing the story of a romance as 'piffle' and including in their private memo on the subject the information that the young man was believed to be 'peculiar'. Letters found on Stappard's body were described at the inquest as of 'a distressing, personal nature' and 'showed that his mind had become unbalanced'.[11] Unbalanced or not, Stappard had a cast-iron alibi for the night of the attack on Evelyn Foster and was swiftly eliminated from the enquiry.

Pursuing Stappard beyond Rochester, then travelling to Elsdon and back, must have occupied a substantial part of Russell's day. In the meantime, Sergeant Robert Shanks had tracked Evelyn's passengers of the previous evening to their respective farmhouses, in order to obtain statements from them. This, too, took several hours. After spending almost eight hours out on the fells guarding the burned-out car, PC Turnbull joined PC Ferguson in the task of taking statements from people in Otterburn itself, while the other constables who had been drafted in presumably dealt with the calls coming in to the tiny village police office, which was already proving entirely inadequate for a major enquiry.[12]

At least one of these officers may well have been exclusively occupied in typing up reports and statements, for although Captain Fullarton James visited the scene of the crime, the Redesdale Arms and Otterburn itself that day, it was his intention to direct operations from his own base in Morpeth, via Supt Shell in Hexham. With both men based well away from the centre of the investigation, it was necessary to retype, in at least quadruplicate, every single piece of information. This was an arduous task, made considerably worse by the chief constable's penchant for issuing memos to all and sundry, as well as marking copy statements with interminable – and often pointless – questions, all of which required a reply. Up to nine carbon copies of some documents still exist in the case archives. By the end of the first day the investigation was already awash with paperwork, and this would grow to such volumes in the days to come, that it would submerge important leads and all but drown the men attempting to pursue the enquiry.

The situation was exacerbated by the obvious truth that the man in charge had no idea how to order or analyse all the information his men were accumulating. At least twice during the investigation, an unknown police officer attempted to compile an alphabetical index of witnesses from whom statements had been taken, but neither of these projects managed to include the name of every witness, and the information contained in all those statements was never formally cross-referenced. That the enquiry progressed as far as it did is undoubtedly to the credit of Inspector Edward Russell and the tiny group of officers under his command, but they were overstretched, under resourced and continually hampered by the dead weight of the donkey who imagined he was leading the team.

In line with normal procedure in the case of sudden death, the police had notified Mr Philip Dodds, the local coroner, who telephoned police headquarters later that day to say that he would open the inquest the next day, on Thursday 8 January, and would require a jury of eight local men. Dodds also suggested that, if they had not already done so, the police should arrange for both the local doctor and a pathologist to undertake a post-mortem.[13] At this time it was not unusual for a local doctor to take sole charge at a post-mortem, particularly in cases of accidental death,[14] however by 2.30 that afternoon, Dr McEachran had already informed the coroner that Evelyn's body was so badly burned that he would be unable to determine whether or not she had been 'outraged', and this made it essential to obtain the services of a specialist in the field of pathology. Fullarton James duly sent a message to Supt Shell, requesting him to make the necessary arrangements.[15]

By 5.40 p.m. the chief constable had also decided that the services of an expert motor engineer would be useful and sent a message instructing Shell to dispatch

PC Francis Sinton to Wolf's Nick the following morning, to show a Mr William Jennings of Newcastle where the vehicle had left the road. Jennings was then to be taken to Otterburn to view what remained of the car, which had by now been taken back to Foster's Garage.

Before the afternoon was out, telephone messages regarding suspicious men were coming in from all over the north of England, with reports of men being detained and required to account for their whereabouts as far afield as Sheffield. Chief constables from neighbouring forces rang to offer assistance, as did the owners of bloodhounds and well-meaning members of the public who had spotted 'suspicious men', many of whom bore no resemblance whatsoever to Evelyn's description of the attacker.[16] The police were also receiving dozens of enquiries from the press and, as well as issuing a formal statement, they decided to take the step of asking for the media's help with the enquiry.

At 4.30 p.m. on 7 January, less than 24 hours after the crime had been committed, the police issued an appeal in the form of a press release.[17] After briefly describing the attack on Evelyn and where it had taken place, the text read:

Will any person who may have been on that road between the hours of 7.30 p.m. and 10 p.m. please communicate with the police at Hexham, or with the Chief Constable at Morpeth. Also will the party who were travelling south from Scotland in a motor car and from which a man whom they gave a lift alighted at Elishaw end, north of Otterburn about 6.30 pm, kindly communicate with the police at Hexham.

Two hours later they sent a further appeal to be broadcast on the BBC radio news. The full text of the appeal was:

At 10.30 pm yesterday a young woman named Foster, driver of a Hackney car, was found badly burned near her car, just off the highway, six miles south of Otterburn in Northumberland, in a very injured condition and she has since died.

Police are anxious to trace a four seater, closed dark coloured car, registration TN followed by four figures, with the last or next to last 2.

The car left the Redesdale Arms near Otterburn at 7.00 pm with three men of the following description:
1. 38 years, 5ft 8in, short dark moustache, very bad teeth, dark hair thin at the front, dark overcoat with broad belt, thin blue striped collar, smartly dressed, Scottish accent.
2. 40 years, 5ft 5in, broad face, prominent cheek bones, very bad teeth, practically none in top jaw, slatey coloured suit, thin blue stripe collar, Scottish accent.
3. 30 years, 5ft 7in, clean shaven, well built, blue overcoat, no hat, Scottish accent.

The men told the manager they were going to London. Any information concerning the car or the men should be communicated to the Chief Constable of Northumberland.

The idea of using a BBC radio broadcast for an appeal

was inspired. It was an approach so innovative that the novelty alone guaranteed headlines in the following day's newspapers, but the positive aspects were diminished by the potentially confusing nature of the two messages being given out. The newspaper appeal focused on a car travelling south from Scotland, which had given a man a lift to a place called Elishaw: a location so obscure as to be unknown beyond the immediate locality, and described as just north of Otterburn – a small village also unfamiliar to most residents of middle and southern England. Even so, there was at least a faint possibility that the woman driver who dropped the man at Elishaw might recognise herself and come forward. However the significance of the man dropped at Elishaw was diluted, if not completely negated, by the radio appeal, which instead of focusing on this man and the vehicle in which he had travelled, provided a specific description of a car travelling to London conveying three men with Scottish accents who had called at a public house, the location of which was again apparently somewhere near Otterburn.

The obvious inference for any member of the public who encountered both messages would be to assume a connection between these two vehicles, and very likely to make the assumption that the same vehicle was being sought in both of them. A woman driver who had dropped a man at the junction of the Newcastle and Hexham roads but was unaware of the location of 'Elishaw end', might well be excused for not recognising herself as the person being sought by the police, who were apparently principally interested in a vehicle carrying three men. Nothing in what Evelyn had said suggested that the car that stopped at Elishaw had contained anyone remotely resembling any of the three men described, or that the car had included a T, an N or a 2 in its registration number. We also know that the actual car in question had not called at the Redesdale Arms and was not travelling to London. As an exercise in locating the vehicle that had dropped the man at Elishaw, the radio appeal was not so much unhelpful as positively counter-productive.

CHAPTER 9

The radio broadcast and press release confusion is an early example of Fullarton James's muddled thinking. The chief constable seemingly never grasped the fact that his most important witness was Evelyn Foster. By the afternoon of the press release, he already had her evidence to hand, and it does not take a great leap of deduction to see that the car containing the three men cannot possibly have been as important to the enquiry as the car that stopped at Elishaw.

In theory, Captain James was the mainstay holding the entire investigation together, as he read a copy of every single statement. His notes and queries survive, but they frequently reveal that his personal involvement was considerably more of a hindrance than a help. Sometimes he could have answered his own questions simply by taking the trouble to properly read the statement in front of him. It fell to one of his officers (often the beleaguered Russell) to respond to all his myriad queries as tactfully as possible – thereby wasting yet more valuable time which could have been employed following up possible leads. What rejoinder might the investigating officers have been tempted to make, when they received a copy of Mrs Murray's statement, on which their boss had written:

'Can the garage man at Redesdale not recall the car of Miss Evelyn Foster? If he can, what car was she in? Was she alone? What time was it?'[1] Alfred Anderson, 'the garage man', had already made a statement from which it was clear that he would have been indoors when Evelyn's car drove by and therefore that he did not see her at all. Even if he had observed her, it is hard to imagine what car she could possibly have been in other than the Hudson. It is difficult to read the reams of nonsense penned by Captain James without wondering if his officers were not occasionally tempted to question the man's sanity.

By the end of 7 January, the small team of policemen in Otterburn must have been close to exhaustion. PC Ferguson was still taking statements after ten that night, while Inspector Russell, who had been roused from his bed in the early hours, was similarly occupied until at least 9.45 p.m. During the course of that first day there is no suggestion that anyone was taking the story told by Evelyn Foster at other than face value, but by 9.30 next morning the team in Otterburn received a telephone message from police headquarters instructing them that 'the word which leads the list under classification of crime must not be used'. In other words, someone within the Northumberland Constabulary was already starting to question whether Evelyn had really been murdered.[2]

This element of doubt may have begun with the arrival of Inspector Russell's initial report at police headquarters. During the course of a hectic day, the inspector had been driven out to Wolf's Nick to see the burned-out car, arriving there at about 3.30 in the afternoon. He described what he found in this first report, which eventually formed part of his statement to the coroner's court.[3] According to Russell, tyre tracks showed that the car had crossed from the west to the east side of the main road, where it had gone down a steep embankment about 4ft 6in deep, at an angle of 45 degrees. The tracks then continued across falling ground until they reached a 'marshy' ditch, about 90 feet from the road. At this point the tracks veered to the left and continued for another 108 feet across rough, heather-covered ground. Though Russell's written report implies that the car travelled in a straight line until it reached the ditch, where it made a distinct turn to the left, he concludes by saying that the car 'had travelled in a semi-circular course' and a curved route is what the official police diagram shows.

Russell noted that though the body and rear of the car was completely burned out, the engine, front lamps, front wheels and tyres were little damaged. The rear wheels and spare tyre, which was normally carried on the back, were all destroyed and nothing remained of the wooden luggage box which was normally on the back, except the metal shelf that had supported it. Standing on this shelf (the luggage box platform), Russell observed a two-gallon Shell petrol tin standing upright at the offside end of the platform, which was not the position of the can when it had been seen in the early hours by PC Proud. The neck of the tin (which was made of a different metal to the body and normally attached by solder, which had melted in the heat) was lying about six inches away from the tin, towards the nearside of the car, while the cap was about ten inches away from the tin in the same direction. The cap appeared to have been removed before the fire began and had definitely not been blown or melted off. Russell also noted the metal clips of the luggage box among the debris and a brass funnel used for transferring petrol from tin to tank.

Underneath the car, Russell found the draining cap from the petrol tank, where it had dropped onto the grass after the heat of the fire had melted the solder that normally helped to keep it in place. The grass and heather beneath the car, and for at least a foot behind it were burned, but Russell noted that there were no signs of scorching along the car's route across the moor and concluded from this that 'the car had been burned where it stood'. (A misguided conclusion, since a moving, burning vehicle does not generally set fire to the ground it passes over.)

Russell noticed smears 'like blood' near the handle of the driver's door and on the nearside mudguard, and similar stains on the grass, which he ordered an officer to dig up and preserve. He also collected various other items of burned clothing found mostly on the nearside of the car, including pieces of Evelyn's brown tweed coat, skirt and suspenders. Her brown scarf was still draped over the nearside headlamp. On completion of his own examination, Russell arranged to have the car taken back to Foster's Garage.

At the invitation of the police, William Jennings arrived at Wolf's Nick at 10.30 on Thursday morning. In 1931 it seems that almost anyone could be labelled 'an expert' for the purpose of assisting in police enquiries. Jennings, as the proprietor of a car showroom and garage, was essentially no more of an expert than, say, Gordon Foster, and while Jennings was well qualified to determine how or why a car would not start, he had no practical experience in assisting at a major crime scene, or interpreting the meaning of car tracks. But in common with numerous other 'experts' at the time, this did not deter Mr Jennings from offering his opinions and interpretations with a confidence that implied they were based upon established forensic principles.

Jennings' examination of the site did provide more information, inasmuch that he noticed some large sandstones embedded in the top of the embankment that bore marks from the passage of the car, and was later able to identify corresponding marks on the underside of the vehicle where it had come into contact with the stones.[4] Jennings concluded that the car could not have been travelling at more than 10mph at this point, or else it would have, at the very least, dislodged the stones. Jennings also thought that if the vehicle had hit the stones while travelling any faster, this would probably have caused it to overturn.

He decided that the tracks at the top of the embankment showed that the steering wheel had been in a right-hand lock when the car went over, whereas at the bottom of the slope the car had taken 'an erratic course', with the front wheels making an arc while the back wheels continued in a straight line. The tracks had then merged again, showing that the steering had been righted, and the car continued to the ditch, which Jennings reckoned to be 16 inches deep and half full of water. On entering the ditch the steering had changed to a more definite left lock and the car then continued in a semicircle for another 30 yards, until it halted with the front wheels coming to rest in 'a dry shallow gutter'.

Jennings decided that though the tracks at the bottom of the embankment showed that the car was out of control, the subsequent realignment of the wheels meant that 'the car seems to have been under a certain amount of control'. His idea that someone was still driving when the car left the road was further reinforced by his belief that the Hudson could not have negotiated the water-filled ditch of its own volition, though he did admit that the remainder of the journey had been across comparatively level ground, and that after escaping the water-filled ditch, the car had come to a halt at the first slight obstacle it met. His explanation of this was that at some point between the water-filled and dry ditches, the driver had 'lost interest'.

When he had finished at Wolf's Nick, Jennings went to Otterburn where he examined the car itself. He found that it was still in low gear, with the engine switched on and the handbrake off. This reinforced his theory that someone had driven the car across the moor, because he dismissed out of hand the idea that the car could have made its 108-foot trip with the throttle in idling position and no one at the wheel. Like Russell, he found no signs of burning on the car's route to its final resting place and also concluded that the fire could only have started after the car came to a standstill on the moor.

It seems painfully obvious from Jennings' pronouncements that he had never actually seen a driverless car on the move, with or without its engine running, because not only can vehicles cover considerable distances under their own steam, but while doing so they often take such a certain course that it can appear to the onlooker uncannily as if there is an invisible hand at the wheel. Piecing together the evidence provided by the tracks and the topography, the argument that the Hudson did not have anyone at the wheel during its eccentric journey across the moor actually makes more sense. As the car went over the embankment, striking the stones, its wheels would have been knocked in various directions so that the steering became erratic, but this would have quite quickly corrected itself, so that all four wheels were moving in unison. The vehicle would have gained momentum from the initial descent of the steep embankment, so that it would actually have been gathering speed as it approached the marshy ditch. Here it would have been slowed by the loss of the favourable incline and the mud would have acted against the steering, presumably introducing a greater degree of left-hand lock to the wheels. Even Jennings admitted that the ground between the water-filled and dry ditches was 'comparatively level and would have offered little resistance', but the encounter with the ditch would have slowed the car enough that, by the time it reached the second ditch, it had insufficient momentum to go any further. The very fact that the car's progress had eventually been arrested by a natural feature should have been suggestive, while the idea that a driver had 'lost interest', simply allowing the car to grind to a halt when it just happened to reach this small, natural depression, with its engine still idling and low gear engaged, is patently absurd.

At the garage Jennings made a very thorough investigation of the car, satisfying himself that it was well maintained and that the fire could not have come about by accident. He found the engine remarkably undamaged and this enabled him to check valves, wiring, and carburettor, in order to eliminate any possibility of self-ignition or backfiring. He also noted that the petrol tank was undamaged, with the filler cap still in place, though the solder had melted from the joint which secured the draining tap, so while the tank had not exploded, its contents would have gradually leaked out and helped fuel the blaze. He concluded that the fire had originated in the rear passenger area and had been set deliberately.

Jennings was also invited to consider the evidence accumulated from on and around the luggage-box platform. He noted that the clips which normally secured the luggage box were of the snap-lever type and in the unlocked position, burned in such a way as to suggest that they had been open when the fire began. He similarly concluded that the evidence of burn marks to the Shell petrol tin and its cap showed that the two had been separated before the fire began.

If the conclusions of Russell and Jennings appeared to cast a pall of doubt over the account provided by Evelyn, it deepened further with the news that afternoon from Roxburghshire Police that their officers in Jedburgh had been unable to trace anyone who remembered a group of travellers taking tea, a man asking about a bus to Newcastle or a man trying to arrange a lift south.[5] Nor had the Northumberland men turned up anyone so far who could corroborate Evelyn's story of what occurred once she had dropped Mrs Murray north of Rochester.

The greatest blow, however, would be provided by the post-mortem examination carried out that same day by Professor McDonald. Though the majority of those involved in the investigation would have to wait several weeks for McDonald's official report, it seems likely that one particular aspect of his examination was conveyed verbally to the chief constable. It would have a profound effect on the enquiry.

CHAPTER 10

The story of the attack had been broken on 7 January by the Newcastle morning papers, but it took until the morning editions on 8 January for most of the national and regional dailies to get their teeth into it. Journalists everywhere seemed to work on the basis that, with hard facts so difficult to establish, a level of invention was perfectly legitimate, and a significant number of them included pure fantasy in their reporting.

The Evening Chronicle informed its readers that Evelyn had only just completed her statement when she died and 'just before breathing her last she gave an agonising cry, "I have been murdered. I have been murdered."'[1] The Scotsman was among many of the papers who repeated this tosh, an invention that has been incorporated into the Otterburn legend ever since, but has no basis in fact. Some papers attributed this particular quote to Joseph Foster. The Fosters certainly spoke to the press, as did various other local people, but comparing press reports to police witness statements, it soon becomes evident that a significant level of misunderstanding or embroidery found their way into the published versions of these comments. Miss Annie Carruthers, the Elsdon schoolmistress, for example, was quoted as saying that on the night of the crime she had been cycling through Otterburn when she was stopped on the bridge by a man answering the description of the assailant, who had asked the time of the next Newcastle bus and then become offensive. Yet on the same day she had allegedly fed this tale to a reporter, Miss Carruthers also made a comprehensive statement to the police in which she makes clear that she was walking to her car rather than cycling, that the man who spoke to her did not answer the description of the assailant and that at no stage in their brief conversation did he become offensive.[2]

On the positive side, the newspaper coverage and radio broadcast had generated numerous sightings of the various men sought, some from as far afield as London.[3] Reports of men who had been sighted in places closer to the scene generated the most interest. Police in Newcastle diligently interviewed witnesses who had sold petrol to strangers, noticed suspicious drunks on the late-night buses, or entertained doubts about their bowler-hat wearing neighbours. Many of these 'suspicious men' were successfully tracked down and identified as innocuous door-to-door salesmen or local grooms on legitimate errands (some grooms, particularly those serving upper-class households, favoured bowler hats). As well as these unrelated sightings, the appeals did also generate interest from at least some of the people to whom they were directed.

Alastair Bull, the driver of the car that had stopped at the Redesdale Arms on 6 January, read the story in the paper on 8 January and came forward immediately.[4] Bull's car was a Morris Oxford saloon, registration no TN8692 and he had been driving from Scotland to London on 6 January. Not long after crossing the border into England, Bull had spotted two men walking south along the road and offered them a lift.

Such an action may seem unusual today, but should be viewed in the context of the times. The famously misquoted statement made in 1981 by Conservative MP Norman Tebbit ran, 'I grew up in the 1930s with an unemployed father.... he got on his bike and looked for work.' Tebbit's father was among those fortunate enough to own a bike. Many men simply walked when heading for a definite promise of employment; many more walked desperately hoping to find any kind of work they could. It was known as 'tramping' or being 'on the tramp', and such men attracted widespread sympathy from all sections of society and this often led to spontaneous acts of generosity, such as the giving of lifts or the provision of a meal. A number of people, mostly men, 'on the tramp' came to the attention of the enquiry, none more poignant than the young couple reported by several witnesses as walking south from the direction of Otterburn during the afternoon of 6 January, pushing their baby in a pram.[5]

Bull was a typical Good Samaritan. Having taken the two men into his car, he stopped at the next hostelry along the road to buy a round of drinks and, on dropping them in Newcastle, he gave each of them a shilling. Unfortunately, when it came to assisting the police, apart from effectively eliminating himself and his companions from the investigation, Bull could offer nothing helpful at all.

On the following day his passengers came forward independently, identifying themselves as Thomas Connor, aged 23, and John Reed, 21, both unemployed and 'on the tramp, looking for work'. Like Bull, Connor and Reed could offer nothing of value to the enquiry.[6]

Some newspapers had carried an additional appeal about a car reportedly travelling at high-speed through Otterburn at approximately 9.45 on the night of the attack and this, too, would prove successful within 24 hours, prompting the arrival of car salesman, Walter Beattie, at Hawick Police Station. Beattie said that on 6 January he had collected a second-hand two-seater Morris Cowley from Darlington, which he had driven back to Hawick the same day. During the journey the car's usual number plates were completely obscured by trade plates bearing the registration 031-K.S. Beattie reckoned that he had stopped for tea at Castle Eden at around 6.30, then driven almost non-stop until he reached home at around 10.50. He estimated his speed at around 25–30mph (which was fast in the context of the roads and weather conditions).

When he crested the hill at the point which he was later able to identify as Wolf's Nick, he had been surprised by the sight of smoke and flames on the moor, to the right-hand side of the road, and had slowed practically to a standstill. However, he said that he did not believe his car or brakes had made any particular noise, and was emphatic that he had not whistled. On opening his window to get a better look, Beattie had seen that it was a car on fire, which was 'practically burned out', with 'just some smoke and small flames around the body of the car'. He decided that the car had probably been alight for some time, estimating that it had been burning for about half an hour, though as he pointed out to the police, he was no expert on such matters. As there appeared to be no one nearby, he assumed that the fire had begun accidentally, and that the car's occupants had either been picked up already or else that he would encounter them walking further along the road, but since he saw no one as he drove further north, he concluded that the driver had already been rescued and that he did not need to report the fire. Based on another journey he had made between Hawick and Otterburn, he estimated that he must have passed the car at approximately 9.50.[7]

Another driver who came forward was Thirumalalai Iyengar, an Indian student who had come to Britain to take up a place at the School of Oriental Studies in London. Prior to commencing his course, Mr Iyengar and two companions had been touring the country, and on 6 January the trio were driving south across the Scottish border, planning to spend the night of 6 January in a Newcastle hotel. In line with the casual racism of the era, Captain James invariably referred to this party in his notes as 'the Hindoo car'; Mr Iyengar's vehicle was a maroon Clyno saloon, registration number MH1000.

Of all the witnesses who came forward voluntarily, Mr Iyengar takes the prize for the vaguest. He and his companions knew that they had driven south from Jedburgh, but were far from certain about very much else. Even driving at a cautious 20mph they had got lost at least once. They did recall stopping to consult the map at the thirty-second milestone (which stands near Shittleheugh Farm, just south of Elishaw) at around 7.45 in the evening and eventually reached Newcastle at about 9.30 that night. Iyengar couldn't remember passing through Otterburn at all, and nor could he recall anything about any other cars on the road, except that he believed a large car with very bright headlights had caught up with him south of Rochester and followed him for a while before it turned off to the right – possibly down the Hexham road.[8]

By interviewing numerous other witnesses, the police eventually established that Mr Iyengar's party had followed the left fork south of Otterburn and ended up in Elsdon, where various people had seen the travellers stop to consult the signpost. Iyengar had then taken the lane to Raylees, where he rejoined the main road. Though offering little in the way of information himself, Iyengar did at least account for one of the vehicles seen on the road that night.

Bull, Beattie and Iyengar had all given their statements to forces in other parts of the country. Meanwhile, the enquiry team in Otterburn were steadily accumulating more information from local people who had been out and about on 6 January, but it was a time-consuming business, often entailing a journey of several miles to speak with witnesses in outlying farms and hamlets, amid

ever-worsening winter weather. Aided by some reinforcements from the Newcastle force, the police also undertook
large-scale searches of the surrounding moorland, pro-
cessed the reports arriving every hour from various other
constabularies, and followed up sightings of mystery men
from all parts of the county. In addition to this, several
officers attended the opening of the inquest before Mr
Dodds in the Memorial Hall in Otterburn.

A crush of newspaper reporters had jostled for places,
but there was very little to report because, after taking
formal evidence of identification, Mr Dodds adjourned
proceedings until 2 February, in order to allow time for
further enquiries. Otterburn was by now overrun with
journalists, the case having proved sufficiently intriguing
to draw the big names from the capital, with even the
notorious F.W. Memory of the Daily Mail putting in an
appearance.[9] With little to say about the inquest, the
press devoted pages to largely imaginary interviews with
local residents, which included such fanciful suggestions
as Otterburn's vicar, the Rev. Brierley, having spoken
with Evelyn not long before she died. A host of other
lively inventions were embellished with descriptions of
the 'desolate moorland' and 'ice-bound roads', with every
shepherd described as 'a lonely guardian of the hills'.[10]

Even at this early stage of the investigation, two other
disturbing elements had also entered the press coverage.
By 9 January some papers were already questioning
Evelyn's version of events, with several of them quoting the
opinions of William Jennings, which clearly contradicted

what she had said about the car being pushed, driverless, into the moorland. A further troubling development lay in the open criticism of the police. The Daily Mail in particular had a strong anti-police agenda and, in murder investigations where no immediate arrest was achieved, the London press invariably turned on the local force involved, questioning their competence and querying why they had failed to call in Scotland Yard.[11] While criticism of Captain James was far from misplaced, any expectation that the Evelyn Foster investigation should have been completed in under 48 hours was surely un-realistic, and the tone taken by the newspapers annoyed the chief constable, which alas only served to intensify his autocratic tendencies.

By unfortunate coincidence, a newspaper report had appeared only the day before the alleged attack on Evelyn Foster, claiming that the Home Office intended to create a 'Scotland Yard in the north', which would bring the con-stabularies in Durham and Northumberland under the control of the chief constable of Newcastle-upon-Tyne.[12] Though there appears to have been no substance behind this suggestion, it would have inevitably infuriated the chief constable of Northumberland and its survival as a news clipping in the Foster file means that he was certainly aware of it. If anything was guaranteed to make Fullarton James even more resistant to the idea of soliciting external help, it was surely the threat that his supremacy in the county police force might be usurped by an outsider.

At this stage, however, the greatest difficulty facing the

investigation lay not in the tone of the press coverage, the threats to Northumberland's autonomy or even the nature of the man leading the investigation, but rather that the police had not located a single witness who could support most of the key elements in Evelyn's story.

CHAPTER 11

By 10 January, doubts about Evelyn's version of events were openly expressed in many newspapers. The Scotsman epitomised the line taken by many: '...the girl stated that she had been attacked... it is understood that the post-mortem may reveal that Evelyn Foster sustained few injuries other than burns... apart from the dying girl's statement, police have found no substantial proof that there was a strange man concerned in the affair ...'[1]

Though the remarks regarding the post-mortem were unattributed, there is a troubling sense throughout the enquiry that the press were being briefed off the record, often to the detriment of the actual investigation.

With supreme irony, on the same day that many newspapers were assuring their readers that the police had found nothing to support Evelyn's story, an important witness came forward in Belsay. Though the local policeman, PC Francis Douglas, had been asking around in the village and surrounding area, he had been unable to find anyone who had been within sight of the main road running through the village between eight and nine on the evening of 6 January – until the appearance of Miss Bessie McDonnell.[2]

Miss McDonnell lodged at The Gate House, which was

on the main road at the extreme north end of the village, and she made a statement explaining that at around 7 p.m. on 6 January she had gone to fetch her milk from Mrs Purves, whose shop was next door to the police station at the southern end of Belsay. The trip to the shop seems to have been a social as well as a practical errand, because Bessie estimated that she did not return home until about 8.30. She had seen no one else about as she walked home, but when she had almost reached the house she saw a car approaching along the main road from Otterburn. She noticed that it was a grey saloon, with very shiny door handles. Just after it had gone by, she heard the brakes screech and glanced back to see that the car was pulling up. She took no further notice, but as she opened the door and stepped into the house, she heard the car turning and after she had closed the door, she heard it driving back in the opposite direction.[3]

Here, then, a glimmer of confirmation of one aspect of Evelyn's story. It is evident that at least one of the investigating officers placed considerable importance on Miss McDonnell's statement, because a paper tag was fixed to the top of it, on which someone wrote: 'Bessie McDonnell Belsay heard car turn'.[4]

Though Bessie McDonnell's evidence had taken a mere three days to appear, it was already too late to sway some opinions, because while outwardly going through the motions of exploring all avenues, it is clear that the chief constable had already made up his mind. Fortunately he does not appear to have confided what he knew about the post-mortem to his junior officers (with whom he tended to deal on a need-to-know basis) and they continued to apply the highest levels of dedication to the task in hand.

On 9 January, Superintendent Shell had suggested a further radio broadcast, appealing for the driver of the vehicle that stopped at Elishaw to come forward. He had also sent out amended information to police forces all over the north of England and southern Scotland, explaining that though the Redesdale Arms car had now been traced, the Elishaw car was still sought.[5]

The chief constable evidently gave his agreement to the radio appeal, because on 10 January the BBC aired the following announcement:

With regard to the message broadcast on Wednesday 7 January relative to the occurrence at Otterburn, the motor car then referred to has been discovered. There is still however one important discovery to be made. It is alleged that from a car which was standing at Elishaw Road Ends of Watling Street, two and a half miles north west of Otterburn, at about 7 p.m. on Tuesday 6 January a man who was anxious to get to Newcastle alighted. Any motorist who on that night may have given a lift to a person who alighted at the above place is requested to communicate with the Chief Constable of Northumberland. Telephone no. Morpeth 204.[6]

The author of the message may well have been the chief constable himself. It certainly seems to reflect the style and tone of his communications and it is noticeable that the language chosen introduces an element of doubt – the attack on Evelyn is described as an occurrence while the car at Elishaw Road Ends is now only alleged to have been there. This followed his 8 January order that instructed Northumberland officers to avoid describing the incident as a murder, and when writing to the police in Jedburgh on 9 January, the chief constable headed his letter 'Otterburn Occurrence'.[7]

From the point of view of his junior officers, one of the most inexplicable aspects of the Evelyn Foster case at this stage must have been the chief constable's attitude to it. Anyone reading his notes and memos can be under no illusions that Fullarton James actively doubted the story told by Evelyn Foster and moreover displayed a peculiar hostility toward this young woman he had never met. On 9 January, having read the statements produced so far, he sent a memo to Superintendent Shell posing a series of questions, every one of which demonstrated his reluctance to believe the story Evelyn had told. It was not an objective analytical exercise: some of his queries represent an almost wilful refusal to take on board information provided by the statements to hand, such as his questioning why Evelyn's family had not been alarmed by her failure to return, when, as Margaret Foster and others had made perfectly plain, the family had in fact become increasingly concerned when Evelyn did not return home.

The chief constable also queried whether there were any 'local lovers' unaccounted for, whether she was in the habit of 'taking strange men for rides' into the surrounding countryside and ridiculing the idea that a taxi ride would be undertaken without the driver first having a sight of the passenger's money. Shell responded in sensible, moderate terms, but nothing seemed to divert the pig-headed certainty that gripped the chief constable.[8]

Fullarton James was particularly obsessed with his theory that a solution would be found in Evelyn's love life. Her ex-fiancé, Ernest Primrose, had been among the first to be questioned, but he had spent the evening at the home of his current girlfriend, Miss Ena Scott, and far from being able to shake his alibi, police interviews with Miss Scott, her father and their neighbours in Seahouses, all confirmed that Ernest's motorbike had been parked outside the Scotts' home and that he had been inside throughout the relevant period on 6 January.[9] With the elimination of Primrose, Fullarton James wanted to know with whom Evelyn had been seen at the Christmas Dance held in Otterburn Memorial Hall and, even more fantastically, required his officers to check whether Evelyn had been seen by anyone at a dance held at Thropton Village Hall on the night she died.[10]

Whereas the officers conducting the investigation at ground level were desperately overstretched, their leader gave every impression of a man with time on his hands. He peppered Shell and, through him, Russell with an endless stream of instructions and queries, apparently prompted by whatever notion of the moment happened to seize him, enquiring, for example, on 10 January, whether any films about murders had recently been shown in the district.[11] He was also fond of issuing enigmatic messages, despatching the men under his command hither and yon, much as an autocratic general deploys his troops. An order issued on 11 January is typical: 'Superintendent Spratt to be at this office at 10.30am, in plain clothes, with his car, and a meal in his pocket.' The order in question was issued at 9.43, allowing the unfortunate Spratt barely 45 minutes to receive and fulfil it.[12]

In spite of blasts of negativity from on high, Inspector Russell stuck to his task, though the handicaps he was working under remained considerable. On 9 January, when he sent his daily report to Superintendent Shell, he was still using the tiny police office in Otterburn as his base, while his junior officers conducted interviews in a room at the Percy Arms. As well as working with inadequate premises, he continued to be woefully short of manpower and, after bringing his superior up to date, he 'respectfully' suggested that intensive enquiries should be made along the main Otterburn to Newcastle road, explaining that 'this will employ more officers than I have at my disposal...' He therefore 'beg[ged] to suggest' that more officers be sent to assist him.[13]

While Russell and his tiny band continued to put in long hours, the work that would naturally be needed in a complex investigation was exacerbated by Fullarton James, who made further demands upon the officers' time by requiring that copies of all statements and messages taken the previous day should be on his desk by ten the following morning – a requirement that not only called for a large quantity of typing, but also entailed an officer travelling from Otterburn to Morpeth and back by motorcycle each day.[14]

One minor improvement in Russell's circumstances came about when Mrs Howard Pease, the absentee owner of Otterburn Towers – then a substantial private house on the edge of the village – generously placed the house at the disposal of the enquiry team, who were able to move into these infinitely more spacious premises on 10 January. The police's removal to Otterburn Towers provoked more colourful outpourings from the press. The Sunday Sun described it as 'a romantic, ivy clad' building and added for good measure 'that there was a rumour that the mysterious man had stayed there on the night of the crime'.[15] If there ever was such a rumour, it is reasonable to conjecture that it probably emanated from a journalist.

His men's occupation of Otterburn Towers was the subject of yet more fussing from Fullarton James, who sent several officious memorandums warning them to be careful regarding damage. He was particularly con-cerned about the effect of muddy boots in the hall, and also ordered the removal of a portable oil stove which his men had been using to warm themselves in the kitchen, but which their chief perceived as a fire risk.[16]

The chief constable responded to Russell's appeal for more manpower by sending instructions that sergeants Robson and Burns should proceed to Otterburn on their motorcycles, taking warm clothing as 'they may have to stay there a few days', together with maps of Northumberland 'and their notebooks for taking statements'.[17] It says much about the state of police training and procedure in Northumberland at the time that the sergeants apparently had to be reminded not only to take their notebooks, but also for what purpose. One imagines that Russell, while delighted to see sergeants Robson and Burns, may have been hoping for reinforcements of more than twice this strength.

During these first three or four days of the investigation, the Otterburn team had already made some headway in identifying drivers and vehicles who had been on the road between the Scottish border and Ponteland on 6 January. As well as Bull, Beattie and Iyengar, several other drivers had contacted the police, describing their vehicles and their journeys. Pedestrians and people who lived by the roadside had also offered information. Bus drivers and their conductors, delivery men, lorry drivers, even the vicar of Kirkwhelpington, had come forward to say where and when they had been on the road that night – and this was just the beginning.[18]

Reports also continued to flow in describing encounters with strange men on trains, mysterious men on foot, and suspicious men lurking in places where they had no business to be. The majority came from people who were simply not in the right place at the right time to be of any help. However, apart from the lone witness in Belsay, nothing else had emerged that specifically supported Evelyn's story, and on 10 January the chief constable held a press conference at Otterburn Towers where he stated that Miss Foster's story contained 'discrepancies' and 'improbabilities', and that her credibility rested on whether or not she had suffered 'blows sufficient to reduce her to a coma' – injuries that could not be substantiated by a qualified surgeon. He told assembled reporters that the police were now awaiting the findings of an examination to be carried out by Dr Stuart McDonald, professor of pathology at Newcastle University.[19] The inherent contradiction within these statements is obvious. On the one hand the police appeared to be awaiting the results of the professor's examination, yet on the other they already appeared to be in possession of them.

The purpose of this exercise is difficult to fathom. With their investigation far from complete and within just three-and-a-half days of a serious crime being reported, the chief constable was publicly casting doubt on the victim's story. Yet in a bizarre twist, the second BBC radio appeal was due to be broadcast within a couple of hours and was to be followed up by a similar appeal in the Monday morning papers. It was almost as if, having given consent to the further appeal for the Elishaw car, the chief constable had then deliberately undermined it in advance. As an example of behaviour which was both disrespectful and tasteless, these comments could scarcely have been better timed, for the Otterburn press conference was held less than 24 hours before Evelyn Foster was due to be buried in the village churchyard.

CHAPTER 12

The funeral had been scheduled for Sunday 11 January, as this was the only day of the week on which all Joseph Foster's employees would be free to attend. As Evelyn's brother Gordon put it to the press, 'they have known her for years and worked alongside her as a sister'.[1]

As the Foster family gathered in The Kennels in readiness to follow the coffin on its short journey to the village church, they must have been aware of the buzz of expectant noise in the street outside. Photographs show the village street packed end to end with an estimated crowd of more than a thousand people. It was not just friends, neighbours and family wanting to pay their respects: curiosity had drawn gawpers from miles around, newspaper reporters and photographers were jostling for vantage points and it was claimed (without any justification) that plain-clothed policemen were among the spectators who lined the main street. Somehow, in the face of their shock and grief, Evelyn's family would have to run the gauntlet of this vast crowd, walking behind their daughter's coffin as it was borne into church by eight Fosters' employees, including Cecil Johnstone, who had found Evelyn on the moors, and Tommy Vasey, who had helped to carry her into the house after the bus had brought her home. Within the family circle it is said that with Evelyn's parents and sisters close to collapse, it was Gordon Foster who managed to hold them all together.

Those few yards must have seemed endless. As the little party emerged from the house, they were confronted by a sea of faces stretching out of sight up the village street. Since the church could only accommodate 150 people, the majority of mourners stood in a howling gale with torrential rain, the women bowed beneath dripping hats and scarves, the men bareheaded. The tiny churchyard was carpeted by more than a hundred wreaths. It can only be hoped that the service, conducted by Rev. Brierley, who had known Evelyn for most of her life, brought some comfort. At its conclusion, the coffin was carried back out into the churchyard and Evelyn was laid to rest in a grave alongside the church gate, which, by a quirk of topography, happens to be almost the only point on the village street that is within sight of both The Kennels where she lived, and the bridge beside the Percy Arms, where she claimed to have met her killer.

While the Fosters mourned their loss, the police operations continued apace. At 8.30 on the morning of the funeral, a small team led by Inspector Russell was back at Wolf's Nick, examining the scene and taking samples of heather and grass. Later that day and well into the evening, they continued to locate possible witnesses and take more statements.[2] The chief constable visited Otterburn again and followed this up with another long memo, suggesting among other potentially fruitless notions: that the investigators should ask the Fosters to hand over whatever papers and letters were among Evelyn's possessions and to 'press with vigour' any points of information regarding 'possible lovers'.[3] The only two young men whose names had been associated with Evelyn in recent years, her ex-fiancé Ernest Primrose and her recent 'boyfriend' George Phillipson, had both already been interviewed and were demonstrably innocent of any part in the affair. Moreover, Evelyn herself had been absolutely adamant that she had never set eyes on her attacker before that night. Fullarton James also queried the identity of a man pictured in Evelyn's photograph album, having got the idea into his head that this was a certain John Angel, who had walked out with Evelyn several years earlier.[4]

PC John Eckford, who was perceived as particularly tactful according to Russell's notes, made yet another visit to the Foster family home, where her parents handed over all letters and papers belonging to their daughter. The family were anxious to help, Inspector Russell reported back to Fullarton James, but having read the letters the inspector considered that they threw no light whatever on the mystery. The family had explained that the photograph in the album was not John Angel, but Evelyn's sister's 'young man', John Wright. Angel was no longer resident in the district and none of the family had heard anything of him for some considerable time.[5]

Responding to other matters raised by Fullarton James, Russell added that he had 'taken up the point regarding possible lovers' but offered no further details, presumably because he had no idea how he was supposed to conjure these non-existent suspects out of thin air. Having addressed various other inconsequential issues raised by his boss, Russell concluded by saying that his men were continuing to comb for information and check the reports of cars coming in.

The newspapers continued to be full of the story, but with every reporter looking for a new angle or sensation, the information they contained was confused, fragmentary and often misleading.[6] Those newspapers which had begun to hint that police were questioning the truth of the victim's story, eagerly seized on the garrulous motor engineer, William Jennings, who had considerably undermined Evelyn's credibility by telling anyone who would listen that he believed there had been someone at the wheel of the car when it left the road. Unlike the expansive Mr Jennings, Professor McDonald had refused to be drawn regarding the post-mortem and told the reporters that, 'I have made no statement of any kind, and shall not say anything until the adjourned coroner's inquest.'[7]

An element of hysteria had entered some of the press coverage, with various papers declaring that isolated moorland communities were in terror of their lives, fearing that 'a homicidal maniac' was prowling the district,[8] while the AA and RAC sounded a slightly more reasonable note in warning motorists against offering lifts to strangers. It is possible that some motorists heeded this warning, but just as many presumably ignored it, for hitchhiking was so much accepted as a standard method of getting around the countryside, not only for those on the tramp but for anyone from soldiers to holidaymakers, that as well as simply flagging a vehicle down, there was even a recognised signal, in which a pedestrian hoping for a lift would wear a white handkerchief wrapped around their right arm.[9]

In the meantime, the police in Otterburn continued to trace and interview anyone who had been out and about on the relevant evening, and, among the many witnesses who apparently had little of value to add, the police had managed to trace one pair of workmen who appeared to be the source of some particularly important information. Albert Beach and his mate John Oliver were the drivers of a steamroller that had been working in the locality. In common with many road men who were required to work some distance from home, Beach and Oliver towed a caravan behind their vehicle, which they set up close to wherever they happened to be working, and for the period which included 6 January this happened to be on the Hexham road, between Blakehope Farm and Elishaw Bridge. After work the two men generally had a wash, then walked into Otterburn, picking up any supplies they needed from the village shops and stopping for a pint at the Percy Arms, before returning home for a late supper.

On 9 January, both men made a statement to Sgt Armstrong, stating that on the evening of 6 January they had left the caravan at about 6.45 and walked down towards the Elishaw bridge, at which point they were passed by a car coming down from the junction with the main road. It was a two-seater Morris Cowley and had been travelling very fast. More importantly, Oliver said he thought, but could not be sure, that he had seen a car standing on the main road above the Elishaw junction a moment before this, and that he was certain this car was not the Morris Cowley which had passed them near the bridge.

Beach took a slightly different view. He, too, thought that he might have seen a car standing at the junction, but decided that, if he had, then it was the Morris Cowley. What is in no doubt is the speed of the vehicle, which had been going so fast that the two men remarked on it to one another. Once over the bridge they had taken a shortcut across the field below Elishaw Farm and while doing so they saw a car going along the main road towards Otterburn. After this they had seen no other cars going in any direction until after they reached the village at around 7.30. They had, however, been passed by a motorcyclist travelling north very slowly and met a workman walking in the opposite direction to themselves, whose boots had got covered in some kind of light-coloured substance.[10]

The evidence of Beach and Oliver was of considerable significance. Here were two men who could see the relevant sections of both the main road towards Otterburn and the route said to have been taken by the mystery man's lift during the crucial period when the 'mystery car' must have been on the road, if it existed, and yet the only cars they had definitely seen were a two-seater, which did not fit with the story of a car capable of transporting both the mystery man and the 'people' who had given him a lift, and a saloon proceeding towards Otterburn, which must presumably have belonged to Evelyn Foster herself. Beach stated firmly that, 'If there had been another car, we would have seen it.'

The man seen walking north from the direction of Otterburn by Beach and Oliver turned out to be a local labourer called Robert Towns. Towns made his own statement the following day, explaining that he had been working at Otterburn Hall, and on finishing work at seven had taken a footpath down to the main road, joining it at a point between the village and the school. He had then taken his usual route home, walking north along the main road until he reached the short cut through the field below Elishaw Farm. This brought him on to the Hexham road, where he walked south-west until he reached his home at Brownriggs. Essentially Towns had taken the same route as Beach and Oliver, but was travelling in the opposite direction. He recalled passing the two men, who were strangers to him, at the gateway to Greenchesters Farm.

He also remembered seeing only two vehicles, both of them towards the end of his walk. The first had been a fast-moving car which had overtaken him just after he crossed Elishaw Bridge, and he had seen the second car a couple of minutes later, when he happened to look back across the fields and saw that a car had pulled up on the main Newcastle road, near Shittleheugh Bridge. He noticed that it remained there for two or three minutes before continuing on its way towards Otterburn.[11]

Owing to the similarity between Towns' descriptions and the vehicles seen by Beach and Oliver, there has been a tendency in the ensuing years to conclude that the cars seen by Beach and Oliver were the same ones seen by Towns, but this is not correct, because these coincidentally similar vehicle movements occurred almost an hour apart. By the time Towns saw his speeding car at Elishaw Bridge and his stationary car on the main Newcastle road, the steamroller drivers had already reached Otterburn. Similarly, when Beach and Oliver saw their speeding car at the bridge, Towns had yet to finish work.

Another witness who was on the road that evening was William Blackham, the village schoolmaster. Mr Blackham was another man who was in the habit of following up his day's work with a well-earned pint, and he told the police that on 6 January he had set out to walk into the village from the school house at around 6.40, arriving in the village at roughly 7 p.m. He had seen only one vehicle – a saloon car which had passed him when he was about half way between the school and the village. (The police worked out that this must have been Alastair Bull's vehicle, which had left the Redesdale Arms shortly before this sighting would have occurred.) Blackham had seen no one between the school and the village, but as he approached Foster's Garage at the edge of the village, he saw Tommy Vasey crossing from the main garage to the buildings on the other side of the road and the men had wished each other 'goodnight'. On passing the Co-op, he met George and Edith Maughan, walking the other way, and they too had exchanged a greeting with him. He had then continued to the Percy Arms, where he stayed until a few minutes before ten.[12]

George and Edith Maughan were also interviewed by the police. George worked for the Co-operative Society, but the Maughans also acted as caretakers for the school buildings, Edith cleaning and George taking care of the fires there each evening. On 6 January they had left their house, Redeside, next door to the Co-op in Otterburn's main street, at roughly seven as usual, and set off on foot for the school. They were walking on the same side of the road as the Co-op and The Kennels, and as they passed the Co-op they met the village schoolmaster William Blackham coming the other way and the trio had exchanged a greeting in passing. A few yards further along the street as they were approaching the church gates, they had seen the headlights of a car approaching from the north, and this car had pulled up outside the Fosters' house. No one appeared to get out and Edith said that she was sufficiently blinded by the lights that she could not see who was inside, or even how many people there were. George said that he could see there was a woman driving, who he took to be Evelyn, though he too was dazzled by the lights and told the police, 'I am not prepared to say that anyone was sitting in the front with Evelyn Foster, but there may have been, I could not see.' As they continued along the road they saw Robert Luke, another of

Foster's mechanics, come out of the main garage. Luke called something to them, and they responded without pausing.[13]

Robert Luke confirmed that he had emerged from the big garage just as the Maughans were passing and had called a greeting to them. He had noticed that Evelyn's car was parked in front of the petrol pumps, but took no particular notice of it and was unable to say whether there had been anyone inside or not. The car was already stationery by the time he saw it, Luke said. After crossing the road he had entered one of the small workshops on The Kennels side of the road, and when he emerged a few minutes later with the piece of wire he had gone in search of, the car was still there. He had seen no one other than the Maughans out in the street.[14]

While they were still walking between the church gates and Foster's Garage, the Maughans had seen another man who was walking south, on the opposite side of the road to them, whom they did not recognise. Apart from this individual they had seen no other people or vehicles at all.

The man seen by the Maughans was quickly identified as John Thompson, a labourer, who lived at Garretsheils. He told the police that while he was walking into Otterburn along the main road from the north, a saloon car with bright lights had overtaken him when he was about 100 yards beyond the village school. When he reached the village a few minutes later, he had seen a saloon car parked alongside the petrol pumps outside The Kennels.

As he passed it he had heard a voice, which he believed he recognised as Evelyn Foster's. It was a 'sharp voice', he said. Unfortunately he did not hear what was said, or actually see the speaker or the person she was addressing. After walking another few yards he had noticed what he took to be two young men, walking in the opposite direction to himself, on the other side of the road. When later confronted with the Maughans, Thompson agreed that he had been mistaken about the gender of one of the people he had seen. (Edith Maughan was wearing leggings to keep out the cold and Thompson had described one of these 'young men' as wearing leggings.)[15] The obvious contradiction in the statements of the Maughans and Thompson is something we will return to later.

The small band of officers under Russell's command at Otterburn Towers, continued to work around the clock to obtain statements from everyone who had been moving through the village on the evening of 6 January.[16] They also began a process of returning to key witnesses, to seek further information. For example, Evelyn's passengers, Mary Murray, William Glendinning and Robert Wilson, were all visited afresh. Some witnesses, including members of the Foster family, made three or four different statements, often to different officers, during the course of the enquiry. While it is sometimes essential to go back to witnesses in order to clarify uncertainties, it is also the case that by the third or fourth time of asking, people's memories are in danger of becoming clouded by what they have heard from other sources, leading to inevitable discrepancies.

The investigators were accumulating a massive amount of information which they had scant time or resources to evaluate. As well as dozens of messages arriving from other constabularies, telephone calls containing information about suspicious men, or news of motorists who had been in various parts of Northumberland from dawn until late at night on 6 January, there were the inevitable sackloads of anonymous letters, offering everything from helpful suggestions to crank messages from the lunatic fringe. Correspondence of this nature was the norm in any high-profile enquiry, but perhaps uniquely, thanks to Fullarton James's insistence on the need for himself and Supt Shell to see every item that came in as soon as possible, officers spent valuable time retyping anonymous letters in quadruplicate. In the vain hope of achieving some order out of this chaos, someone was also regularly typing and retyping updated lists of witness statements. The investigation was effectively drowning under a self-inflicted tidal wave of paper.

On 12 January, PC John Eckford conducted the first interview with a man who was destined to become Chief Constable Fullarton James's star witness. William Kirsopp-Reed farmed at Old Town, a mile and a half south-west of Otterburn. Then in his early forties, Mr Kirsopp-Reed was well respected locally, already the honorary secretary to the Otterburn Parochial Church Council, a position he would occupy for close on 40 years, and he would soon be appointed a magistrate. More significantly from the point of view of the Foster enquiry, he was the owner of the one vehicle Evelyn said she had recognised on her drive south to Belsay. Given that Mr Kirsopp-Reed had been mentioned by name in Evelyn's 'statement', it is surprising that the police do not appear to have got round to questioning him until five days into the enquiry.

PC John Eckford initially visited Kirsopp-Reed at Old Town to obtain a statement, but the evidence he obtained was considered of sufficient importance that Mr Kirsopp-Reed was invited to Otterburn Towers the following evening, to be questioned further by Supt Shell. Essentially the farmer from Old Town told both officers the same story. On 6 January he had driven from Gosforth to Old Town, setting off at about 6.45 in the evening. It was a journey he made regularly and he knew that it always took him around an hour and ten minutes to get home. He recalled that there had been a saloon car travelling south, which he met only about 200 yards north of Belsay. When approaching Bradford Bank (a section of the road a couple of miles north of Belsay) he had noticed a stationary car, facing north, with its lights switched off. (Several witnesses reported this car. It was believed to contain a courting couple and was never traced.) About 40 to 50 yards north of Ferney Chesters, at about 7.25, by which time he was following another car, he had met a large saloon coming south. The car he had been following turned off at Mirlaw Road End and it too was never traced. Just before Harle Post Office he had met a large lorry with very poor headlights, and close to the post office itself, one of Tait's buses. Apart from this he was adamant that he had seen no other vehicles at all. An unknown hand, which bears a strong resemblance to the chief constable's, has written 'Very important' on the file copy of Kirsopp-Reed's original statement and the words: 'I did not meet any other car', have been heavily underlined, as have the words: 'I know Evelyn Foster's car. I did not see it.'[17]

In the car with him that night had been his sister, Margaret, and his young son. The police also took a statement from Margaret, who corroborated every detail, except for placing the encounter with Tait's bus slightly further south than had her brother.[18]

On the same day that Supt Shell met with William Kirsopp-Reed, PC Turnbull had travelled down to Tait's bus garage and interviewed Robert Harrison, the driver of the bus which was demonstrably the one reported by the Kirsopp-Reeds. When asked to describe the vehicles he had seen en route south to Belsay, the driver replied that he had noticed one saloon car travelling north near Ferney Chesters, but apart from this single vehicle, he did not remember any other cars.[19]

Harrison had already been interviewed by PC Sinton three days earlier and had given him exactly the same information. These statements from the Tait's bus driver should have given the chief constable food for thought, but they did not. By the time the police spoke with Harrison on 13 January, they had already interviewed enough witnesses to have established that Harrison must have passed more than one car between Knowesgate and Belsay, and should have concluded from this, even if they had not realised it before, that a person's not remembering seeing any cars is not the same as there being no cars. Similarly, it does not appear to have occurred to anyone that the chances of the Kirsopp-Reeds being able to accurately remember every single vehicle that had passed them in the course of a routine journey undertaken almost a week before were remote to non-existent. Unfortunately, Captain James was not interested in witnesses like Harrison, who stated that they could not recall which vehicles they had seen on any particular night. What he wanted were people full of misplaced confidence in their ability to recall absolutely everything they had seen.

More evidence that seemed to damage Evelyn's credibility had emerged from enquiries at the Percy Arms, where John Scott, the barman who had been on duty from 6 to 8.30 p.m. on 6 January, assured Sgt Archie Robson that there had been no strangers in the bar that night and that no one had entered enquiring after a lift.[20] Gladys Tatham, the landlord's daughter, told the police that she had been dealing with newly arrived guests and keeping an eye on the main entrance of the hotel, but had seen no one enter the premises who could possibly have been the man described by Evelyn Foster.[21] Both Scott and Mrs Tatham were also absolutely certain that Evelyn herself had not called at the hotel that evening.

Two witnesses who did see the Hudson motor car

south of Otterburn that night were easily able to identify it, because both were Foster's employees: they were John Robson, driver of the Foster's bus service which had left Newcastle for Otterburn at around six on 6 January, and his conductor, Oswald Young. Their journey had followed its usual timetable and by 7.22 (the driver recalled checking his watch when he pulled up) they had reached Raylees, where they paused briefly to drop off a bundle of evening newspapers. Young got off the bus and crossed the road with the papers, leaving them on a wall to be collected as usual, and while he was doing so Robson saw a car approaching from the direction of Otterburn and dimmed his lights. As it came closer he recognised the vehicle as Evelyn Foster's Hudson, but he was unable to see anything of the occupants. He noticed that the car was being driven very cautiously and estimated its speed at no more than 10mph. Further confirmation that they had encountered the car at 7.22 was provided by the bus's arrival on time in Otterburn at 7.30, as it normally took them seven or eight minutes to get there from Raylees.[22]

The bus conductor, Young, told the police that after crossing the road and leaving the papers on the corner, he had to wait for the oncoming car to pass him before he could cross back to the bus. When he got back on board, either he or Robson had commented that it was 'the boss's car' and Robson had asked if he'd noticed who was driving it, but Young said he had not been able to see.[23]

One more potentially important witness had given a statement that sounded a grim note. Sydney Henderson, a shepherd, came forward to say that while walking on the road between Harwood Head and his home at Harwood Gate, he had noticed a fire blazing on the moor near Wolf's Nick, about two miles across country. Henderson's vantage point and direction of travel suggest that he would have spotted the flames fairly quickly. He estimated that he had first noticed the fire at 8.45 and said that by the time he had reached his destination, some 15 minutes later, it was already burning less brightly.[24]

CHAPTER 13

Every major London daily had despatched a reporter to cover the Evelyn Foster case, and now that the funeral was over reporters began hounding the police again, desperate for something new to print. On 13 January, F.W. Memory of the Daily Mail presented himself at police headquarters, demanded to speak with the chief constable and informed the duty officer that he would not leave until he had done so. When the officer returned with word that the chief constable was unavailable, Mr Memory 'became very unpleasant' and had to be 'shown off the premises'.[1]

Reporters from another trio of London papers made a more successful approach, sending a telegram direct to Captain James, protesting about the 'extraordinary attitude' being displayed to newspaper reporters by 'some of your subordinate officers', which was 'creating a strong impression that the investigation into Miss Foster's death is being mishandled... [We] believe this cannot be on your instruction and therefore suggest you may like to meet with the undersigned...'[2]

This flagrant appeal to the chief constable's vanity did the trick, and he granted the three men (from the Evening Standard, Daily Herald and Daily Express) an interview the same day, in addition to calling another press con-ference that afternoon at Otterburn Hall.[3] Here the chief constable told reporters that his men had found nothing concrete to support the story of an attack and said that the police had abandoned any further searches on the moors. Rather than using this opportunity to make a further appeal for the car in which Evelyn claimed that her at-tacker had been conveyed from Jedburgh to Elishaw, Fullarton James instead emphasised that the driver of this elusive vehicle had failed to come forward.

In their coverage the following day, several papers took the view that after the nationwide publicity in the preceding week, the driver of this vehicle could not avoid knowing that they were sought by the police and that therefore, if this person existed, they were unlikely to come forward now. While this appears to have been a generally held opinion at the time, there was the possibility, dis-cussed earlier, that the particularly detailed description of Alastair Bull's car and its occupants, which had been reproduced word-for-word both in a radio broadcast and in practically every daily paper in the land, was given more emphasis, with the result that many newspapers reported requests for information regarding the 'Elishaw car' in terms that did not fit the particulars provided by Evelyn Foster at all.

It was the same situation on 13 January, when the majority of papers commenting on the driver's failure to come forward wrote of a male driver, and many confused the issue still further by having this male driver drop the wanted man at a whole selection of places that were nowhere near Elishaw Road Ends. The Scotsman, for example, has a male driver leaving his passenger 'close to the spot where Miss Foster's body was found'. It would therefore be hardly surprising if a female driver, who had never taken the road on which police interest seemed to be exclusively focused, and had no idea of the location of 'Wolf's Jaw', as several of the papers persisted in referring to it, failed to appreciate that it was her to whom the police wished to speak. Numerous papers completely failed to explain the Elishaw connection and, after attending the latest press briefing, were more interested in explaining to their readers that the police were now 'paying more attention to the theory... that the girl's mind may have been disturbed'.[4]

Though the majority of London papers followed the line that the mysterious assailant had probably never existed, at least one voice was raised in dissent. No doubt still infuriated by his treatment at their hands, F.W. Memory used his 13 January column in the Daily Mail to decry the activities of Northumberland Police, ridiculing them for being unable to state definitely whether or not Miss Foster had been murdered, and himself coming down firmly on the side of murder. Evelyn's account, he wrote, 'was a plain, straightforward story of what had befallen her, and no one hearing it could doubt its truth'. For good measure, Memory included a description of the bowler-hatted man and was one of the few reporters to reiterate accurately that, according to Evelyn, the man had been dropped at

Elishaw by a woman driving a saloon car.[5]

In the meantime, whatever the man at the top may or may not have believed, Inspector Russell's team continued the investigation with a determination that lends particular irony to any suggestion that these 'subordinate' officers were the ones guilty of mishandling the affair. As each fresh witness statement was obtained, the team sought and interviewed anyone mentioned in it, gradually building up a complete picture of who had been in the Otterburn area that night, on foot, on their bicycles, or in buses and cars; frequently returning to re-interview witnesses for confirmation on specific issues. They interviewed each of the people who had been present when Evelyn made what passed for a statement in the hours before she died. Unfortunately, no one from the investigation spoke with key witnesses such as Dr Miller and Nurse Lawson until 15 January, by which time they were being asked to recall the details of something they had heard more than a week before, and this was equally true of some drivers and pedestrians. The Fosters' neighbour, Mrs Jennings, who had been in the sickroom from shortly after Evelyn was brought home until well after midnight, was overlooked to the extent that she was not asked to make a statement until 27 January.[6]

This delay was presumably due to the lack of manpower, as, in their efforts to leave no stone unturned, the Otterburn team even looked into allegations that a young woman had been assaulted on the outskirts of the village a couple of years prior to the attack on Evelyn.

The episode in question had involved a girl who had come to Otterburn to work in the Percy Arms, and who had narrowly escaped molestation by a soldier who had been stationed at the army camp near Rochester. Fortunately, the girl's screams had attracted the attention of some of the men working in Foster's Garage, and they had run outside and successfully intervened. The victim was traced back to her home in Newcastle and questioned, while her attacker was identified and eliminated from the enquiry.[7]

Hospitals in the area were contacted and asked for details of anyone who had been admitted suffering from burns, but this drew a complete blank.[8] In response to various suggestions from both members of the public and the chief constable himself, enquiries were made regarding various films that had been shown in the area, and a popular novel about a murder involving a burning car.[9] When it came to a possible inspiration for setting fire to the vehicle, no wild goose was left unchased.

The general public's enthusiasm to help was unabated. Unfortunately, for every caller who was helping to add to the picture of vehicle movements in the wider Otterburn area on 6 January, there were others who merely wanted to tell the police that they had inside information (often via dreams or spiritualism), which unquestionably proved that the fire had been started by Evelyn as a scam to rescue the Fosters from their 'money problems'. Anonymous letter-writers levied similar allegations. 'It is Spring Heel Jack,' wrote one self-appointed comedian. 'He has burnt several cars in the neighbourhood, then comes back to claim the insurance money.'[10]

On 15 January there was a glimmer of a break-through, when word came in from the Roxburghshire Constabulary regarding some potentially interesting witnesses in Jedburgh. Initial enquiries in the town had produced nothing to substantiate Evelyn's story that the man and his companions had eaten tea together there, but this fresh information led to a journey over the border for Sgt Armstrong and PC Eckford.

On 16 January, Armstrong and Eckford interviewed Thomas Hughes, the proprietor of the Royal Hotel Jedburgh, waitress Helen Wood and John Mackenzie, one of the regular customers.[11] According to this trio, two men and a woman had entered the hotel at some time between 12.30 and 1 p.m. on 6 January and enquired about lunch. The group were English and spoke with what Mackenzie and Wood described as a cockney accent, though the landlord thought they sounded more like people who came from the Midlands. The three strangers had drinks in the parlour before going upstairs to the dining room for their meal of soup, beefsteak pie and pudding. They had not appeared in any hurry and after settling the bill, which came to 10s 6d, and leaving a one shilling tip, the travellers had departed at around 2 p.m.

The English customers did not make a positive impression. After enquiring about lunch, one of the men had wondered aloud whether the landlord had understood what he said, which not surprisingly did not go down well with Mr Mackenzie, who told him that the landlord had understood him well enough. Miss Wood, who served their meal, said they 'weren't pleasant, like usual customers', and had seemed displeased with the lack of choice on the menu. Thomas Hughes summed up the opinion of all three witnesses, saying that they were 'not the class of people who normally motor', though all three were 'well dressed'.

The witnesses were divided over whether there was any suggestion that one of the number might have been a stranger to the other two. Miss Wood did not feel any of them showed signs of being a couple or siblings, but her boss took the opposite view, assuming they were all related and noting that they all spoke with the same accent. Mr Mackenzie thought it possible that one of the men (the one who settled the bill) did not know the others, basing this impression mainly on the fact that the woman and the other man had done most of the talking.

Both Hughes and Mackenzie were able to describe the three visitors in surprising detail considering that ten days had gone by. Helen Wood's recollections were less precise, but supported theirs. According to these descriptions both men had been around 5ft 7in and the woman slightly shorter. The men had been in their thirties, the woman slightly younger. The man who had taken charge of ordering both the drinks and lunch, and had subsequently settled the bill, was slightly taller and broader than his male companion, had dark hair and was somewhat red faced, whereas the other man had been fair and rather sallow. (Unlike the menfolk, Miss Wood thought the younger man 'good looking'.) Both men had worn dark overcoats, bowler hats and navy suits. The woman, who was slightly stout, had worn a brown or fawn two-piece costume of some kind, and either a matching or darker-coloured hat.

Had these descriptions been available from the outset, it is possible that they would have been given the same prominence as that of Alastair Bull and his companions, not least because the dark-haired man was a relatively good match for Evelyn's assailant. However, though enquiries were subsequently made in Hawick – the one place definitely mentioned by the travellers – no further trace of them was found.[12]

Having taken these statements, Armstrong and Eckford returned to Otterburn,[13] and though the press got hold of the story about the three diners and hailed it as a possible new lead, the police took little further interest in them. They were probably right not to do so, because though there were some similarities between the party which had travelled in the Elishaw car and the one taking lunch in the Jedburgh hotel, there were plenty of discrepancies, too. According to Evelyn, the man had missed his bus and taken tea in Jedburgh, whereas the group in question had eaten lunch, the timing of which would have left ample opportunity for one of their number to catch the Newcastle bus. More significantly, it took not much over an hour to reach Otterburn from Jedburgh, so even if the group were travelling across the border into England – and there had been nothing in their conversation to suggest this one way or the other – they would have been many miles further south than Elishaw by six o'clock that night.

The most important point about this evidence, however, was that when the Roxburghshire police had visited every Jedburgh hostelry on 7 January, they had naturally included the Royal Hotel, which stands in a prominent position in the main street, and on that occasion no one had been able to recall any strangers entering the premises the previous day: not until reading about the case in 13 January's Edinburgh Evening News had Mr Hughes remembered these customers and decided to contact the police about them.

The episode of the Royal Hotel is illustrative of the uncertain waters that the investigation was now forced to navigate. Scarcely anyone they interviewed by this stage of the enquiry would not have read all kinds of things about the case in the newspapers, and the things they read would necessarily have helped form their overall view of what had taken place and could have subconsciously altered their own recollections. There can be little doubt that this group of English travellers had taken lunch in the Royal Hotel at some point in the recent past, but the likelihood is that their visit did not occur on 6 January.

The day after the Jedburgh expedition, the police caught up with another witness who was destined to attract considerable public interest. John Kennedy, a county council workman who lived in Knowesgate, had walked to choir practice in Kirkwhelpington and back along the Newcastle to Otterburn road on 6 January, but in spite of repeated appeals he had not come forward during the first ten days of the enquiry. Within the case files there is a strong suggestion that, like a number of witnesses, Kennedy seemed more interested in getting his 15 minutes of fame in the press than he was in providing information to the police.

Kennedy told the police that when choir practice was finished on 6 January, he and his wife had walked home along the main road to Knowesgate.[14] They had been walking north for some distance and, as they were rounding a bend known as Easton's Corner, they were overtaken by a car travelling exceptionally fast. It was a saloon car with a 1 and a 3 in the registration number. The significance of this was considerable, because both the timing of Kennedy's walk – choir practice had finished just before 8 p.m. – and the registration plate – Evelyn's car registration was TN8135 – were suggestive.

Some sections of the press immediately leapt on this as a positive sighting of Evelyn's car driving north from Belsay. The chief constable, on the other hand, was immediately sceptical about Kennedy,[15] querying why it had taken him so long to come forward and pointing out that, on his own admission, Kennedy had been among the sightseers who had walked up to have a look at the Hudson car before it was removed from Wolf's Nick, and that he therefore already knew its number plate. He also noted that whereas Evelyn's statement implied that the man had driven slowly, the car Kennedy had seen had been travelling exceptionally fast.

Fullarton James at once set out to identify the car Kennedy had seen with a vehicle other than Evelyn's Hudson, and he soon found one which he felt was a match. A local farmer, Dennis Herdman, had been out in his Morris Cowley saloon, registration BR6123 on 6 January.[16] After visiting Hexham market he had driven to Kirkwhelpington, arriving at 5.45 and remaining in the village until 8.10, when he drove home to Hawick Farm. This journey entailed him turning on to the main road at Kirkwhelpington and leaving it again at Knowesgate, where he took the left-hand turn towards Woodburn.

Herdman told the police that he did not recall passing any vehicles or pedestrians during the few minutes he was on the main road, and this has generated suggestions that Herdman's was therefore not the car seen by Kennedy. The most important point, however, was that both Mr Herdman's car and Mr and Mrs Kennedy were indisputably travelling north along this short stretch of road at the same time. Herdman would have needed to be at least 15 minutes earlier or 30 minutes later than his stated timings in order to have made this journey without overtaking the Kennedys on the main road, and there is nothing to suggest that this was the case.

After the flurry of interest created by Kennedy, the numbers of new witnesses needing to be interviewed began to decrease to the point where various officers were able to undertake house-to-house enquiries in villages and hamlets along the route, mopping up any local information which had so far eluded them.[17] The press continued to follow the story, but while the local reporters (no doubt with an eye to the fact that they needed to work with the Northumberland Constabulary long after the Foster case was closed) sprang to the defence of the police, pointing out that it was not in the interests of the enquiry to reveal everything that was discovered, stressing the thoroughness of the officers involved and criticising 'complaints about secretiveness from people who should know better',[18] the London newspapers took a different line, shouting their usual refrain, that Scotland Yard ought to have been called in. The majority of papers were now saying that there was nothing to support Evelyn's story, with the Daily Express sounding the gloomily prophetic note that: 'It is now almost certain that a definite solution will never be reached of the riddle of Miss Evelyn Foster.'[19]

Most reports now focused on the level of doubt among the police officers as to the veracity of Evelyn's story, but F.W. Memory of the Daily Mail continued to follow a different tack. After receiving the cold shoulder from the chief constable, the Mail's man on the spot had evidently managed to have a chat with some of the officers working in Otterburn, and while reprising his customary mantra that Scotland Yard should have been called in, Memory added that his criticism of 'Northumberland police chiefs' was 'no reflection on the admirable work of the two police officers of Newcastle CID'. 'These officers have – with painstaking care – accumulated evidence which can have no doubt that Miss Foster was the victim of foul play, but as of this afternoon, the Northumberland Constabulary was still professing "an open mind" on the subject.'[20]

This rare breach in what was normally presented as a united front among the investigators went pretty much unremarked elsewhere, but F.W. Memory had exposed the tip of a very big iceberg: the man running the investigation was thinking and working along completely different lines to the junior officers who were actively engaged in evidence gathering. Captain James had made up his mind about Evelyn's story at an astonishingly early stage, and it seemed that nothing was going to divert him. This left the team working under Inspector Russell – not just those on loan from Newcastle CID – in the awkward position of pursuing an investigation led by a man who took a diametrically opposite view of the situation to their own, and trying to produce some evidence which would force their senior officer to change his mind.

In the 1930s junior officers did not question their superiors, but around the second or third week of the enquiry, PC John Eckford prepared a lengthy response to various queries that had come via Supt Shell from Fullarton James. It is likely that Eckford was chosen as the author of the report because he was on loan from the Newcastle force and therefore immune to the future wrath of the Northumberland chief constable. This document leaves no doubt where Eckford – and presumably his colleagues in the Otterburn enquiry team – actually stood. Eckford's report is clear, well-reasoned and intelligent: it cannot be interpreted in any possible way other than that the Newcastle CID man believed that Evelyn Foster had been murdered.[21]

Shell's original queries do not survive, but the questions can be inferred from Eckford's replies. It is apparent that the chief constable was still adopting an entrenched position – either that Evelyn had fabricated the story of an attack to cover up her own actions in firing the vehicle, or that, if there had been an attack, it had been perpetrated by a 'local lover'. There was no actual evidence to support either of these ideas and Eckford pointed out, among other things, that if the man had been local it would be fair to assume that he would have known the road and therefore chosen a better spot to mount his assault, because the point on the road where Evelyn claimed that the attack had taken place gave no warning of vehicles approaching from the south. He reminded the senior officer that Evelyn had been asked repeatedly whether she knew her attacker and had stated very firmly that she did not.

'These assertions given under such tragic circumstances would require some very definite evidence to the contrary, before it could be said that it could not be accepted as correct,' Eckford wrote. He also firmly rebutted suggestions that it was somehow evidence against Evelyn that she did not have to account to her father for each individual fare, and similarly dismissed a variety of other irrelevant points. He ended his three-page report on an unequivocal note: 'The whole of her conversation with the doctors, relatives, etc., is not contradicted by any direct evidence obtained so far.'

CHAPTER 14

PC Eckford's eminently sensible, evidence-based reasoning cut no ice with Fullarton James. Whereas Eckford saw no evidence for disbelieving Evelyn's story, Captain James took the opposite view and considered her story full of 'inherent impossibilities'.[1] It cannot be denied that there was little in the way of corroboration for Evelyn's story, and that certain elements of it appeared unlikely, but the chief constable took his scepticism to extremes, sometimes performing mental gymnastics to justify his disbelief. He ridiculed the idea that anyone having got as far as Belsay would then want to turn back towards Otterburn, asking even if they did, why they should wish to take the wheel from a 'competent driver': objections that may be perfectly valid when applied to a normal, rational person bound for Ponteland, but which fail to allow for the thought processes of a passenger capable of attacking a young woman, then setting fire to her.

There is no doubt that Evelyn's story of the man grabbing the wheel and continuing to drive the Hudson for a distance of some ten miles while she was crushed against the driver's door sounds unlikely, but the arrangement of the car's pedals and steering wheel meant that it was by no means impossible. However, Fullarton

James ridiculed this scenario on the grounds that Evelyn was 'a physically strong girl', which suggests a wilful failure to comprehend that in a struggle between a young man who stands around 5ft 6in to 5ft 8in and a young woman measuring a mere 5ft tall, the latter is unlikely to come off best. The chief constable went on to say that, even if the man had taken the controls, Evelyn could at any time have stopped the car by using the brake, putting out the headlights, getting out of the side door or touching the horn to attract attention. Scarcely a moment's pause is required to appreciate that wrestling for control of the brakes, switching off the lights or throwing yourself from the door of a moving vehicle are not exactly to be recommended on an unlit country road in the middle of nowhere.

Determined to pour scorn on every aspect of the story, the chief constable also queried the likelihood of the man alighting from a car at Elishaw, 'just as the only taxi in the district happened to go by'. This is of course to miss the point by a mile. The man had no way of knowing that the approaching vehicle was a hire car, and having already been fortunate enough to receive a lift from an ordinary private motorist, he presumably hoped to repeat the experience by flagging down whatever vehicle happened to come along. Fullarton James also questioned again the notion that 'complete strangers' would be transported long distances, without a hire car driver first seeing the colour of their money, when in fact this was and remains the norm.

In the chief constable's defence, there was some material that supported his doubts. He returned constantly to the point that William Kirsopp-Reed knew what Evelyn's car looked like and had not seen it. Then there was his 'expert mechanic', William Jennings, who insisted that the Hudson had been deliberately driven onto the moor, and cited the lack of burned heather along its course as evidence that the car had not been set alight until after it came to a standstill, both of which contradicted Evelyn's story that the car had been set alight while it was still standing on the road. Of still greater significance was the point Fullarton James underlined heavily in at least one of his memos – how could this mystery man have walked 300 yards down the main village street, then waited around for 15 minutes without being seen by anyone?

Throughout January, Fullarton James continued to barrage his officers with notes and memos concerning the case, many of which contained half-baked assumptions and illogical conclusions. (To add to the irritation value of these messages, the chief constable could never let the smallest typing error go by without drawing attention to it.) It is one thing for a policeman to be genuinely mistaken in his interpretation of evidence, but quite another for him to attempt to suppress evidence in order to gain official acceptance of his personal theories. For reasons it is no longer possible to understand, the chief constable of Northumberland had developed a prejudice bordering on obsession concerning the Foster case. Whether this reflects the pig-headedness of a man who, having acted on a hunch, refused to lose face by backing down, or whether for misogynistic reasons which we can no longer even conjecture, Fullarton James was convinced that Evelyn Foster had lied and was determined that the official inquest verdict would confirm this.

In a case of suspicious death it was customary for the coroner to work pretty much hand in hand with the local police force. All important information would be shared, with the coroner given full discretion on which witnesses should be called and which evidence needed to be taken to establish cause of death. This scenario clearly did not suit Captain James at all, and as early as 17 January he was discussing with his senior officers which evidence should be sent to the coroner and which withheld. He sought advice on the legal niceties from his subordinate Superintendent Wright, who appears to have been something of an expert in dealing with the local coroners. Wright reassured his chief that, unlike Mr Percy, another of the Northumberland coroners, Mr Dodds was 'not so anxious to see statements', but, presumably mindful of the impropriety of the situation, after skating around the point and agreeing that the coroner probably only needed to see statements about 'facts showing cause of death', Wright eventually concluded by stating: 'I am not prepared to say how much the coroner should be told.'[2]

The entire correspondence between the coroner and the chief constable no longer survives, but it is obvious from

Above: Evelyn Foster in a studio shot and posed alongside one of the cars she would have driven prior to acquiring the Hudson.

Left: The Kennels, Otterburn, home of the Foster family.

Above: Cecil Johnston and Tommy Rutherford, the bus driver and 15-year-old conductor, who found Evelyn on the moor.

Below: Police measure the distance the car had travelled from the road.

Above and Left: The burned-out Hudson as it was found on the moor. The angle of the images makes the car appear much closer to the road than it actually was.

Right: Gordon Foster (left) and Joseph Foster (right) walking to the inquest. The identity of their companion is uncertain.

Above: Police officers at the crime scene. The tallest of the trio may be Inspector Russell.

Below: As the investigation got under way, friends of the Chief Constable were allowed to inspect the site.

Above, left and bottom: The photographs and diagrams produced at the inquest failed to show the sharp bend where the car left the road.

Above right: the road emerges from the south through the gap known as Wolf's Nick.

Above left: Facing north from the same spot we see the sharp bend just below Wolf's Nick, where the car left the road.

Elishaw Road Ends approached from the Hexham road. When descending from Brownriggs to Elishaw Bridge, traffic moving along the Jedburgh to Newcastle road is clearly visible.

By the time a pedestrian has reached Elishaw Bridge, not only the passing traffic, but even the much taller road signs have completely vanished below the horizon.

Looking north from the bridge beside the Percy Arms. The hotel now occupies the entire row of buildings, but this was not the case in 1931.

Looking south from Evelyn Foster's grave, which lies beside the entrance to the churchyard. The large guest house in the foreground was the Co-Operative Stores in 1931. Going south, the building with the prominent front porch is the Memorial Hall and the sign for the Percy Arms can be seen beyond that.

Looking north from Evelyn's grave, The Kennels is just visible – behind the trees on the opposite side of the road.

Right: Confidential telephone message from Police Headquarters dated 8 January 1931, instructing that 'the word which heads the list under classification of crime must not be used'. In spite of this directive, an unknown hand has subsequently written 'murder' in the margin.
(Northumberland Police Archives)

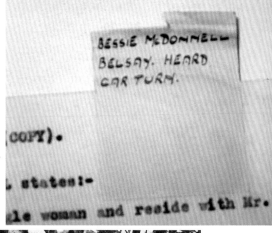

Right: Bessie McDonnell's tagged statement. This important testimony went unheard as Miss McDonnell was not called to give evidence at the inquest.
(Northumberland Police Archives)

Left: Evelyn Foster's grave

what remains that very few of the statements collected by Otterburn team ever found their way to Mr Dodds. On 28 January, Fullarton James sent just 16 carefully selected statements to the coroner, accompanied by a note headed 'Observation on Statements', which directed the coroner's attention to particular aspects of the evidence telling against Evelyn Foster's story. [3]

Philip Dodds wrote back the following day, thanking the chief constable for his comments, but requesting copies of the statements provided by John Kennedy and 'the man who saw Miss Foster's car while crossing a field' (Albert Beach). Both men had been quoted in various newspapers as having seen the Hudson car during its travels on 6 January, so the coroner not unnaturally thought them relevant to the enquiry. It was a polite, tactful letter, which gave no indication of the degree to which the coroner may have found it irregular or disturbing that he was only becoming aware of potentially important witnesses via the medium of the press. [4]

Instead of providing copies as requested, Fullarton James responded next day [5] by informing the coroner that 'the car seen by Kennedy is accounted for', and putting forward various arguments as to why the other statement Mr Dodds had requested was irrelevant. Since the coroner was perfectly entitled to see any statements he asked for, the chief constable was not so much overstepping the line as leaping several yards beyond it, and though further correspondence on this particular issue has not survived in either the police or coroner's files, Mr Dodds must have successfully pressed the point, because he did eventually receive the statements in question, and both Kennedy and Beach were called to give evidence at the inquest.

It is not hard to imagine what effect all this was having on the team of officers still at work in Otterburn. Whereas they appear to have been intent on sourcing corroboration for Evelyn's story, the chief constable constantly demonstrated the opposite mindset. When the Evening Chronicle reported on 21 January that Joseph Foster intended to offer a reward to anyone who could give information about the woman motorist who had given the assailant a lift, an official police spokesman immediately threw cold water on the idea, saying that 'a motorist who has chosen to remain anonymous for a fortnight is unlikely to be induced by a reward'.[6]

To say that the original search of the crime scene had lacked competence was a considerable understatement. Bits and pieces of evidence had been collected on the first day of the investigation, more fragments of burned clothing were found during the course of further searches, and as late as 26 and 29 January the police returned to look over the ground yet again, though it had by now been contaminated with the passage of literally hundreds of reporters, sightseers and policemen.

The remnants of Evelyn's burned clothing – both that found at the scene and what she had been wearing when taken home – were initially handed over to Professor McDonald, who had been appointed to carry out the post-mortem, and they were then passed on to Professor Dunn, whose speciality was chemical analysis.[7] The clothing was cross-checked with a list provided by Mrs Foster, which detailed what her daughter had been wearing when she left the house that evening, and is indicative of Evelyn's comparative wealth and stylishness. She had set out that night in a cotton silk camisole, celanese knickers, pink corsets with suspenders, a white silk vest, a grey-and-red check skirt in Otterburn tweed with fawn bodice, a pair of brown silk stockings, a cinnamon-and-brown knitted woollen jumper, a dark brown herring-bone pattern Otterburn tweed coat, a brown-and-yellow striped scarf, brown shoes and a close-fitting brown felt hat with a brown ribbon on the side of it.[8] When she returned home she was still wearing what remained of these garments, with the exception of: her coat, which Evelyn said she had shrugged off, of which only a small burned portion was ever discovered; her knickers, a small piece of burned fabric with elastic attached that was found at the scene; her scarf, which had been discovered by a visiting reporter in the early hours of 7 January and was relatively undamaged; and her hat, which was never found. The police concluded that the clothing she had been wearing on the most badly burned sections of her body had been completely destroyed.[9]

Professor Dunn and his colleague Professor Briscoe, sometimes assisted by Professor McDonald, carried out a series of inconclusive chemical experiments on the items provided, principally in the hope of determining what accelerant had been employed by the fire starter. The trio came up with very little concrete information, apart from observing that the remnants of Evelyn's clothes smelled faintly of petroleum, or a petroleum distillate such as paraffin, and that a mysterious 'waxy substance' that had impregnated virtually all the fabrics was probably melted human fat. The one useful outcome of all this was that tests carried out on the glass bottle discovered by PC Ferguson not far from the burned-out car proved it to have contained nothing more sinister than a small amount of a flavoured sugar solution, which was not consistent with any alcoholic or flammable substance. This suggested that the bottle was an unrelated piece of litter, left behind by picnickers at some point in the past.[10]

Professor McDonald's original role had been to conduct the post-mortem, which he had carried out on 8 January, assisted by his son and Dr McEachran, who had originally treated Evelyn's injuries in Otterburn. There was then an inexplicable delay of almost a fortnight before the report was officially made available to the coroner on 21 January.[11] This delay is somewhat troubling when viewed in the light of the chief constable's attitude and coupled with the leakage of information to the press, both of which suggest that McDonald and Fullarton James were involved in some kind of off-the-record tick-tacking. In 1931, forensic science was in its infancy, and it was a period when 'experts' could and did drift into areas in which they had no particular knowledge or expertise, teaming up with the police to undertake less-than-scientific experiments, sometimes geared to obtaining pre-ordained conclusions.[12] Today a pathologist stays rigidly within his own discipline and bases his report on his own findings, with few opportunities to play at Sherlock Holmes, but the conduct of investigations in the early 1930s was very different.

McDonald's remit should have been to provide a strictly impartial report based solely on the evidence he found during the post-mortem on Evelyn Foster's body and his subsequent laboratory work on her organs, but a full week after conducting his initial post-mortem, he had been taken on a visit to the crime scene and soon afterwards he teamed up with chemistry professors Dunn and Bristoe to undertake some experiments designed to demonstrate the effects of burning various substances against human skin.[13] There is no question but that McDonald became involved with aspects of the investigation that had nothing to do with him, raising the possibility that he allowed himself to become part of a team supporting the most senior police officer's theories about the way Evelyn Foster had met her death, rather than providing a strictly neutral, impartial set of conclusions.

The pathologist's report, when it finally arrived, began by noting that Evelyn was a rather small woman, approximately 5ft tall, but with good muscular development. She had died as a result of shock after suffering extensive burns.[14] The police were well aware from the outset that Evelyn had suffered fatal burns. What inevitably interested them far more was whether Professor McDonald's examination supported her story of being attacked and sexually assaulted. According to the pathologist's official report, he had examined the body carefully for signs of violence, but explained that 'over the burned areas, superficial injuries or scratches could not possibly have been recognised'. Her facial features had been obscured by burns, but he had noted 'some bluish discoloration about the root of the nose and upper part of the eyelids'. McDonald had therefore dissected the lower forehead and found evidence that 'suggested a slight amount of superficial bruising', though his dissection of the eyelids had shown nothing indicative of bruising.

As well as this suggestion that Evelyn might have been hit in the face, the report contained further support for Evelyn's version of events, inasmuch that McDonald suggested that the distribution of the burns meant that Evelyn had been sitting down for at least part of the time when she was on fire, and that the small, round patches of burning on her upper body were consistent with something flammable splashing onto her clothing. This fitted with Evelyn's story of sitting in the rear of the car when some kind of liquid had been thrown onto her and set alight. However, McDonald found less to support the accusation of sexual assault. As there was no obvious sign of laceration in the genital area, the professor had removed the whole of the genito-urinary organs in one piece, in order to carry out a full dissection and microscopical examination.

It might have been assumed that the reason everyone had been waiting 13 days for the professor's report was to enable him to include his findings in respect of these dissections, but that was not the case. The dissections had been carried out immediately, but for reasons best known to himself Professor McDonald did not officially reveal his conclusions regarding the critical question of sexual assault until a second report dated 26 January.[15] Here, he recorded that he had found no injury at the outer lips of the genital passage, except some swelling 'which may be the result of superficial burns'. The hymen had not been ruptured and the vagina above the hymen 'showed appearances normally seen in a virgin'. There was no evidence of sperm in the genital or vaginal passages, though there was evidence that Evelyn was in the early stages of a menstrual period. McDonald concluded that there was 'no evidence of violation'.

It is likely that at least some of the officers who had been earnestly pursuing the investigation, particularly DC Eckford, who had consistently stood out in favour of Evelyn's story being true, must have hoped that the eventual arrival of the pathologist's report would mark a change of attitude at the top. (It is clear from Eckford's report mentioned in Chapter 13 that he and his immediate colleagues had not been made privy to the post-mortem findings.) If so, then Professor McDonald's conclusions must have been a blow to the workforce in Otterburn Hall and, in the final days of January, as the resumption of the inquest approached, though the men still stationed in Otterburn continued to put in the hours, there is a sense that the investigation began to lose its way.

CHAPTER 15

The sufferings of the Foster family during this period cannot be understated. It was bad enough that one of them had been snatched away in the prime of life, after sustaining hideous injuries, and each member of the family had then been repeatedly forced to relive these events in order to provide the police with the fullest possible information. The natural instinct for any family might be to withdraw and grieve, but there was no refuge into which they could retreat, for the village where they lived and worked had become the centre of a major investigation, constantly besieged by reporters and sightseers, with their daughter's funeral transformed into a massive public event.

Worse still, they began to lose faith in the police operation and in particular the public appeals, which had blatantly focused on the wrong car. As if this was not enough to contend with, there had been a rising crescendo of doubt and innuendo regarding the circumstances of Evelyn's death, with newspapers questioning her veracity and even her sanity, and since the Fosters' address was now public property, anonymous letters were arriving daily from all over the country, each of them opened and read by Joseph Foster in the vain hope that they would contain some helpful information. Alas, large numbers of correspondents had written only to abuse the family, accusing them of attempting insurance fraud.[1] In these circumstances it is little wonder that as the resumption of the inquest approached, feelings were running high in Otterburn.

The inquest recommenced on Monday, 2 February 1931, in the Memorial Hall.[2] The way in which Mr Dodds had crossed swords with the chief constable over the availability of witness statements suggested that he was not prepared to simply accept the Fullarton James line on the case; but perhaps Dodds' attitude had more to do with standing on his rights and dignity than a determination to keep an open mind, because the first session had barely got underway before it became apparent that, so far as the outcome was concerned, Mr Dodds was entirely in agreement with the most senior police officer involved in the case.

Before calling any witnesses, the coroner took the somewhat unusual step of cautioning the jury that Evelyn Foster's 'statement as given to her mother' was 'not to be taken as a statement of fact'. The jury needed to consider the evidence presented to them, Mr Dodds said, 'to see if it is true'. This was perfectly fair so far as it went, inasmuch that no witness statement can ever be automatically accepted as an absolute statement of fact, but as this fundamental principal applied to all the statements heard at the inquest, the effect was to commence proceedings by suggesting that the credibility of Evelyn's statement was particularly open to doubt.

The first witness was Mrs Margaret Foster. In response to the coroner's questions, Mrs Foster went over the events of the evening, and the story her daughter had told on her deathbed. It was a prolonged grilling, during which many of the issues Mr Dodds focused on seemed scarcely relevant to the bigger picture: for example, whether Evelyn had said that the man himself had hailed her or whether she said that she had been hailed by the people in the car.

After enduring an hour and 40 minutes of questions from the coroner, Mrs Foster faced a further interrogation from Mr Smirk, the unfortunately named solicitor who had been retained to represent Northumberland Constabulary. While assuring the witness that he only put these questions in order to find out how Evelyn had died, it must have been apparent to everyone in the room that the Newcastle solicitor's actual intention was to undermine not only Evelyn's story, but Mrs Foster herself, at every possible opportunity. For example, he noted that Margaret Foster now said that Evelyn had described the strange man as 'a bit of a knut', whereas in her original statement, Mrs Foster had merely said that Evelyn described him as well dressed. By now Evelyn's mother was visibly upset, and since 'knut' was contemporary slang for a snappy dresser, the general meaning of the two expressions was exactly the same and had no bearing whatsoever on how Evelyn had died. In spite of this, Smirk pressed the point, forcing the admission from the witness that, although she had made several statements to the police, she had never used that particular expression until now. Smirk presumably hoped to create sufficient doubt about Margaret Foster's evidence that the jury would infer that she herself was an unreliable witness, thereby casting an even greater cloud of doubt over the whole proceedings. It would be the first of numerous attempts to discredit the Fosters during the three-day hearing.

What Smirk perhaps failed to allow for was that Otterburn was a small, close-knit community. The inquest jury was made up of local men, who would have known enough via the village grapevine to be aware that, while some of the details might be hazy, there was no real dispute about the basic gist of Evelyn's story. Nor did the story attributed to Evelyn rely merely on the memory of Margaret Foster, because it had been attested to by half-a-dozen others who had heard it at the same time. Smirk's attempts to lead the jury down this particular avenue were therefore a complete waste of time.

In all, Margaret Foster spent a gruelling two hours in the chair, which would have been hard for any witness, but especially so when required to identify the charred garments worn by a daughter on the last night of her life, and faced with questions about matters so intimate that any respectable woman of the period would have blanched at the prospect. On the night that Evelyn had been attacked, her mother had been reluctant to ask for details of the assault, even in the privacy of the girl's own bedroom with only a handful of people present. Now she was being asked to deal with subjects to which no decent woman would normally allude in front of her entire local community, a group of hostile interrogators and the national press.

In his report, Professor McDonald had included the information that Evelyn was in the first stage of a menstrual period, claiming that a bit of charred wadding found at the scene had the appearance of a sanitary towel. It is not easy to see what direct bearing this had on Evelyn's death, and in an era when public mention of gynaecological issues was normally avoided wherever humanly possible, the decision to question Mrs Foster on this issue raises another disturbing indicator on the direction taken by the coroner, because the only possible relevance of Evelyn's period lay in the then widely held perception that women who were menstruating were more likely to behave irrationally or to commit crime.[3]

In line with the 1930s' climate of euphemism, when questioned on the subject, Mrs Foster avoided uttering such forbidden words as period or menstruation, and spoke instead of Evelyn's 'courses', stating firmly that Evelyn was not usually upset or in any way different to normal at these times.

Euphemism would have its moment again when Mr Smirk returned to Mrs Foster's evidence regarding the alleged sexual assault.

'When you asked her whether the man had interfered with her, did she understand that you meant outraged?' he asked.

'Yes.'

'There is no doubt about that?'

'No,' Mrs Foster replied.

We can have no way of knowing whether Margaret Foster appreciated how much was riding on this answer. At this point it is worth returning to the coroner's initial warning that Evelyn's statement could not be accepted as a statement of fact. Surely, if it was dangerous to accept as fact what a witness had described about their own experiences, it was even more dangerous to accept the premise that one witness could necessarily read the mind of another. Smirk asked whether Evelyn had understood the expression 'interfered with', to mean 'outraged', which in turn was code for 'raped'. Even if she had managed that three-stage translation, we then have to assume that Evelyn, a 29-year-old virgin, understood − to borrow yet another euphemism − what was then known as 'the facts of life'. In reality, no one but Evelyn herself could have answered that question, so in answering in the affirmative for her daughter, Margaret Foster was making a considerable assumption.

In 1931, it was extremely unusual for an unmarried woman to know anything at all about 'the facts of life'. Information on the subject was not widely available; films and books were strictly censored and there was no television. Sex education in schools did not exist and sex itself was seen as an entirely inappropriate subject to be tackled at home, even between husbands and wives, let alone with their sons and daughters. Particularly enlightened mothers sometimes offered their daughter a brief lowdown on what to expect (a 'little talk' generally saved for the eve of the wedding), but what evidence we have suggests that the majority did not. The world of sexual intercourse was so well hidden behind a wall of euphemism and silence that many young women were all but unaware of its existence, and those who did exhibit curiosity by asking a mother for information were liable to be fobbed off, or scolded for straying into an area where 'nice' young women had no need to pry. Well into the 1950s, some women were still embarking on marriage with absolutely no knowledge of what sexual intercourse entailed.[4]

For a girl who had grown up in a respectable, middle-class home, it was not only possible but entirely normal to remain completely innocent of any sexual knowledge at all. Evelyn would have been completely reliant for information on her mother, who does not come across as the sort of ultra-modern, enlightened woman who would have explained 'married life' to her daughters as a matter of course.

Why, then, did Mrs Foster answer as she did? Had there perhaps been some half-hearted attempt on her part to explain things to Evelyn? An awkward exchange, during which Margaret Foster felt that she had done her duty, but which had left Evelyn ignorant of the full picture?

Whatever Mrs Foster had or had not told Evelyn, she cannot possibly have known whether Evelyn understood that, to her mother and the chief constable, being 'interfered with' constituted a specific sexual act of which Evelyn herself had no previous personal experience. The closest Margaret Foster could have got to an accurate answer was that she believed or thought that Evelyn understood her meaning. The fact that she did not say this suggests that Margaret Foster never stopped to think the thing through. She had asked her original question in the highly charged atmosphere of Evelyn's bedroom, and having received Evelyn's reply, that she had done her best to fight the man off – indeed had fought for her life – Mrs Foster simply assumed that Evelyn had confirmed her worst fears, reacting with dramatic distress, rather than pausing to question whether Evelyn understood the expression in precisely the way that she did herself. From that moment onwards, Evelyn's being raped by the man was an accepted fact so far as Margaret Foster was concerned, though in reality the question she had asked was open to a whole variety of other interpretations.[5]

It is important to consider, too, that when Margaret Foster asked the question, 'Did he interfere with you?' the immediate reaction from Sgt Shanks was to attempt to obtain some clarification of precisely what was meant by this allegation. Whatever the words conveyed to Margaret Foster, they evidently did not have the same rigid definition for the policeman from Bellingham.

Evelyn lived in an era when nice girls adhered to a strict code of conduct. Routinely warned not to let men 'touch' them or 'allow liberties', young women were aware that there were some men who might attempt to do unspecified, shameful things, which they were not under any circumstances to allow. Girls who broke the code brought shame on themselves and on their families, and a girl who 'gave in' to a man was always at fault. Women who 'got into trouble' were inevitably perceived as culpable, condemned for 'leading a man on' or 'letting him go too far'. (Uncertain how far constituted 'too far', many young women were dubious about permitting any intimacy beyond holding hands.) Small wonder that Evelyn fought for her life when a strange man attacked her, then shoved her into the back seat of a motor car – surely a definite indication that some of these unspeakable things were about to take place.

While Fullarton James equated 'interference' with nothing short of actual rape, the police definition of sexual assault today is much wider: it can constitute any kind of unwelcome physical contact considered sexual in nature.[6] It seems likely that, in her innocence, Evelyn's definition of 'interference' was equally wide. The experience of a man fumbling up her skirts, perhaps discovering the dread and shameful secret that she was wearing a sanitary towel, would have been deeply distressing, and more than enough for her to feel that she had been 'interfered with'. Numerous unwelcome actions on the man's part could have constituted interference, without the loss of Evelyn's virginity, but to Margaret Foster, as to Fullarton James, the allegation was confined to a single issue. Margaret Foster therefore claimed that her daughter alleged she had been raped, but the medical evidence proved that she had not.

Unfortunately, Evelyn's mother gave the chief constable

and his hired gun precisely what they were looking for. Here was confirmation that Evelyn Foster had levelled a definite accusation of rape that was not substantiated by the medical facts. Margaret Foster had as good as told the court that her daughter was a liar.

CHAPTER 16

Evelyn's mother was not the only member of the family to be questioned at length that day. Joseph Foster also spent a long period in the witness chair.[1] After he had taken Mr Foster through his recollections of the night of Evelyn's death, the coroner turned his attention to the Hudson, taking particular interest in the question of its insurance value. Though the vehicle indisputably belonged to Evelyn, it was insured under a block policy covering all the vehicles owned by Foster's Garage. Joseph Foster explained that the insurance company were well aware that the car belonged to Evelyn, but the introduction of the insurance arrangements introduced a vague sense of irregularity. This increased when it emerged that if the car caught fire indoors, the amount insured would only be £450, whereas an offsite, outdoor fire elevated that sum to £700, which was considerably more than the car was worth. Had the coroner chosen to call a witness from the insurance company, they would no doubt have clarified this by explaining that block policies covering multiple vehicles often contained quirks of this nature, and that in the event of a claim it was most unlikely that the insurance company would actually have paid out a settlement anywhere approaching this maximum sum.[2]

Unfortunately, the coroner made no attempt to illuminate the issue any further and instead, having established that – on the face of it at least – the car was worth more burned out on the moor, than it was in full running order on the road, he then questioned Mr Foster regarding the road tax on the vehicle. Having been primed by a memorandum from Supt Shell some 48 hours earlier, Mr Dodds was well aware that the road tax on the Hudson had run out on 31 December.[3] Joseph Foster agreed that the road tax had been overlooked and not been renewed until 15 January, when he himself had renewed it for three months. It was another apparently damaging admission, giving a smidgeon of support to the suggestion that the Fosters had conspired to fire the car for the sake of the insurance money – after all, why tax a car on 1 January if you knew its days were numbered?

The coroner also seemed keen to undermine the contention that Evelyn had been in business on her own account. If that was the case, why had she asked her father to quote the fare to Ponteland?

'It just naturally happened. She always asked my advice.'

In spite of Mr Dodds' reservations, other aspects of the

evidence implied that Evelyn enjoyed a healthy level of independence from her father. Asked about his daughter's earnings, Joseph Foster said that he was unable to provide any information because she took care of that side of things herself, and the notebook in which she had kept details of her fares had been discovered almost completely destroyed in the body of the car, which was where she normally kept it. He was, however, able to assure the coroner that Evelyn had no worries and in particular no financial worries. She had a healthy balance of £481 4s 8d in her bank account and a further £8 5s 4d in the Post Office.[4]

When Mr Smirk took his turn at questioning the witness, he again acted like a prosecuting barrister, underlining points that told against the accused. Having taken Mr Foster back to Evelyn's return from Elishaw, and confirmed yet again that the man had not come up to the garage 'to enquire for the car as one would have expected him to', Smirk concluded by saying: 'There is no question about it, that you did not see the man?'

'No,' Evelyn's father replied.

Though this sort of showboating at the expense of the bereaved relatives may have had the desired impact on-out-of-town reporters, it was unlikely to have elicited the approval of the jury, who knew the Fosters and cannot have enjoyed the spectacle of their cross-examination by the police solicitor.

In many respects the Foster inquest was a peculiar affair, not least when it came to the selection of witnesses chosen to appear. The correspondence between Philip Dodds and Fullarton James proves that Mr Dodds simply called everyone from whom he had received a statement, whether they had anything particularly relevant to add or not. In fairness to Mr Dodds, he could not call witnesses that he did not know about, and some of his comments do suggest that he had no idea of the quantity of evidence which Fullarton James had chosen to withhold.

Margaret Foster, who could relate the story told by Evelyn herself, and Evelyn's father, Joseph, who could tell the court a great deal about the car, were obvious choices to give evidence, as were Professor McDonald, who had carried out the post-mortem and Professor Dunn, who had analysed what remained of Evelyn's clothing and various items recovered from the scene. William Jennings, the chief constable's 'expert' on motor cars, Dr McEachran and Cecil Johnstone, the driver who had discovered her on the moor and brought her home, had equally clear roles to play, but the relative significance of the other witnesses was less obvious.

Of the three taxi passengers who had travelled north from Otterburn with Evelyn that night, only Mary Murray was called to give evidence. Her testimony contrived to produce a sense of deserted roads, where the passage of any car would be a noteworthy event – a somewhat misleading picture, as we will see.

Sydney Henderson testified to seeing the fire across the moors while he was walking home, though this added little to the sum of knowledge, as no one was in any doubt that a car fire had occurred at Wolf's Nick at some time that evening. In similar vein, Walter Beattie was required to travel all the way from Hawick in order to describe how he had pulled up to get a better look at the blazing car, though this offered nothing in the way of evidence regarding how Evelyn had come to be dying on the moors.

The logic behind calling Robert Harrison, who had been driving a southbound Tait's bus from Knowesgate on 6 January, is initially even harder to fathom. Harrison's bus left Knowesgate at 7.30 bound for Newcastle, and he made no claim to having seen Evelyn's car. From the point of view of constructing the scenario favoured by the chief constable, however, Harrison was an excellent witness because he too gave the impression of a deserted road, where he could definitely recall seeing only one car. This, in turn, provided a neat bit of support for the chief constable's favourite witness, William Kirsopp-Reed, because Kirsopp-Reed would say in his evidence that he had passed a Tait's bus which was travelling south, and since Harrison could only remember seeing one car, the farmer and the bus driver were inadvertently helping to create a picture in which every vehicle had been accounted for.

In reality, the police had traced and questioned a number of other drivers who had been on the road that night, but whose statements Fullarton James had not chosen to pass on to the coroner. Similarly Bessie McDonnell, the witness who had actually seen a car matching the description of Evelyn's turning in Belsay at around the time it must have done if Evelyn's story was true, was never called to give evidence. This was an appalling omission and one of the clearest indicators of the chief constable's agenda, but with the coroner presumably unaware of Miss McDonnell's evidence, the court heard instead from Robert Harrison and William Kirsopp-Reed, whose accounts of their journeys appeared to completely undermine Evelyn's story.

Just as Margaret Foster had fallen into the error of saying that Evelyn understood 'interfered with' to constitute rape, William Kirsopp-Reed also allowed his testimony to be twisted in a way that it should not have been. What the Old Town farmer's evidence really amounted to was that though he was familiar with Evelyn's car, he had not specifically noticed it as he drove home on 6 January, which did not in any way rule out his having passed the car without recognising it. What the chief constable wanted him to say was that the car had definitely not been on the road between Wolf's Nick and Belsay that evening, and Mr Smirk was primed accordingly.

Though Kirsopp-Reed tried to temper his evidence by suggesting that he might not have remembered every vehicle that passed him, even stating that the large fast-moving car he and his sister recalled meeting just north of Ferney Chesters could have been Evelyn Foster's car, Mr Smirk was ready and waiting to trap him. Having asked the farmer whether he was sure of his times to 'within five minutes' as he had originally told the police, Smirk then ridiculed the notion that Evelyn's car could have been seen at 7.20 – the time Kirsopp-Reed had placed this sighting – when the Hudson car had also been positively identified by the Foster's bus crew at 7.22 at Raylees, some half-a-dozen miles further north.

Smirk then excelled himself by settling the question of how Evelyn could have known that the Kirsopp-Reeds were on the road that night, by asking the farmer whether Miss Foster or anyone associated with her could have known that he was going to Newcastle that day, and receiving confirmation that Gordon Foster had probably known about this expedition in advance, thereby setting up the obvious inference that Gordon could then have mentioned it to Evelyn.

On the face of it, any neutral party might have assumed that the inquest jury were being offered every possible sighting of Evelyn and her car that night. George Maughan, John Thompson and Robert Luke each took their turn in explaining how they had seen each other and the car itself, either immediately before or immediately after it had arrived back in Otterburn. Each of these witnesses only helped to emphasise the invisibility of the mysterious stranger – for here were three people who had passed close by the car that night and yet none of them were able to say that they had seen the mystery man – a point pressed home repeatedly by Mr Smirk. Like Kirsopp-Reed, George Maughan tried to lessen the damage, pointing out that it had been too dark for him to see whether there had been anyone in the car with Evelyn, but Smirk forced one witness after another to confirm that they had not seen this man.

With hindsight it is obvious what effect the chief

constable hoped to achieve by putting forward the witnesses that he did. The idea that he was actively suppressing any evidence at all that supported Evelyn's story is shocking, but it is difficult to find any other explanation for his failure to call Bessie McDonnell, or his initial reluctance to provide the coroner with a copy of Albert Beach's statement when requested to do so. After all, if someone as peripheral as the bus driver Robert Harrison was thought to have a relevant contribution, then Albert Beach, who had seen two cars at Elishaw Road Ends at around the time when Evelyn was theoretically meeting her mystery passenger, was surely worthy of the coroner's notice, yet the coroner had to argue it out with the chief constable in order to see Beach's statement at all.

Beach presented a potential problem for anyone who wanted to demonstrate that the Elishaw car and the mystery man were figments of Evelyn's imagination, because his claim to have seen two cars, one which had sped past him on the Hexham road, and the other, presumed to belong to Evelyn, travelling along the road towards Otterburn, introduced an untraced, Hexham-bound car into the evidence. However the car Beach had seen travelling towards Hexham was a two-seater and therefore the wrong size and shape to be a match for the car which Evelyn said had dropped the man at Elishaw, and better yet Beach was adamant that he had seen only two cars, which effectively ruled out the possibility of there having been a third vehicle from which the mystery man could have emerged.

The real problem for the anti-Evelyn camp lay in the statement provided by Beach's mate, John Oliver, which contained a far more important piece of information, for as well as describing the speeding two-seater that passed them at Elishaw Bridge and the car seen a couple of minutes later along the main road, Oliver had introduced a possible third vehicle into the equation – the car parked at the Elishaw junction – and though Beach thought this had been the two-seater that passed them at the bridge, Oliver believed it had been a different car. Fullarton James lit on a simple solution. Beach and Oliver were among numerous witnesses who had provided more than one statement to the police. The original statements had been taken on 9 January by Sgt Armstrong, and it was on this occasion that Oliver had explicitly stated that he believed the car standing at the junction and the car seen near the bridge were two different vehicles. Sgt Armstrong took further statements from the men on the following day, but on that occasion he was principally interested in sorting out what time the men had left the van. Required to provide copies of the workmen's statements, Fullarton James forwarded the statements taken on 10 January, which conveniently omit Oliver's dissent regarding his mate's opinion of the car parked on the main road. This could have been the result of dealing with chaotic number of statements, but may equally have been blatant duplicity. Whichever was the way of it, instead of the roadmen providing some limited backing for Evelyn's story, Beach's testimony was effectively taken alone and so did yet more damage.[5]

It was doubly unfortunate that the only other 'missing witness' Philip Dodds had spotted in the newspaper was John Kennedy, the labourer who had been overtaken by a car on his way home from choir practice in Kirkwhelpington, because Denis Herdman's evidence leaves no doubt that the car Kennedy had seen belonged to him, and having been forced to hand over Kennedy's statement, the chief constable naturally provided Herdman's too, and the farmer from Hawick Farm was called as a witness. Matching his testimony up with Kennedy's can only have served to reassure the coroner that Fullarton James had withheld these statements solely because the car seen by Kennedy had not the slightest relevance to the case.

For anyone who hoped to find support for Evelyn's story however, the most damaging witnesses of all were the experts. Professor Dunn took a very long time to deliver conclusions that can be summarised in a matter of two sentences. None of the stains found on the car door handles, heather or anywhere else had tested positive for blood. A glass bottle found about 12 feet from the rear of the car during the initial police search had proved to contain nothing more sinister than the dregs of a soft drink, and, finally, Evelyn's clothing showed clear evidence of having been in contact with some form of petroleum distillate.

Inspector Russell had already explained at length about the discovery of the open petrol tin, found lying on the rack where the luggage box had once been, and with the news that Evelyn's clothing bore traces of petrol, the conclusion that the contents of the petrol can had been used to start the fire was somewhat inescapable. This, of course, appeared to directly contradict Evelyn's story of the accelerant coming from a bottle produced from the man's pocket.

The medical testimony was even more damaging, for Professor McDonald's report gave no credence whatsoever to Evelyn's allegations of sexual assault. The evidence relating to a possible physical assault was more complex, but, astonishingly, McDonald managed to transform information that should have told in favour of Evelyn into something that told against her. Several of the witnesses who saw Evelyn when she was brought home had remarked on the obvious swelling around parts of her face, commenting that her eyelids were bluish and swollen and that one eye had been swollen shut. Burns can cause swelling of tissue and in McDonald's words, 'the facial features, especially the eyelids, were obscured by burning,' but his report went on to state that there was 'some bluish discoloration about the root of the nose, and the upper part of the eyelids, and on dissection of the lower part of the forehead above the nose suggested a slight amount of superficial bruising.' Apart from this there were no other external marks to suggest that Evelyn had sustained any injuries apart from burning, but 'over the burned areas, superficial injuries or scratches could not possibly have been registered'.

Anyone adopting a neutral perspective might well summarise this as follows. Due to the burns it was impossible to detect any sign of physical assault to most of Evelyn's body. Therefore the absence of any marks of physical assault in these areas cannot help us to determine what occurred one way or the other. However, the area where Evelyn said she had been hit in the face showed various signs of bruising. If Evelyn was lying about the assault, some other explanation for this bruising needed to be sought.

That Mr Dodds had adopted a less than neutral approach can be detected in his asking McDonald: 'There is absolutely no trace of evidence of bruising of the face?'

Jaws presumably dropped collectively when McDonald, having previously read aloud his own report quoted above, which describes the presence of bruising, responded, 'There is none.'

'If it had been severe, you would have found it?'

'A quite severe injury I should have found.'

Dodds, evidently wishing to reinforce the point even further asked: 'If the girl was knocked down and stunned by a blow, you would probably have found some trace?'

McDonald agreed that he would have expected to.

And then from Dodds, 'There was no sign of outrage?'

'No sign at all.' As if to further underline the unreliability of Evelyn's story, McDonald then volunteered that there was no sign of Evelyn's arms being nipped, as she had claimed, without bothering to add that as his own report had already made clear, the burns to Evelyn's arms would have obscured any evidence of nipping, something which in any case would not necessarily leave any lasting, visible marks.

Between them the professor and the coroner were creating a thoroughly misleading picture, and the demolition job the coroner had embarked upon gathered further momentum when he asked McDonald whether, if the girl had stood with her left leg on the running board and her right leg on the step into the car, then thrown petrol into the back of the car and set fire to it, could the flames have 'come back and blinded her'? In his report the professor had stated plainly that the position of Evelyn's worst injuries made it obvious that she had been seated during at least part of the fire, whereas in the scenario now being suggested by the coroner, it was likely that Evelyn's face and upper body would have suffered the worst of the initial flames and most unlikely for her buttocks and thighs to have taken the brunt of the fire, but rather than explaining that what was being proposed was inconsistent with Evelyn's injuries, McDonald responded with a disingenuous level of ambiguity, saying, 'I think it quite possible. Though I cannot quite understand, if that were the explanation, why there should have been such localisation of the burns.'

At the end of the coroner's questions the point regarding the blows Evelyn claimed to have received was revisited by the police solicitor, Mr Smirk, and McDonald obediently fell into line again, saying that he had 'found no evidence of the girl being struck'. This was too much for at least one member of the jury, Reverend Brierley, who asked the pathologist, 'In your examination of the face, you say there was a bluish discoloration. Does that suggest bruising to the face?'

McDonald's response was the most disgraceful example of double-speak and nonsense with which the jury had been confronted so far. 'Yes. There was really no evidence of bruising by a blow.' A halfway decent, neutral coroner might well have asked the professor to explain what on earth he meant by this. If there was bruising to Evelyn Foster's face and the professor was confident that it had not been the result of a blow, then how did he account for its being there? In what circumstances could a young woman's face become bruised without having sustained some kind of blow – whether it be from an inanimate object, or an assailant's hand?

By now, however, the jury must have realised that Mr Dodds was anything but neutral.

The final witness was William Jennings, whose evidence was understandably lengthy. Jennings described the condition of all the various parts of the car in the loving detail of a man thoroughly immersed in automobiles. He confirmed that the fire had not been the result of any mechanical failure and had undoubtedly started in the rear of the vehicle. He explained that the petrol tank had not exploded, but rather that the solder holding the draining tap in place had melted, enabling the petrol to leak out under the vehicle and thereby help to fuel the blaze. He reiterated his belief that the fire could not have started until the car had reached the position where it had been found on the moor, and that someone had been at the wheel until it arrived there.

Once Jennings had undermined Evelyn's version of how and when the fire had begun, the coroner turned to Evelyn's claim that the man had taken control of the car and asked Jennings whether he thought it a possibility that the man would have been able to drive the car for ten or twelve miles as described. Initially, Jennings proved helpful to the coroner again, saying: 'It would be a very difficult thing to do if she acquiesced... and almost impossible if she resisted.'

The question of how the man had managed to wrest control of the car from Evelyn is complicated because we have no way of knowing to what degree he did so, or how far he is actually supposed to have driven. However, it would not have been terribly difficult to grab the steering wheel of the Hudson, because in common with many cars of the time it had a large steering wheel which extended at least a couple of inches beyond the centre point of the dashboard. In addition, unlike later car designs, the front seats formed a continuous bench and there was no barrier running down the centre of the foot-well, though the tall gear lever which came up in the middle of this space would certainly have been a nuisance to anyone attempting to operate the pedals from the passenger's side of the seat.

Mr Dodds was evidently hoping that Jennings would follow McDonald's example, by utilising a follow-up question to underline the implausibility of Evelyn's story, but when he was faced with a second question on the point, instead of dismissing the idea out of hand, Jennings admitted that someone could drive the car like that, 'but he would not be in a comfortable position.'

Mr Dodds tried again: 'Do you think a man would drive a car of this horse power very far on a dark night in this position?'

Jennings again said that it was possible, adding the doubtful rider that it was 'a question of control'. At this point, the coroner perhaps decided that he was not going to get what he hoped for out of the witness, because he adjourned the proceedings so that the jury could be taken outside to inspect a Hudson car brought along for the occasion. They were permitted to sit inside and test out for themselves whether or not it was possible for someone to take control of the car while the previous driver remained scrunched up against the right-hand door. On their return to the building, the coroner summed up the evidence as he saw it, before inviting them to retire and consider their verdict.

CHAPTER 17

The jury can have been in no doubt as to what verdict was expected from them. The various claims made by Evelyn, that the petrol tank had exploded, that someone had pulled up near the burning car and whistled, that the fire had been started using the contents of a bottle produced from a man's pocket, had been all shot down by the sworn testimony of independent witnesses.

In his summing-up, the coroner had given them a very clear idea of his own position. Instructing them that they could put aside accident or suicide,[1] he told them that they must decide whether it had been murder, or else that 'the girl' had set fire to the car herself and been burned accidentally in the process. If it was the latter, then the jury needed to consider why she might have done so. 'Was it the insurance money?' Mr Dodds asked, again tossing the misleading sum of £700 into the arena. Or, on the other hand, the coroner suggested, 'there were cases of persons obsessed with the idea of notoriety'. It was a suggestion that typified the approach of both the coroner and the chief constable, for while neither of them was prepared to accept Evelyn's own story without some firm corroboration, both men had not the slightest difficulty in introducing theories of their own (and farfetched theories at that) for which not a shred of evidence existed.

The coroner's 'review' of the evidence had swiftly turned into an exposition of all the reasons to dismiss Evelyn's account. 'It strikes me as a little peculiar,' he said, 'that a man comes down from Jedburgh with some people, has some tea with them, and tells them that he is going to Newcastle, and they did not continue their friendship with him and give him a lift to Hexham. There he would have been more certain of getting a connection by train or omnibus than the definite uncertainty of leaving him at Elishaw, on the chance of getting an omnibus in Otterburn.'

Such speculations may have appeared plausible to the out-of-town reporters, but the Otterburn jury would have known perfectly well that had the man caught the Newcastle bus in Otterburn (a bus he had missed by less than 30 minutes), he would have reached Newcastle considerably sooner than if he had made the 20-mile detour south-west to Hexham and picked up some transport there. Taking the man on to Hexham would only have become helpful once it was apparent that he had missed the Newcastle bus – something that was not established until after they had flagged Evelyn down at Elishaw.

Mr Dodds said he found it 'astonishing' that no one had seen the man walk down the street in Otterburn, after being dropped at Fosters' garage. 'He was supposed to have gone into the inn, but no one had seen him there', though 'there were no cars outside the inn, so he would have had to go inside to enquire'. At this point one wonders how many of those sitting in the Memorial Hall began to divine just how far Mr Dodds was over-egging the pudding. No evidence had been presented one way or the other at the inquest as to whether there had been cars parked outside the inn, and there may well have been local people present who knew that Dodds was incorrect in his surmise that there were none.[2]

Not content with his inaccurate remarks regarding the absence of parked cars, Dodds now decided to exaggerate the case against Evelyn still further by drawing to the jury's attention the point that, 'Mrs Foster had always insisted as far as possible on Evelyn being accompanied by somebody on long journeys, particularly on a dark night'. In reality, Evelyn did not normally take a third party with her on 'long journeys', and though Mrs Foster preferred it if Evelyn took a companion when her fare was a lone male stranger, she had never suggested that Evelyn was 'always' accompanied in such circumstances – on the contrary she had told the police that Evelyn had previously driven strangers alone at night.

'It was suggested that she take Phillipson,' the coroner went on, 'and she said, "All right, Mum." She did not take him, though Phillipson was in the village at the time.' Again the implication of this remark was misleading, suggesting that it would have been the simplest thing in the world to have taken Phillipson, when in fact Evelyn had no way of knowing whether the young man was in the village and, if so, where he might be located.

Moving to the journey beyond Otterburn, Mr Dodds

said that there was no evidence to show that Evelyn had ever travelled as far as Belsay that night. Five witnesses who had been on the road between Raylees and Belsay had been called and only one of them said he had seen a car, and he could not identify it as Miss Foster's car. 'She had never been seen on the outward journey between those two places.' As for the girl's statement that the man had thrown something from a bottle or a tin over her, 'no trace of anything inflammable, except petrol, had been found on her clothes...

'Was it likely,' Dodds asked, warming to his task, 'that a stranger would carry a bottle or a tin of petrol on him? According to Miss Foster's statement, the car must have been on fire on the road – could it then have been driven across the moor? Such a thing is absolutely impossible. It is nonsense. If the man had taken the car off the road, he would have run the risk of breaking his own neck as it went down the embankment. It is impossible to conceive that he would do it.'

The coroner elaborated further regarding the open petrol tin, saying that this was the obvious source of the accelerant for the fire. 'It has been suggested that she might have been standing with one foot on the step and one foot on the running board, pouring petrol on the cushions and when she lighted it, the flames came back and caught her . . . Was not the position of the burns consistent with a theory of that description?' (It is surely much to the credit of the jury and spectators that no one shouted aloud at this point, 'No – they were not!')

There was no direct evidence that the burns had been caused by a third person, the coroner said, and it would be 'improper to bring in a verdict of that description', unless they were 'satisfied beyond doubt as to how they were caused'.

The jury retired to consider their verdict, over which they deliberated for two hours and ten minutes. On their return, to the coroner's evident annoyance, the foreman declared that their verdict was wilful murder against some person or persons unknown.

As if unable to believe his ears, Mr Dodds asked whether they had found 'that some individual had wilfully poured petrol over her and set her on fire?'

'Yes,' said the foreman, 'we do.'

A knot of villagers waiting outside to hear the verdict cheered and applauded when it reached them. The coroner and the chief constable were less well pleased, with the former telling a waiting reporter that 'such a verdict can only have been arrived at by total disregard of the medical, scientific and expert evidence'.[3] Fullarton James's reaction to the verdict was identical, though whether or not he actually told reporters outside the Memorial Hall that the verdict went against the evidence and that he was satisfied that neither the car nor the assailant existed, as reported by the Daily Express, is open to debate.[4]

The gentlemen of the press were as taken aback by the verdict as had been the coroner. The News Chronicle,[5] though moderate in its tone, expressed concern about the verdict being unsupported by the evidence, writing that the 'jury of Otterburn villagers... refuse to accept that Miss Foster could have been capable of saying anything which was not true', adding that 'if the jury had composed of people from some other area, the verdict would probably not have been one of murder'.

This was the reaction to a greater or lesser degree within the majority of the newspapers, and some were scathing. J.M. Holland of Empire News[6] penned a particularly vicious piece, ridiculing the jury and writing of Evelyn herself that:

...women and particularly pure women who are approaching their thirties are prone to do queer things at times... Miss Foster was pure and chaste, but she still seems to have had definite opinions on a matter that cannot be discussed in a public newspaper... to my mind we should have heard a good deal less of this case if a woman of twenty-eight had not been constantly spoken and written of as a girl.

Holland provided a particularly vile example of an openly misogynistic society, but he was far from alone in suggesting that 28-year-old virgins were automatically to be suspected of mental instability if they accused a man of molesting them. This particular article tells us much about the attitude of many men towards not only women in general, but specifically to young women believed to have falsely cried 'rape'. If Holland was right and Evelyn had set the fire herself, she had nevertheless paid a terrible price, suffering an awful death, perhaps as a result of some temporary mental illness, yet Holland was merciless in his attack on this harmless young woman. Similarly, it is impossible to read Fullarton James's thoughts about the case without appreciating that he had conceived a deep loathing for Evelyn Foster, which became such an obsession that he even avoided, wherever possible, dignifying her with a name.

Revolting diatribes aside, Holland also raised some points of genuine concern. According to several journalists, one juror had told reporters after the inquest, 'I know that you take the oath and are sworn to return a true verdict, but I'm a local man and have knowledge of the facts which will not come out in evidence.' Another juryman said, 'I have a perfectly open mind, but I have known Evelyn Foster all her life and you're not going to persuade me she made that story up. She was a good, clean, pure girl and I cannot imagine for a moment that she would invent that yarn on her deathbed.'[7]

Though the good faith of these men is unquestionable, their remarks only served to underline that a verdict had been returned that ran contrary to the evidence produced. Holland wrote, 'It shakes my faith in the jury system . . .'[8] On the face of it, he had a point.

CHAPTER 18

The jurors quoted in the newspapers appeared to suggest that when arriving at their verdict, they had taken into consideration not only their personal knowledge of the victim, but also 'facts which will not come out in evidence'. It is hardly surprising that they were vilified for this by numerous newspapers, since these supposed 'facts' cannot have comprised of much more than gossip and hearsay, whereas their verdict should have been based solely on the information presented at the inquest. However, this was an exceptional case, in which the jurymen must have been aware that they were working under the disadvantage of not being made privy to the bulk of the evidence which the police had accumulated in the month since Evelyn Foster's death. If that information had been made available to them, would it have strengthened or shaken their belief in Evelyn's story?

When, in 2012, I was granted unique, privileged access to the police files on the Foster case, I was able to consider Evelyn's account of what happened that night against the material accumulated by the police, in its entirety.

A key point in Evelyn's story is that the man got out of her car at Foster's Garage and walked down the village street to the Percy Arms. It has been surmised that if the man had already decided to scam Evelyn for the fare, then her story is in no way disproved by the fact that he never entered the Percy Arms, but the complete absence of any witnesses able to testify to his presence in the street itself cannot be explained away so easily. If Evelyn's story is true, then unless this man owned a cloak of invisibility, he must have walked along the main street and waited for several minutes near the bridge, in plain sight of any passers-by.

It would later be suggested that the police, out of prejudice or ignorance, suppressed evidence of this man's presence in Otterburn that night, calling only those witnesses who would testify to having not seen him, rather than those who had observed a stranger.[1] This is completely incorrect. It is true that some witnesses did report sightings of men whom they did not recognise in the village that night, but the police records reveal that they managed to identify and eliminate every single person who was seen by anyone else in Otterburn during the crucial period. It was a gargantuan task of cross-checking and re-interviewing, but by the end of January they had pieced together the evidence obtained from everyone who admitted to being out and about in the village that evening, and far from suggesting that there had been an unknown man lurking in Otterburn, the eyewitness testimony appeared to bear out the chief constable's theory that the mystery man simply did not exist.

Stories of local people encountering an unidentified stranger had found their way into the newspapers from the earliest days of the enquiry. There was the report in some papers that Annie Carruthers had encountered a man on the bridge at around 7 p.m. and he had initially asked her about the bus to Newcastle, but then become so abusive that she had hastened away in considerable alarm. In reality, this was a misconstruction of the schoolmistress's evidence, presumably cobbled together by a journalist who had only half listened to what she had to say.

In Miss Carruthers' statement to the police, she said that she had encountered two men much earlier in the day, who had made a lewd or insulting remark as she passed them in the road – from other statements made to the police, it is actually possible to identify these men and eliminate them completely. Then, at around 6.30, she had been approached by another strange man at the top of Mill Lane, who had asked her about the bus to Newcastle. There had been nothing remotely sinister about this encounter and the police established that he was in fact a workman named Henry Park, who was waiting for the Foster's bus to take him back to Newcastle, where he lived.[2]

A second woman, Mary Ferry, is reported by Jonathan Goodman as having been alarmed by a man near the bridge, when she called to collect a parcel from the Percy Arms at 7.15.[3] The origin of this tale is again the Chinese whispers reproduced by various newspapers and now incorporated into the folk memory of the case, for while it is entirely possible that Mary Ferry did one evening collect a parcel from the Percy Arms and then undergo an unnerving encounter with a strange man who was lurking near the bridge, this event definitely did not take place on 6 January 1931 – had it done so she would surely have informed the police of the details when they took a statement from her on 8 January. Miss Ferry gave a full account of her movements to the police, which included seeing the same workman as Annie Carruthers at around 6.15, but did not include any reference to collecting a parcel from the Percy Arms or to seeing a man lurking near the bridge at 7.15, a time by which Mary Ferry, according to her witness statement, had long since returned home.[4]

Goodman also set much store on the evidence of George Sinclair, manager of the Otterburn Co-operative Store, who told the police that he saw a man emerging from the post office doorway whom he did not recognise. The existence of this stranger would have lent considerable support to Evelyn Foster's story, and the competence and integrity of Northumberland Police has been called into question in not calling George Sinclair as a witness at the inquest – but the police were right to discount Sinclair's evidence as unimportant. It has often been assumed that the man seen by Sinclair had been lurking in the shadows provided by the doorway of a closed shop, but the Otterburn post office remained open until 7.30 that night. This fact immediately transforms the man from a suspicious lurker in a darkened doorway, to an ordinary customer emerging after a transaction – and so he was. The man seen by George Sinclair was identified by the police as John Murray of Monkridge, who had arrived in Otterburn to spend the evening at the home of some friends in Mill Lane. Murray gave the police a detailed, coherent account of his movements, which includes the fact that he was in the post office from 6.40 to around 6.45, and that as he left the post office he saw Mr Sinclair. George Sinclair's timing of his trip across to the post box fits precisely with Murray's period in the shop, and this not only served to eliminate the 'suspicious stranger', but also demonstrated that by the time any suspicious stranger arrived in the village with Evelyn Foster, George Sinclair had already posted his letter and was back at home.[5]

If you take a walk through Otterburn on a chilly January evening today, there is a fair chance that you will go unobserved. Mass ownership of cars has drastically reduced the number of errands undertaken on foot, and scarcely anyone in rural employment ends their working day by walking home. Few people nowadays habitually leave the house to purchase fresh milk, or an evening paper, nor do they need to seek entertainment beyond their own front doors, but life was very different in the 1930s. On 6 January 1931, there appeared to be no lack of potential witnesses on Otterburn village's street, the bitter weather notwithstanding. The regular bus services brought clusters of arriving and departing passengers at roughly half-hour intervals. The shops and garages were open for business, disgorging their customers and staff in ones and twos. The Memorial Hall not only attracted a regular crowd who came to play cards, darts and dominoes, but that evening it also played host to a committee meeting which was scheduled to begin at 7.30. Three separate pairs of overnight guests arrived at the Percy Arms, while the bar was steadily filling up with all the regulars, the blacksmith, the school master, the rabbit catcher...[6] Northumberland Police located and interviewed more than 30 individuals who had travelled along at least part of the village street between 6.30 and 7.30 that evening, and many more who had been out and about either earlier or later. Significant numbers of these witnesses confirmed one another's presence – but not one of them corroborated the presence of Evelyn's supposed assailant, and when the entire jigsaw of statements was pieced together, not one person remained unaccounted for, except of course, the bowler-hatted stranger.

However, establishing a clear timeline is a vital part of any enquiry, and, unlike detective fiction, where pocket watches are stopped by a fatal blow, precisely timed church bells ring out as the murderer passes by, railway trains, factory hooters or the ever reliable 6.30 bus provide exact timings for critical events, in real-life witnesses generally have to estimate their timings. It is comparatively unusual for a witness to be able to recall at precisely what time anything took place.[7]

The most accurately timed sighting of Evelyn's car was provided by the Foster's bus crew, John Robson and Oswald Young, who placed the Hudson at Raylees at 7.22.[8] As their bus arrived on time at Foster's Garage at 7.30 and the journey normally took them about seven minutes, the two men were probably right about the time. To reach Raylees by 7.22 Evelyn must have left Otterburn no later than 7.15, if she was averaging around 20mph, and even earlier if John Robson was correct in estimating her speed at no more than 10mph (though this is a notoriously tricky thing to assess in respect of a vehicle travelling towards you).

The crucial point here is that anyone out and about in the village before 7.00 or much after 7.15 cannot possibly have observed Evelyn Foster or her passenger, but when reading the copious notes made by Fullarton James and his officers, is becomes clear that the police never fully appreciated this point, and therefore never attempted to narrow down, precisely when the murderer must have been in the village street and who had been on the spot to observe him. In fact, they came at the question from a completely different angle. Faced with numerous statements that mentioned unidentified men seen in Otterburn that evening, they set about putting a name to every person who had been seen by anyone else, comparing witness accounts one against another, until they had meticulously matched up and identified every man who was seen that evening. It never occurred to them to turn the question on its head and endeavour to establish whether it was possible for someone to have passed down the street at any given time without being seen.

Among many letters received from members of the public who were trying to help, the chief constable received one from a personal friend, Sir Claude Morrison-Bell, whose home, Highgreen Manor, lay roughly five miles west of Otterburn.[9] The baronet had been driving home with one of his daughters on 6 January and recorded that he had passed through Otterburn at around 3.30 that afternoon. Having taken the trouble to describe the various cars and pedestrians he could remember, Sir Claude explained that he was writing in response to the newspapers appeal, and while 'sorry to bother you, when you are so busy, thought the possibility of what one might call negative evidence, might be of some use in this ghastly affair'.

Though there was nothing else of any significance in the letter, its author was absolutely right to place value on what he termed 'negative evidence'. Sometimes what people do not see can be every bit as important as the things they do. Unfortunately, Fullarton James had no concept of this at all.

CHAPTER 19

At this point it essential to return to what can be established about Evelyn Foster's arrival in Otterburn at around 7 p.m.[1] Previously published accounts have necessarily relied on what took place at the coroner's inquest, where a very limited number of witnesses were called and confusing questions from the coroner and police solicitor sometimes led to confused responses from the witnesses. The original witness statements taken immediately after the event provide a much clearer picture of those vital moments surrounding Evelyn's return.

The word 'moment' is an important one. When a car draws up as someone is walking by, it is so fleeting that, when asked to recall it later, it is almost inevitable that minor discrepancies between witnesses will arise – in particular, at which split second you noticed or spoke with a third party – none of which alters the fact that you were there and you did see the car arrive. The return of the Hudson occurred at one of those points in the evening when several witnesses happened to converge on the same spot within the same couple of minutes. They were: Tommy Vasey and Robert Luke, who were both working in Foster's Garage; William Blackham, the schoolmaster, who was walking into Otterburn for an evening pint at the Percy Arms; John Thompson, a farm labourer who lived at Garretsheils and was walking into Otterburn to visit a friend; Eleanor Wilson, who worked for the Fosters, in the office which was part of The Kennels; and George and Edith Maughan, who were walking from their home in the centre of Otterburn to the village school.

The Maughans told the police that they left home at roughly 7 p.m. Walking towards Foster's Garage, on the same side of the road as The Kennels, they recalled meeting two separate people coming the other way, both of them walking on the opposite side of the road: the first was Mr Blackham, the schoolmaster, but the second man was a stranger to them. They also saw a car approaching from the north which drew up alongside The Kennels, just as the Maughans reached the building. (All witnesses agreed that Evelyn parked outside The Kennels that night and not, as has sometimes been suggested since, outside the big garage on the opposite side of the road.)

George Maughan could see that a woman was driving and assumed that it was Evelyn, but he did not notice whether she had a passenger. His wife could add nothing further on this point, and both said they were somewhat blinded by the bright headlights. They heard no voices and did not see anyone get out of the car. As they passed the big garage Robert Luke came out of the main doors and shouted something across the road to them, but it was a cold night and the Maughans hurried on, with Edith Maughan calling out no more than an acknowledgement.

Robert Luke was one of several men still working on

the broken-down Bean bus, and he was crossing the road in order to fetch a piece of wire from one of the smaller sheds on the same side as The Kennels. Just prior to doing this he had heard the church clock strike seven – something he had remarked on to his co-workers in the garage (this is confirmed in statements by his workmates, so there can be no doubt that he did not cross the road until after he heard the clock strike).[2] Luke told the police that as he emerged from the main garage he spotted the Maughans on the other side of the road and called out jokingly to them about 'sweethearting again'. He thought that Mrs Maughan had called out something in reply, but had not caught what she said. Luke then crossed the road, walking directly behind the Hudson car, though he did not notice whether there was anyone inside.

William Blackham, the school master, confirmed that he had seen the Maughans, but said that he did not see the Hudson car standing in front of The Kennels when he walked by. This makes perfect sense, because the Maughans encountered Blackham between their home and the garage, so Blackham would have walked beyond The Kennels before Evelyn's car arrived. Further support is given to this sequence of events by Tommy Vasey, who had popped out of the garage a moment or two before Robert Luke in order to obtain a bolt needed for the repair of the bus, and as he crossed the road he had seen and greeted William Blackham.

Vasey's excursion to obtain the bolt is confirmed by Eleanor Wilson, Foster's clerk, who signed it out of the stock for him, something she thought took place at about 6.55. Miss Wilson told the police that though she had not actually seen Evelyn Foster arrive home, she had heard her. According to Miss Wilson, she heard someone approach and knock on the kitchen door at about 6.50 (the kitchen door was close to the door to the office). At the time the kitchen door handle was broken, so the door had to be wedged shut from the inside to keep it closed. A voice had called out, 'Who's there?' and Evelyn said, 'It's me, hurry up' or 'look sharp'. Miss Wilson then heard the door open and a snatch of voices talking in the kitchen, though she could not hear what was said. She finished work and left the office soon afterwards, estimating her departure at seven. When she left The Kennels, the Hudson car was standing alongside the petrol pumps in front of the house and there did not appear to be anyone about. Her route to her lodgings at Home Farm took her up the lane opposite The Kennels, so she did not walk along the village street.

On the face of it there is an oddity in this account, because Eleanor Wilson places the arrival of Evelyn Foster in the kitchen at 6.50, before the arrival of Thomas Vasey in the office at 6.55. However, this doesn't necessarily present a problem. Eleanor Wilson was due to finish work at around seven and she mentions in her statement that she had checked her watch and noticed that it was 6.50 before Evelyn Foster's arrival. One of the perils of attempting to establish a timeline is that witnesses, often encouraged by the interviewing officer, tried to peg an event to something definite and tended to express small intervals between events as 'about five minutes later', which neatly places each separate occurrence to the nearest five-minute interval. When dealing with a series of things occurring within a short space of time, this can be fatally misleading. We can be reasonably certain that Eleanor Wilson was wrong about the time of Evelyn Foster's arrival, because the other witnesses without exception place it soon after seven. Given that we are dealing with a sequence of events that probably took up less than four or five minutes in total, it is perfectly feasible to assume that Thomas Vasey emerged from the big garage, greeted William Blackham and crossed the road very shortly before Evelyn Foster drove up. Vasey entered the sheds in search of his bolt and in the meantime the Hudson arrived, Evelyn got out and was heard by Miss Wilson, seeking admission to the kitchen. A moment or two later Vasey appeared in the office, bolt in hand, wanting the clerk to sign the item out, and very soon afterwards she realised that it was home time, put on her outdoor things and left.

This would mean that when Vasey re-crossed the road with his bolt, the Hudson must have been parked outside The Kennels, but in his statement Vasey said that he could not say whether the Hudson was there or not, pointing out that it was such a commonplace sight, he would have taken no notice either way. Robert Luke took a similar line, explaining that though he had spotted the Hudson parked outside the house when he crossed the road for a length of wire, he didn't take any particular notice of it, because the presence of the car was nothing out of the ordinary.

So far the evidence of each witness dovetails neatly — that is until we reach John Thompson, the labourer who was heading into the village from Garretsheils. Thompson told the police that a big saloon car with bright lights had passed him when he was about 100 yards south of Otterburn School and that, when he reached the edge of the village, he saw the Hudson (a car he recognised as belonging to Evelyn Foster) parked outside The Kennels and he also heard Evelyn Foster's voice (which he said he knew) talking to someone, though he could not see her or the person she was addressing. As he continued into the village, he met what he took to be two young men walking in the opposite direction, one wearing 'leggings'. Though Thompson did not know the Maughans and the Maughans did not know Thompson, the police later brought the two parties together and each was satisfied that the other was the person or persons they had encountered that night.

Unfortunately, the line of questioning taken at the coroner's inquest muddied the testimony of these witnesses, leading some people to arrive at an ingenious theory whereby George Maughan may have actually walked past Evelyn Foster's killer in the village street that night.[3] Comparing Thompson's account with everyone else's, it is apparent that he was not gifted with a precise memory. The implication of his statement is that it was Evelyn's car that overtook him when he was about 100 yards south of the school, but that is evidently incorrect as it contradicts the combined testimony of everyone else. Thompson is therefore demonstrably mistaken about precisely where and when he first saw the car.

Moving to his encounter with the Maughans, though George Maughan and John Thompson both became confused when questioned at the inquest, in their original accounts it is clear that they agree they passed each other in the village street just south of Foster's Garage, and this makes it impossible for both men to have walked past the car while it was stationery at the Fosters' gate, but a minor tweak to Thompson's evidence would render this sequence of events perfectly logical.

Thompson would have been passed by a car between the village and the school, because Alastair Bull's car was travelling south from the Redesdale Arms during this period (William Blackham also mentioned being passed by this car as he walked towards the village). Having remembered seeing a car, Thompson must have subsequently assumed that it was the one being driven by Evelyn Foster. The Hudson was not there when Blackham walked past the garage, but was seen approaching and pulling up by the Maughans, so Evelyn's car cannot have been there when Thompson walked past The Kennels, but it did arrive a few seconds later. Thompson lived locally and was used to seeing the big Hudson parked in that spot. By the time he was interviewed on 14 January, it would have been all too easy for Thompson to visualise the car there, particularly when he thought he recalled that the car had passed him on his walk into the village.

Singularly among the witnesses, Thompson claimed to have heard a voice he said he recognised as Evelyn's. It is probably significant that he did not see the speaker and seems to have had no idea where this voice was coming from. He was not close enough to catch what was said, and if Evelyn's voice had been sufficiently loud to carry to Thompson, it would be very odd if it had not also reached Mr and Mrs Maughan or Robert Luke, who were both closer to the car than he was. What seems much more likely is that the voice Thompson heard belonged to Edith Maughan, who called across the street to Robert Luke while Thompson would still have been within earshot.

In any real-life investigation, it is extremely unusual for the recollections of all eye witnesses to match in every detail – so unusual that to a seasoned police detective, such perfect synchronicity would imply collusion – but minor details aside, this group of seven witnesses bear one another out in all important aspects, and place Evelyn and the Hudson back at The Kennels very shortly after seven. Pinning down the time of her arrival was immensely important when it came to establishing which witnesses in Otterburn could have seen her attacker as he made the two-minute walk from one end of the village to the other. In fact, timing was everything.

CHAPTER 20

Fixated on the fact that not one single witness had been found who could confirm the presence of Evelyn's passenger in Otterburn, it apparently never occurred to Fullarton James that although the police had witnesses who had seen the car arrive, not one of these witnesses had actually observed Evelyn Foster get out of the car. In spite of this, Evelyn had unquestionably got out of the car within a short time of arriving home. Logic suggests that Evelyn's passenger would have left the car at the same time as she did, which means that if no one happened to be around to see Evelyn vacate the driver's seat, it naturally follows that there would be no witness to see her passenger either. Similarly, although it is an incontrovertible fact that Evelyn Foster must have filled the car with petrol, got back into the car and driven down the village street, not one single person observed her at any stage in this process either. The original investigation was so focused on Evelyn's passenger that they completely failed to appreciate the significance of her own 'invisibility'.

As well as looking at the question from the wrong angle, the police made another mistake in that they tended to look no further than the estimated times provided by their witnesses, taking them at face value even though comparing these statements against one another would have shown that some people's estimates had to be a long way out. Only by making a detailed comparison of every statement against every other statement and aligning the movements of witnesses is it possible to produce an accurate set of timings for each individual. Today this could have been achieved using a computer, but in 1931 the police would have needed to devise a paper-based system.

In order to establish precisely where everyone was and at what time, I constructed a two-metre long diagram of Otterburn village's street and the immediate approach roads, using moveable slips of paper to represent all the various witnesses.[1] By comparing who had seen whom and correcting the various time anomalies, this exercise eventually mapped every witness's movements in the village street for the period between 6.15 and 7.45. The result of this detailed examination of all the data collected some 80 years earlier is that a small window emerges in which, by the direst of chances from the point of view of the investigation, there was a perfect opportunity for Evelyn Foster's assailant to stroll down the village street unseen.

It is clear from the contemporary statements that no one had the Hudson in view at the moment when Evelyn and her theoretical passenger got out. Assuming that this passenger existed, we can surmise that he left the car and walked along the village street at a few minutes after seven. By this time the big doors of the main bus garage had been closed against the cold for some time, so the men still working on the broken-down bus inside would not have seen him. We also know that William Blackham had passed The Kennels before the car arrived and was probably ensconced in the Percy Arms before our suspect set off in that direction. John Thompson had also gone by and his business in the village did not take him any further than the row of cottages midway along the street, so he, too, was indoors well before the man could have caught him up, while the Maughans had walked out of the village, in the direction of the school. Robert Luke and Tommy Vasey would both have re-crossed the road while the Hudson was still outside The Kennels, but they did not see Evelyn getting out of the car and the gentle curve of the village street ensures that someone standing outside Foster's Garage or The Kennels cannot see all the way down to the Percy Arms, so once Evelyn's assailant had walked a few yards up the road, he would not have been visible to anyone crossing from one set of buildings to another.

There had been considerable activity along the village street between 6.30 and 7 p.m., with George Sinclair slipping out to post his letter and seeing John Murray leaving the post office, and various witnesses on their way home from work, but all these people were already back indoors or else walking away from the village before seven.

Another flurry of activity took place at around 7.30, when the start of the committee meeting at the Memorial

Hall, or 'Institute', coincided with the arrival of the Newcastle bus, bringing with it the evening papers. At this point half the village appears to have emerged on some errand or another, but of course we know that by this time Evelyn Foster and the Hudson were long gone. After cross-checking all the witness statements, the vital fact emerges that amidst all this activity hardly anyone was out in the main street between 7.00 and 7.20, and only one person's statement initially suggests that they may have been in a position to observe anyone waiting beside the bridge between 7.00 and 7.10.

This potentially important witness was John Geddes, who lived at Bank Foot Cottages in East Otterburn. Geddes was due to attend the committee meeting at 7.30 and says he set off from home at a couple of minutes after seven. He recalled seeing two people on the short walk between his home and the Memorial Hall, one of which proved to be a man called William Thompson, who was walking out of the village towards the Elsdon junction, and the other was Annie Brown, who was walking home after calling at East Otterburn Farm.

Geddes believed that he had arrived at the Memorial Hall by 7.10. (The walk from his home takes no more than three or four minutes.) This made Mr Geddes a tremendously important witness, because his short journey apparently took him across the bridge during the vital period when Evelyn's attacker would have been waiting there. The trouble is that these times don't work when compared with the other witnesses. Annie Brown estimated that she did not leave East Otterburn Farm until about 7.10 and her timings are supported by Edric Hedley, who was running late for the meeting in the Memorial Hall and did not arrive until after 7.30. Hedley had encountered William Thompson on the road to Elsdon at about 7.20 and, factoring in the time it would have taken Thompson to cover the distance between being seen by Geddes and Hedley, it is clear that John Geddes could not have seen Thompson much before 7.12.

Geddes was probably a mere five minutes out regarding the time he reached the Memorial Hall, which still places him tantalisingly close to the period when the mystery man is supposed to have waited on the bridge, but even if Mr Geddes did cross the bridge and walk past the Percy Arms between 7.05 and 7.15 this is of no help to the enquiry, because when questioned by the police he was unable to recall whether there was anyone waiting there, telling Inspector Russell, 'I cannot say if I passed anyone between the Institute and Miss Brown or not.'

In making this assertion Geddes throws up another important truth. Contrary to the optimistic expectations of Fullarton James, every witness did not enjoy perfect recall, and neither was Otterburn such a sleepy backwater that a stranger, perhaps smoking a cigarette outside the Percy Arms, would have been so very remarkable or noteworthy. Two married couples and a couple of auditors working in the area were staying at the hotel that night, all of them strangers to the district. Earlier in the day the Tyneside workman, Henry Park, had been doing some jobs at Otterburn Hall. Travelling workmen like steam-roller driver Albert Beach and his mate came into the village after work to use the shops and the pub. There was no reason for Geddes to single any of these people out for notice and, by the time he was questioned on 20 January, a whole fortnight after the event, he gave the police his honest answer: he could not remember whether he had seen anyone that night or not. Far from confirming that Evelyn Foster's mysterious passenger did not exist, Geddes testimony merely underlines the lack of evidence one way or the other.

There is nothing to suggest that the police even realised what a potentially important witness John Geddes could have been. They did not speak to him until they took his statement on 20 January, and there is no indication that they returned to ask him further questions, or tried to confirm what time he had passed the Percy Arms that night. The point that Geddes is the only witness who even appeared to have been in the right place at the crucial time to have observed Evelyn's attacker completely es-caped them.

Another interesting snippet of evidence exists in the note made by PC Ferguson when he took the telephone call that originally summoned him to The Kennels that night. The times provided by Mr Foster during that initial conversation must necessarily be estimated, but they were no more nor less estimates than anything subsequently provided by other witnesses, and moreover have the ad-vantage of being made on the night of the event, rather than several days later. According to Ferguson's note, Evelyn set off north with her Rochester-bound passengers at 6.30, returned home with her tale of picking up a fare at Elishaw at 7 p.m. and she 'picked him up again in the village at 7.15'. Here, then, an underlining of the vital point that the mystery passenger undoubtedly spent less than 15 minutes in Otterburn, arriving soon after 7.00 and departing again by 7.15, it being the work of less than ten minutes for Evelyn to enquire about the fare, go out and refuel the Hudson, return to the house to confirm the cost of the fare, set off to pick up her passenger and drive south, and all of this accomplished during the one period that coincides perfectly with there being not a single person in the right place at the right time to see the mystery man.

Plenty of other witnesses were out on the street again as the time approached 7.20, the first of whom was George Phillipson, who popped down to the shop in East Otterburn for a couple of minutes, then walked back up the street with John Jackson. Jackson was another man due at the Institute at 7.30 and like many witnesses, Jackson was slightly out with his timings, but by comparing all the statements from around this time, it can be determined that Phillipson cannot have left his lodgings until 7.15 at the earliest.

At this stage we return to Sir Claude Morrison-Bell's 'negative evidence'. Not one of these witnesses, Geddes, Brown, Jackson or Phillipson, saw the Hudson as it passed through the village, and Phillipson in particular would have been likely to notice Evelyn's car. All of this apparently negative evidence is suggestive in quite the opposite way to that which Fullarton James interpreted it. Far from producing a stream of witnesses who were on the street but did not see the 'invisible man', in reality they throw up a gap in the evidence lasting roughly ten minutes, during which there was no one to see a stranger walking up the street and waiting at the bridge; no one to see Evelyn getting into her car, driving a few hundred yards, then pausing to collect her passenger as arranged.

Though there is nothing concrete in the Otterburn evidence to support Evelyn's story, neither is there anything that remotely disproves it.

CHAPTER 21

Chief Constable Fullarton James initially appears to have believed that he could create a complete record of the cars that travelled along the relevant stretches of road that night simply by asking everyone on the road, pedestrian and driver alike, to describe all the cars they had seen, then matching them one to another. While this is precisely what any good detective would attempt, common sense suggests that the process was fraught with difficulties. The road in question was a main route into Scotland and, while there was by no means a constant stream of traffic, nor was this a quiet country lane where a strange car might have stood out.

Reconstructing the passage of traffic along a rural road over several hours is an exceptionally difficult task. Any reader tempted to accept Fullarton James's premise that a majority of witnesses will have total recall, may like to experiment by privately keeping count of all the vehicles they meet during a half-hour drive along a relatively quiet rural road, then asking the other occupants of the car to describe the vehicles they have noticed. Without being warned in advance that they need to memorise what they see, the majority will invariably fail to remember some of the passing traffic even if asked to do so immediately afterwards, and the chance of accuracy decreases when people are asked to provide this sort of information up to several days later.

An additional problem lay in the fact that many of those questioned were people who regularly walked or drove along the same stretches of road and would therefore have a problem separating out which memories belonged to one specific (and for them entirely uneventful) journey. It was inevitable that some witnesses would be mistaken about which particular night they had seen things, and matters were further compounded by the fact that, among the relatively small community involved, some witnesses had inevitably discussed what they had seen with one another before providing the police with a formal statement, which introduced the possibility of being influenced by other people's recollections.

The most significant issue, however, is that anyone attempting to piece together the data obtained from their witnesses needs to do so in the most open-minded and objective way possible, but, as we have already seen, Fullarton James made up his mind about what had taken place at an extraordinarily early stage and then approached the investigation with the objective of proving his own theory.

During January 1931, the chief constable compiled numerous lists of cars, coupled with the times and places where they were seen, and concluded that this proved Evelyn Foster was lying in respect of various aspects of the night's events. He noted that Evelyn's car had been observed by a number of witnesses on its initial journey north, but that no witnesses had come forward to say they had seen a vehicle which could definitely be identified with the Hudson south of Raylees, while the one witness who knew the car and must have passed it if Evelyn's story was true, said that he had not seen her car that night. From this, Fullarton James concluded that Evelyn had never gone anywhere near as far south as Belsay, but instead had pulled off the road and waited in some obscure spot until the time was right for driving a short distance to Wolf's Nick and firing the car.

As for the car that had allegedly dropped Evelyn's assailant at Elishaw, the chief constable decided that, just as had been done with the evidence regarding men seen in Otterburn village street, if he could account for every car seen on the road between Rochester and Elishaw during the early part of the evening, he could prove that the mystery car did not exist.

Unfortunately, both the conclusions he reached and the process by which he arrived at them were hopelessly flawed, for while the chief constable seems to have satisfied himself that he accounted for all the vehicles that had been observed – including some that remained unidentified because their drivers never came forward – he only achieved this by cherry picking the statements of motorists and pedestrians that seemed to fit together, ignoring any inconvenient statements that were not a good fit and completely failing to take into account factors such as the relative speeds at which cars were moving along the road. It was a highly selective and thoroughly misguided process.[1]

Eighty years on, I approached the question in considerably more detail, drawing up a large diagram of the Newcastle road, extending from just short of the Scottish border to some distance south of Belsay, and again used moveable slips of card to represent every single witness who claimed to be on the road that night, cross-checking every aspect of the descriptions of vehicles, pedestrians or cyclists and the times they were said to have been in their reported positions. Only by undertaking this labyrinthine process, taking into account every piece of witness testimony, was it possible to plot these multiple journeys, undertaken at widely differing speeds over a period of several hours. The process was complicated by the fact that a significant number of drivers never came forward, so that it is not always possible to determine at what point a vehicle either joined or left the main road. In addition, the vast majority of witnesses were working with estimated times, which cannot be taken at face value. In spite of this, it was possible to establish two important points – firstly that some of Fullarton James's original vehicle identifications were undoubtedly wrong, but, more importantly, that Evelyn Foster's story could be true.

The undisputed facts of the initial journey north are that, during a period between roughly 6.30 and 7.00, Evelyn drove north as far as Birdhopecraig Farm and then back south again as far as The Kennels. During this period, the car Evelyn alleged she had encountered at

Elishaw must have been travelling south down the road through Rochester and presumably passed Evelyn as she drove north.

More than 40 witnesses, some on foot, some cycling, some driving and one in a horse-drawn cart, testified to being on or within sight of the main road between Otterburn and the Scottish border between 6.30 and 7.30 that evening. Their testimonies are frequently complementary, with many recognising one another or easily identified by the descriptions given.

One of them was the splendidly named Lancelot Robson, who responded to the original police appeal with the information that he had driven south along the stretch of road in question on 6 January, stopping for petrol in Otterburn at around 6.30.[2]

As he drove past the Redesdale Arms, Robson had noticed a Morris Oxford parked in front of the inn. This was Alastair Bull's car, which left the Redesdale Arms at approximately 6.40. By his own estimate, Bull was travelling at around 30mph, so it would have taken him about eight minutes to reach Otterburn, and in Otterburn the police found two separate witnesses who either heard or saw a car travelling south through the village at around 6.50–6.55.[3]

At this point, however, we find another significant bit of 'negative' evidence that the police completely overlooked. Albert Beach and his mate John Oliver left their van at 6.45 and supposedly had the Newcastle road in their sights constantly from then until 7.30. If this is correct, then they must have been in sight of the road when Bull's car drove south along it, yet they made absolutely no mention of seeing a vehicle that can be matched with Bull's. On the contrary, they insisted that the only car they saw travelling along the Newcastle road was the lone saloon assumed to have been Evelyn's.[4] While Beach and Oliver's failure to recall Bull's car does not provide us with a positive sighting of a four-seater that could have deposited our mystery man at the AA box, it does demonstrate the lack of wisdom in placing too much reliance on witnesses who claimed not to have seen things.

Beach and Oliver's failure to remember Bull's car represents a significant omission, because if the two men failed to remember Bull's car, how many other vehicles had also slipped their mind? Beach and Oliver fall ever deeper into the abyss of doubt once the spotlight is focused on the latter part of their statements, because after seeing the single car identified by the chief constable as Evelyn's, the two men finished crossing the field and continued to walk along the main road for another 30 minutes, claiming to have encountered no other vehicles except a motorcyclist, who they met near the school as he was riding north along the main road. Beach said that they particularly noticed the way the man was travelling very slowly, because of the road conditions. This cautious progress suggests that the motorcyclist was not travelling very far, and was therefore a local person who was likely to come forward, but in fact he was never identified. Not only did the motorcyclist himself fail to come forward, but no other witnesses reported his presence on the road, though there were numerous people from whom statements had been taken who could not have avoided being passed by this motorcyclist, if he existed.

While it is possible that the motorcyclist just happened to go unnoticed by everyone else, it is equally possible that this was a memory that actually belonged to a different walk into the village, undertaken on a different night. Combining the absence of Bull's car with the presence of the mystery motorcyclist places the information provided by Beach in a somewhat uncertain light, casting doubt on a key witness whose confident assertion regarding the number of cars travelling along the road that night has been relied upon for more than 80 years.

Returning to Evelyn's travels north of Otterburn and the evidence of one of her passengers, Mary Murray, it seems that while the Hudson paused to offload firebricks at Horsley shops, Mrs Murray saw a car go by, travelling south. Neither of her fellow passengers noticed this car, though William Glendinning spotted a cyclist going south, whom he correctly identified as Douglas Nelson. Douglas went unnoticed by both Mrs Murray and the third person in the car, Mr Wilson.[5] By simply comparing these three witness statements, it should have become obvious to Fullarton James that not everyone sees or recalls everything that happens. However, the chief constable was happy to accept witness testimony as 100 per cent accurate, providing it supported his own line of thinking.

The car lights reported at Horsley by Mrs Murray

could have been Alastair Bull's car, leaving the Redesdale Arms, and the chief constable decided that this was the case, thereby neatly eliminating a vehicle which might otherwise have been a possibility for the car containing the mystery man.

When Evelyn reached the village school in Rochester, she had to pull in to the side to allow a southbound car to pass. Both her remaining passengers recalled this car, describing it as a large saloon with very bright lights. Its driver was never identified, but for Fullarton James the identity of the car was obvious. Beach and Oliver said they had seen only two cars pass the Elishaw junction, one of which was presumed to have been Evelyn's, so the other – the car seen speeding across Elishaw Bridge towards Hexham – had to be the 'Rochester school car'. The workmen had told the police that this was a two-seater car, but in spite of the obvious discrepancy between this and the 'large saloon' seen at the Rochester school, the chief constable decided that it must have been the same car, which meant that all cars reported travelling south at the relevant time had been accounted for – a conclusion considerably wide of the truth.

The evidential waters were further muddied by the way in which some eye witnesses took little convincing that, if they had seen any vehicle travelling up or down the road during the early evening, then it must have been the ill-fated Hudson. Several witnesses north of Elishaw claimed to have 'recognised' Evelyn's car, and Fullarton James appears to have accepted their identifications without question, but these 'positive identifications' need to be put into context. The roads were unlit. Witnesses on foot were likely to be dazzled by approaching car headlights and, by the time statements were taken, everyone was agog with the shocking news of Miss Foster's awful death. It was known that she had driven as far as Birdhopecraig Farm, and therefore only natural that anyone on the road that night would automatically assume that a car which they recalled passing them that night was hers – even when it very clearly was not.

Among the 40 people who walked, cycled, drove along or happened to be standing beside the road between Elishaw Road Ends and Carter Bar between 6.30 and 7.30 that evening, the single most compelling fact is that witness after witness demonstrably undercounted the number of vehicles that passed them. Numerous witnesses who must have been passed by vehicles whose presence on the road was well attested told the police that they did not remember seeing any vehicles at all that night. Witnesses who were walking or driving with a companion proved to be the least reliable.

Unfortunately, Fullarton James simply ignored the issue of undercounting and kept himself busy matching each vehicle anyone had mentioned with another vehicle known to have been on the road, making things fit even when they obviously did not. A southbound car observed travelling well north of Rochester at roughly 6.55 by butcher George Ashford was assumed by the chief constable to be the same lone vehicle reported by a Wilfred

Leighton and Mary Murray, who were respectively cycling and walking north along the road. The chief constable's vehicle analysis ascribed all these sightings with the car being driven by Mr Iyengar – a vehicle which became his default match for numerous sightings of saloons up and down the road that night.[6]

This was another tempting conclusion, because as Iyengar drove south he must have passed each of these witnesses in turn. However, the car Ashford described (he had to move in to let it pass) was a four-seater car: a 'fast tourer' with flickering headlights. Mrs Murray described the car she saw as a four-seater with 'good headlights', while Leighton described a light-coloured two-seater. This does not sound like the same car. In fact, it sounds like two or quite possibly three different cars.

By cross-checking the times provided by each of these witnesses against those provided by everyone else, it is possible to determine with a reasonable degree of accuracy where each of them would have been on the road when they met this car. Assuming that the car was travelling at a reasonably constant speed, it is difficult to believe that each of them can have been overtaken at the point they suggest by the same car. Of course, the witnesses could have been mistaken about where exactly they saw the car. Perhaps Wilf Leighton was erroneous in his assertion that the car was a light-coloured, two-seater, but once we have accepted that in order to make this evidence fit, one witness must be wrong about where they saw the car and another must be mistaken about its appearance, is it not equally reasonable to speculate that the discrepancy arises because they have each remembered only one of at least two vehicles that passed them that night, and therefore that what we have here is not one car, but two? In addition, since butcher Ashford was making deliveries, which necessitated him constantly joining and leaving the road for several minutes at a time, it is entirely possible that he would not have seen every vehicle which was travelling in each direction, so his evidence of only seeing one car in no way rules out the possibility of other cars travelling south which he did not see.

Despite all the evidence to the contrary, the chief constable clung doggedly to his assertion that he had accounted for all the vehicles driving south towards Elishaw during the 6.30–7.00 period, and therefore that the vehicle that supposedly dropped the mystery man at Elishaw had simply never existed.

The Northumberland Police did an excellent job in tracing, interviewing and often re-interviewing witnesses who had been on the road north of Elishaw, managing to account for everyone seen out on foot that night. However, even as he was pretending to the press and the coroner that all vehicles had been accounted for, privately Fullarton James knew perfectly well that at least some of the drivers who had been on the road at the relevant time had not come forward. In spite of having this information to hand, the chief constable never acknowledged that not coming forward, just like undercounting, was probably the norm. With the exception of Alastair Bull (to whom an appeal was specifically directed), Thirumalalai Iyengar and Lancelot Robson, no non-local drivers came forward to account for any of the vehicles that travelled north or south along the 15-mile stretch of road including Elishaw during the early evening of 6 January. This silence probably encouraged Fullarton James to conclude that scarcely anyone had travelled along the route that night, when what he ought to have realised was that his appeal for information had failed. The reasons for this were twofold: firstly, a natural reluctance on the part of many members of the public to become involved, but more significantly because the appeal was bungled.

The police's initial, well-publicised appeal for a car carrying three men, which had stopped at the Redesdale Arms, had placed undue importance on a vehicle that had no bearing on the case and whose occupants were able to offer nothing useful. Had they focused the same level of attention on an appeal for the right car – a car probably driven by a woman, carrying at least one other passenger, which had travelled south through Rochester then turned down the road towards Hexham – it is just possible that the occupants of the mystery car might have come forward.

By the conclusion of his enquiries, Fullarton James believed that any possibility of this mystery car had been eliminated, but is that what his evidence really demonstrated?

CHAPTER 22

Apart from Evelyn Foster, how many cars actually travelled up and down the road running through Rochester towards Elishaw Road Ends that evening?

We know that Lancelot Robson was driving home from Hawick on 6 January and stopped in Otterburn to buy petrol at about 6.30,[1] and though he had noticed the car parked outside the Redesdale Arms when he drove by, he recalled nothing else on the road north of Otterburn except two men on foot. Robson's accurate description of a Morris Oxford (Bull's car) at the Redesdale Arms narrows the time when he passed the inn to between shortly after 6.00 and around 6.30, which is an important period when it comes to piecing together everyone's movements. In spite of this, the police took no interest in Mr Robson, presumably taking the narrow view that he would have been on the road too early to have seen the mystery man, and therefore had nothing of value to add.

Robson reinforces the point about 'negative evidence' still further. His presence in Otterburn went completely unreported, so that the fact of his being there at all survives only in a single telephone message, which has lain unremarked in a closed file for more than 80 years. The two men he saw on foot cannot be clearly identified, though it is possible that they were local men John Anderson and William Pringle, who were walking north from the Redesdale Arms to Woolaw at a time when Robson must have passed them, but like so many witnesses, Anderson and Pringle could not recall seeing any cars at all.[2]

The next southbound car we can be sure of is Bull's Morris Oxford, which left the Redesdale Arms at approximately 6.40. When he went outside to start the engine, Bull thought he noticed a car facing north at 'the nearby buildings', which were, in fact, Horsley shops.[3] The car seen by Bull must have been Evelyn Foster's, since this was the only car that stopped there at the relevant time and this makes it possible that Bull's was the car observed by Mary Murray, while she was waiting in the Hudson at Horsley.

The progress of Bull's car from the Redesdale Arms through Otterburn is well attested by a whole variety of witnesses.[4] While we can definitely pinpoint the car driven by Thirumalalai Iyengar at a particular time and location, because the students stopped at the thirty-second milestone in order to identify their precise whereabouts and checked their watches at the same time, noting that it was 7.40. Corroboration for this is provided by Robert Towns, who was walking along the Hexham road, on his way home from work and saw the car pulled up there, from across the fields.[5]

One southbound vehicle in particular should have been the focus of attention: the car that passed Evelyn's near Rochester's school. This encounter took place when

Evelyn still had to make two drops before turning round, so the 'Rochester school car' would have reached Elishaw a good five to ten minutes ahead of her, though it cannot possibly have reached Elishaw before Beach and Oliver set out from their van at 6.45. Can the 'large' car seen at Rochester's school really have been the 'two-seater' seen by Beach and Oliver? Or could it be the case that the two-seater was a completely different car that went unnoticed by the passengers in the Hudson, while the 'Rochester school car' was one of the relatively long list of vehicles forgotten by Oliver and Beach?

In spite of all the evidence to the contrary, the chief constable decided that the police were dealing with just three southbound cars during the critical period. The Hudson, the 'Rochester school car' and Bull's car (the undisputed existence of these three cars in no way led him to distrust Beach and Oliver's insistence that they had seen only two cars). Ignoring how Evelyn's passengers had described the car they had seen at Rochester, he decided that the two cars seen by Beach and Oliver were the 'Rochester school car' and the victim's own car, leaving no possible candidate to fill the role of the mystery car.

The truth is that neither the police in 1931, nor anyone examining the evidence today, can ever be absolutely sure exactly how many cars drove south past the Elishaw junction that evening. We cannot be sure that either or both of the two cars observed by Beach and Oliver can be conclusively identified with any of these three cars, or if they too represent cars never identified. What can be said with certainty is that of all the cars en route between Carter Bar and Elishaw between 6.30 and 7.30 that evening, not one car was reported by every witness who was in a position to have seen it, and, more importantly, that the majority of cars went unnoticed or were forgotten by at least some of the people in a position to have seen them. Some vehicles went unremarked by as many as half-a-dozen witnesses, with at least two southbound vehicles, a car with flickering headlights seen north of Ramshope at 6.55 by butcher George Ashford, and a light-coloured two-seater reported by Wilf Leighton north of Rochester at about 7.15, not spotted by anyone else at all. Lancelot Robson's car went completely unreported, in spite of numerous witnesses being in a position to have seen it, while a car with distinctive headlights, one bright, one dim, was not recollected by anyone other than a quartet of young men who stood chatting outside Rochester post office.[6] On the balance of probabilities, it is therefore perfectly possible for the car that dropped the man at Elishaw to have existed.

At this stage it is important to consider the statements provided by one particular pair of witnesses, on whom considerable reliance was placed in support of a theory espoused by the late Jonathan Goodman.[7] Matthew Wallace, a 19-year-old apprentice butcher, and Alan Bell, his unemployed friend, told the police that they set out from their homes in West Woodburn at between 7.10 to

7.15 on the evening of 6 January and cycled to Rochester Camp, a ride of some eight miles along a steeply undulating route, which took them about an hour-and-a-half. After spending 20 to 30 minutes at the camp they made the return journey, which for some unspecified reason seems to have taken them considerably longer. Both youths were 'absolutely certain' that they were not passed by any vehicles at all for the entirety of their outward or return journeys.[8]

On the face of it that is quite a claim – not a single car for an hour or more each way. Their certainty led Jonathan Goodman to believe that the car seen at Elishaw Bridge by Beach and Oliver at approximately 6.55 must have turned off before reaching West Woodburn. (In fact, a car travelling fast that had reached Elishaw by 6.55 could have been through West Woodburn before Wallace and Bell set out.) However, there was also the speeding car reported by Robert Towns, and this vehicle was travelling along the cyclists' route at a time when they should have seen it, but for some reason they did not.

The 'undercounting' problem is not the only issue. The oddest aspect of the boys' evidence is that unlike pretty much everyone else who travelled on the Elishaw to Rochester stretch of the road that evening, the Woodburn cyclists apparently met no one at all, not the paperboy Douglas Nelson, or two other teenage friends, Edward Stappard and Hugh Tully, or any of the other local people who were on the road until well after the cyclists should have passed them en route to Rochester Camp. In spite of there being plenty of possible witnesses, there is not the slightest corroboration for the Woodburn cyclists having been on that particular stretch of road that night.

It is far from unknown for people to approach the police – often in good faith – having been mistaken about precisely when they undertook a particular journey, and coupled with the lack of confirmation for the ride supposedly undertaken by Wallace and Bell, there is good reason to suspect that this may be the situation facing us here. Both boys made their statements on 12 January, which allows for the possibility that they were mistaken about the date. A less charitable explanation is that they had had time to formulate a story that would gain some attention from the press, who did in fact take considerable interest in them.

Neither lad explains why they rode all the way to Rochester Camp and who, if anyone, they saw when they got there. The only vehicle they noticed en route was George Ashford's van, parked at the Redesdale Arms, but since Ashford was a regular visitor at the inn his presence at that hour might reasonably have been assumed, while the only person the youths claimed to have seen during the entire journey was William Johnstone, whom they said they met cycling in the opposite direction to them at Dyke Head, a couple of miles north of West Woodburn. In fact, Johnstone had already provided the police with a statement indicating that he was nowhere near Dyke Head at this time.[9]

Determining the timing of their journeys was

necessarily difficult. The majority of cyclists interviewed in the enquiry seem to have averaged around 10mph. Wallace and Bell's route included some steep uphill sections, but even so it is difficult to believe that their average speed would have been only half as fast as everyone else that evening. At an average of 10mph, they should have taken less than an hour to cover the ground from West Woodburn to Rochester Camp, but they both believed the journey had taken them at least half as long again, with the return journey supposedly taking longer still. At any speed between 5 and 10mph, they could scarcely have avoided seeing and being seen by several pedestrians and at least one other cyclist who were indisputably on their route. While numerous witnesses failed to recall some of the people they had seen, and were not always remembered by everyone who must have seen them, the 'Woodburn Cyclists' stand in a class of their own for both invisibility and amnesia. They seem, at best, unreliable witnesses and at worst untrustworthy ones.

Though there is uncertainty about the actual numbers of vehicles travelling south via Elishaw Road Ends between 6.45 and 7 that night, this is a long way from being able to suggest that the presence of the mystery car at Elishaw is proven. Of course, a definite sighting of an 'extra' car would take us a lot closer and among the dozens of witness statements provided to the police, there is just one possible sighting of this extra car and it came from the steamroller driver, John Oliver.

Oliver essentially confirmed everything that his mate, Albert Beach, had told the police, with the exception of two significant points. The first dispute between the two men lay in the timing of their walk, with Beach initially stating that they left their caravan at 6.25, while Oliver insisted that he had checked his watch and the time was actually 6.45.[10] The police eventually determined that Oliver was correct about this, which does tend to suggest that Oliver was the more observant of the two, but by a quirk of fate it was his mate's name which appeared in the newspapers and thereby came to the coroner's notice, with the result that Mr Dodds specifically asked to see Albert Beach's statement but was less interested in John Oliver's. This becomes more significant when we reach the second matter on which the men diverged.

Both men had recalled that as they walked north from their caravan towards Elishaw Bridge they were passed by a dark blue, two-seater car, which Oliver firmly identified to the police as a Morris Cowley. Before noticing this car, they both thought that they had glimpsed a car standing up on the main road at the junction. Beach told the police that he thought this car was the one which had sped past them shortly afterwards, but Oliver did not agree, saying, 'I am certain the second car [the one seen parked at the junction] was not the one we met on Elishaw Road.'

At Elishaw we are not dealing with a flat landscape and perfect sightlines, but with steeply sloping terrain. After leaving their caravan, Beach and Oliver had to walk north until they crossed Elishaw Bridge, then take a short-cut across a field in order to reach the Newcastle road. From their starting point on the Hexham road, the junction at Elishaw Road Ends would have been in sight, and it would therefore have been possible to see any vehicles at the junction, but once the men began to descend towards Elishaw bridge, the junction and any cars parked there would have gradually vanished, and then remained out of sight while the workmen headed across the fields. It is therefore perfectly feasible that a car standing at the AA box could have remained there for some time, with Beach and Oliver none the wiser, and if Evelyn Foster's car happened to encounter this waiting car during the five minutes or so that it took Beach and Oliver to complete their descent to the bridge and start crossing the field towards the main road, they would have been unaware of it.

It is perfectly reasonable to conjecture that a car was already waiting alongside the AA box when Beach and Oliver left their van, not least because both men thought they had seen a car there. If the car was standing at the junction between 6.45 and 6.50, it cannot possibly have been Evelyn's car, though the 'Rochester school car' could easily have made it to the junction within that margin. The car would have 'disappeared' within minutes of them embarking on their walk and could have continued to wait at the junction, out of their sight, until Evelyn's car arrived – also out of their sight. (The Morris Cowley which sped past the men near the bridge would have been of no interest to the occupants of this waiting vehicle, if they wanted a Newcastle-bound car.)

If Evelyn Foster had approached the junction and been flagged down during this period, there is no possible way in which Beach and Oliver could have witnessed her arrival, or seen what transpired in the moments it took to explain the situation, and for her to accept this new passenger and drive away again. However, Evelyn's car would have emerged into their line of sight soon after she drove on again, becoming the southbound car which Beach and Oliver reported seeing as they crossed the field.

The question remains as to how the two men could have failed to notice the other car, when with the transfer of the passenger complete, it turned onto the Hexham road and resumed its own journey. It is a question to which there is more than one solution. First, it is possible that the men did see the car, but subsequently forgot about it, just as they forgot about various other vehicles that night, however, there is an even more likely explanation, so obvious that it is well-nigh incredible that the officers on the spot at the time never seem to have thought of it.

By the time they saw what was in all probability Evelyn's car, Beach and Oliver were crossing the field with their backs to the Hexham road. In all likelihood, they were focusing more on where they put their feet, than on any traffic passing along a road several hundred yards behind them, and unless they turned to look back for some reason, the men would not have been able to see the car. Even if they heard the distant car engine, it is unlikely to have provoked their interest, and it is possible that the sound was masked by the simultaneous passage of the Hudson heading along the main road, or by their own voices if they were talking to one another.

Under the circumstances, it would almost be more surprising if the men had noticed this car on the road running behind them than that they failed to do so. It would also be an astonishing coincidence if a car had happened to stop at the junction just where Evelyn said it had and yet be unconnected with the events she described. The fact that Beach and Oliver reported a car standing in the right place at the right time is a vital piece of evidence that gives credence to the first part of Evelyn's story.

CHAPTER 23

Is it possible to find anything substantiating what Evelyn said about her ordeal, or even the drive she claims to have undertaken all the way south to Belsay, then northwards back to Wolf's Nick?

Attempting to reconstruct this section of the journey is even more complicated, because unlike the route north of Elishaw, the road from Otterburn to Belsay offers multiple minor junctions where vehicles can join and leave the road. To add to the difficulty, not everyone on the road that night came forward, and many of those who did had problems recalling the times when they had started or finished their journeys. The police traced almost 30 drivers who had been on the Newcastle road at some point between Otterburn and Belsay between 6.30 and 10.30 that night, and, in addition to these drivers, they took statements from a similar number of witnesses who had walked along stretches of the road, or who had seen or heard cars passing by. It was an impressive effort, but the untold story lies with the large number of drivers and vehicles that were never identified. Far from establishing a complete picture of what was happening on the road that night, the police were working from a picture that had numerous holes in it. Today, every snippet of information would have been used to compile as full a picture as possible of all known vehicle movements, but though Fullarton James drew up several lists of cars travelling north and south between Otterburn and Belsay, the magnitude of the task proved beyond him, and he again resorted to recording only what he perceived as useful matches, without worrying about any obvious discrepancies.

In mitigation, we know that the chief constable and his men were in over their heads. Russell's team at Otterburn were essentially foot soldiers, entirely taken up with the sheer slog of following up leads and taking down information. There was a hole at the centre of the enquiry where a criminal investigation department should have been, and without this Fullarton James did not have the manpower or expertise that the investigation required. Lack of manpower had been an issue from the outset, and when examining the statements relating to events that had taken place on the fatal evening, it becomes obvious that whereas the officers had diligently tracked down everyone mentioned in the statements relating to activity in Otterburn village itself and on the road leading north towards the border, they had been unable to carry out anything like such a comprehensive operation in respect of the road leading south. Overworked and under-resourced, Russell's team had simply been unable to pursue every possible lead across this much wider geographical area.

This lack of thoroughness is particularly apparent on examination of the statement given by Fullarton James's star witness, William Kirsopp-Reed. According to Mr

Kirsopp-Reed and his sister, they had followed a car north virtually all the way from Belsay, which had eventually taken the turn for Mirlaw. This car was never identified, yet in Margaret Kirsopp-Reed's statement, she mentioned that she thought she recognised the car as belonging to a local doctor, Dr Goodall, who lived at the first property along that road.[1] Whereas every paperboy and person who popped out to post a letter in Otterburn or Rochester was tracked down, there is no statement in the files from Dr Goodall, and no memo regarding any approach being made to him. He slipped the net, yet if his car was on the road that night, the doctor was a potentially vital witness.[2]

It was not just Margaret Kirsopp-Reed's evidence about Dr Goodall that was missed. It became the official position that the only definite sighting of Evelyn's car driving south of Otterburn was the one provided by the bus crew at Raylees, but when the information from every statement is used to build up a complete picture, it emerges that this was probably not the case.

We know that in order to get to Raylees by 7.22, where she was seen by the bus crew, Evelyn must have left Otterburn at around 7.15 and there is a possible sighting of Evelyn's car just outside Otterburn by Annie Brown, who left East Otterburn Farm at around 7.10 and soon afterwards thought she was overtaken by a car heading out of the village. Support for Annie comes from William Thompson, who was walking not far ahead of her, because he independently said that he thought he saw a car pass him, driving south.[3] Fullarton James would no doubt have argued that it did not matter whether this was the Hudson or not, because the police already knew that Evelyn had driven as far as Raylees, however, these sightings are important because they all help us to understand the timeline.

The likelihood that this was Evelyn's car only emerges after the relative positions of all known witnesses and vehicle sightings have been cross-checked and plotted – an exercise which was not contemporaneously undertaken. No other cars apart from Evelyn's are definitely known to have been driving south through East Otterburn at around this time, and the next vehicle to do so belonged to a man called Walter Brydon, who was driving from Otterburn to Elsdon a good 15 to 20 minutes later.[4] As this car left the main road at the Elsdon turn off, it cannot have been the car which was seen much further south by our next important witness, a farmer called John Telfer.

Mr Telfer only drove a short distance along the main Newcastle road that night, joining it at the Knowesgate crossroads and driving north 'for about ten minutes' until he reached his farm at Ottercops, a little way north of Wolf's Nick. As he was driving along this section of the road he remembered being passed by a car coming south. He estimated that he reached home at around 7.45 and thought that he had seen the car about five minutes before that.[5] The chief constable made no attempt to factor the car seen by John Telfer into the equation, noting in the margin of the statement 'this is too early to be EF car, or else he is wrong about the time'. Having been dismissed in this peremptory fashion, the statement was presumably disregarded, but there are sound reasons for thinking that this could have been another sighting of Evelyn Foster, not least because there is no evidence that any other southbound cars were on this stretch of the route at this particular time (Bull and Robson were long gone while Iyengar had only just reached Elishaw).

The bus driver John Robson told the police that he thought Evelyn was driving extremely cautiously when he saw her at 7.22, and put the Hudson's speed at a mere 10mph, but the bus conductor, Oswald Young, contradicted this, saying that Evelyn was driving at 'a steady speed', which hardly suggests anything so abnormal as 10mph.[6] An experienced driver who knew the road as Evelyn did was most unlikely to have been crawling as such an exceptionally slow rate – even Mr Iyengar, on his own admission a cautious driver and poor navigator, managed to average double that. Though the chief constable chose to focus on Robson's suggestion that Evelyn's progress was peculiarly slow, most of the cars on the road that night averaged 25mph and Evelyn was considered a 'fast driver', so it is far more likely that for most of the southbound journey she travelled at around 28–30mph. If Evelyn had driven at just under 30mph from Raylees, this would have placed her on the length of road where Telfer saw his southbound car at somewhere between 7.30 and 7.35, which is extremely close to his rough estimate. While this doesn't take us anywhere near Belsay, it does suggest that Evelyn was making steady progress in that direction, driving south, just as she said she did.

This brings us inevitably to the testimony of William Kirsopp-Reed and his sister, Margaret. They were indisputably driving north from Belsay at a time when they were guaranteed to see Evelyn's car if it was heading the opposite way. Mr Kirsopp-Reed and his sister were no doubt sincere and well intentioned people, but even the most sincere and well intentioned are capable of being mistaken. Unfortunately, this was not a possibility that Fullarton James allowed for: on the contrary, he seems to have believed that people could summon up a complete and wholly reliable recollection of every aspect of a 20-mile journey when asked to do so several days after the event. In his notes and memos, the chief constable returned again and again to the fact that William Kirsopp-Reed had said that he did not see Evelyn Foster's car that night.

There exists more than a suspicion that the chief constable was a snob.[7] Kirsopp-Reed was a well-respected, middle-class farmer. To Fullarton James he represented a man of the better sort, and, if he said that he had not seen Miss Foster's car, who could possibly doubt him? It was only natural that he should be elevated into the role of star witness – the local gentleman who could prove that Evelyn Foster was lying.

Presumably Fullarton James thought that the presence of Margaret Kirsopp-Reed in the car, and the way that she corroborated everything her brother said gave added credence to his account, but an experienced officer today would be more likely to suspect collusion on discovering that a brother and sister living under the same roof shared an identical recollection of this 20-mile drive, and would therefore place considerably less reliance on its absolute accuracy, as it is most unlikely that two witnesses would independently remember exactly the same things.

The biggest problem, however, was that the chief constable fell into precisely the same trap as he had done with Beach and Oliver. He never tested the Kirsopp-Reeds' statements against anyone else's in order to expose any clear errors or omissions. In their remarkable display of sibling unity, William and Margaret had both seen all the same vehicles in all the same places on the road, with the single minor discrepancy that Margaret placed the sighting of a southbound Tait's bus a little further south than did her brother.[8]

The Tait's southbound bus provides us with our first clue about the reliability of the Kirsopp-Reeds' evidence, because not only was there a Tait's bus travelling south at this time, there was also a Foster's bus, driven by Cecil Johnstone. It left Otterburn at 6.40, averaged 20mph and arrived in Belsay at 7.30.[9] According to William Kirsopp-Reed's statement, he passed through Belsay no later than 7.15 and if this was so then he must have met the Foster's bus a few miles north of Belsay – yet there is no mention of this in his statement. Similarly, a motorcyclist called Ernest Robson was riding south from Knowesgate to Belsay between 7 and 8 p.m., but the Kirsopp-Reeds failed to recall him, too.[10] It has to be said that any witnesses who don't notice an object as large as an omnibus cannot be deemed 100 per cent reliable.

This was of course entirely lost on the police because they never undertook the full-scale cross-referencing of every single statement, which would have established not only which vehicles had been seen by various witnesses, but also which vehicles they had missed. The undue emphasis placed on William Kirsopp-Reed's testimony had an extremely damaging effect on the whole enquiry. The 'fact' that Mr Kirsopp-Reed had not seen Evelyn directly led to the theory that she had never driven as far as Belsay at all.

However, there is another crucial aspect of William Kirsopp-Reed's evidence that became lost at an early stage. Pencilled at the bottom of one typewritten copy of the statement he made to Supt Shell on 13 January are the words, 'I knew Evelyn Foster's car, but I don't think I would have recognised it in the dark.'[11] This vital qualification was never incorporated into his official statement, and though Kirsopp-Reed tried to indicate at the inquest that it was less a question of his saying that Evelyn Foster's car had definitely not been on the road than of his saying that he did not remember seeing it, the damaging way in which his original statement was worded – 'I know Evelyn Foster's car. I did not see it.' – could not be undone.

When the Kirsopp-Reeds' statements are compared with those of other motorists and pedestrians who were on the route at the same time, several glaring discrepancies appear. First, we have the meeting with Tait's bus, not far from Harle Post Office. According to the timings provided by the farmer and his sister, this occurred at around 7.25, but that is absolutely impossible, because the bus did not set off from Knowesgate until just after 7.30, had stopped to pick up passengers in Kirkwhelpington, and would not have reached Harle Post Office until around 7.40–7.45 at the earliest.[12] The timings provided by William Kirsopp-Reed are not therefore 'accurate to within five minutes', as he was repeatedly asked to assert at the inquest, but out by a factor of at least 20 minutes. This is underlined by his omission regarding the Foster's bus, which he should have seen if he had travelled through Belsay at 7.15, but would not have seen if he came through after 7.30.

Mr Kirsopp-Reed was mistaken in his timing of the journey and this places his sighting of the large, fast saloon car near Ferney Chesters, dismissed by Mr Smirk at the inquest as being far too early to have been the one driven by Evelyn Foster, into a whole new light. With this in mind, we need to revisit what the brother and sister from Old Town had to say about this car. They saw this southbound saloon while they were following a car that left the main road at the turn for Mirlaw. Kirsopp-Reed told the police that the oncoming saloon had dipped its lights for the first car, but evidently had not realised there was another car following, because the driver then returned them to full beam, which dazzled the occupants of the second car. This would obviously have made it more difficult for the Kirsopp-Reeds to get a particularly good look at the offending saloon.

It is also suggestive that when Evelyn told her mother about the cars she remembered seeing, she mentioned the Kirsopp-Reeds' car in the same breath as a car that she 'thought she knew'. This suggests that these two cars were in some way linked together in her memory. The car the Kirsopp-Reeds were following was thought by Margaret Kirsopp-Reed to have been recognisable as belonging to a local doctor, in which case it is highly likely that Evelyn would have been familiar with this car, too.

A car sounding very much like the one seen near Ferney Chesters by the Kirsopp-Reeds was also recalled by Miss Eva Morrison, who had been visiting her parents at Harnham Buildings, with her boyfriend Sidney Henderson. She described 'a large car with powerful headlights' which passed them shortly before they caught Tait's bus at around 7.45 at Harnham Gate.[13]

The chief constable decided that the southbound vehicle seen by Miss Morrison and the Kirsopp-Reeds must have been Alastair Bull's car. That might have been a reasonable assumption had the Old Town farmer been correct about the time, but was a disastrous mistake in the light of Kirsopp-Reed's considerable margin of error and did not fit with the timing of Miss Morrison's catching the bus, either. To make matters worse, Fullarton James seized on the fact that another witness, Alfred Thompson, had turned off at Mirlaw that evening and decided that this was the vehicle which the Kirsopp-Reeds had been following, though a full reading of Thompson's statement demonstrates unequivocally that this cannot possibly have been the case. (This misplaced assumption may explain why no one ever bothered to check up on Dr Goodall's movements.)[14]

It is perfectly feasible that the car seen by Miss Morrison and the Kirsopp-Reeds was Evelyn's car, travelling a few minutes ahead of Tait's bus. She would therefore have arrived in Belsay at around 7.50 to 7.55, and at this point the reconstruction of the journey hits a problem. The police had collected a handful of witness statements from people who were in Belsay at around that time, none of whom saw Evelyn, while Bessie McDonnell, the one witness who claimed to have seen a car turning in the village, placed the incident a good 30 minutes later.

The police had acquired so many statements from witnesses in Otterburn that it is possible to cross-reference everyone's movements and thereby to correct the numerous misleading estimates of times provided, but unfortunately no such interviewing programme was undertaken in Belsay. This means that neither Mr Gallagher, with whom Bessie lodged, or Mrs Purves, from whom she bought her milk, were asked what time they thought this vitally important witness had arrived and left from their premises. The times provided by Bessie herself read very oddly, because she allows an hour and a half to encompass an errand which should have taken less than a third of the time.[15] The walk between Bessie's lodgings to Mrs Purves' premises would have taken her no more than five to ten minutes at most. Her estimate suggests that she knew she had spent some time chatting in the shop, but was this for well in excess of an hour? There is a distinct possibility that Bessie was wrong in her time estimates.

The position of Bessie's lodgings is significant. She lived in a cottage called the Gate House on the main Newcastle Road, at the junction of the roads to Otterburn and Bolam. Belsay is a small, strung-out settlement, with the Gate House at its northernmost extreme, beyond the village school. The angle of the road is such that anyone standing at the bus stop near the post office could not have seen someone standing at the Gate House and vice versa.

Witness statements establish that there were three people waiting to catch the Tait's bus, at least one of whom, Alice Ord, told the police she had sheltered in the post office out of the cold until the bus arrived.[16] To Bessie, walking home with her milk at a theoretical 7.55 rather than 8.30, once she had left the arcade of shops behind, there would have been 'no one standing about'.

Bessie was almost home by the time she saw the car approach and pass her. At this point the car would still not have been within sight of the shops and cottages at the heart of the village. Miss McDonnell told PC Douglas that she heard the car's brakes, glanced over her shoulder and saw it pulling up. By the time she had got inside and closed the door, the car had executed a complete turn and was heading back in the opposite direction. From this it is clear that the car Bessie saw went no more than a matter of maybe 50 yards beyond the junction where she lived and would therefore never have been within sight of anyone in the centre of the village.

Evelyn's claim to have 'gone as far as Belsay' tended to conjure up a picture of the Hudson screeching to a halt in the centre of the little village, alongside the distinctive arched shop fronts which line the eastern side of the road, but taking into account the layout of the village and the position of the one witness to this manoeuvre, it becomes clear that Evelyn never made it to the village centre, though she did indeed get 'as far as Belsay'.

Bessie McDonnell is an immensely important witness. Her estimated times did not fit with Evelyn's story, but as the police should have been well aware, witnesses who have no particular reason for remembering a time could be anything up to half an hour out, and in one other respect at least, Bessie McDonnell's statement is particularly compelling: because if she did see this car turning in the village – and why should we doubt her – then it remains completely unaccounted for. No driver apart from Evelyn herself came forward to say that they had executed this unusual manoeuvre in Belsay that night, and nor does there seem any obvious explanation for anyone to do so.

Stage by stage, witness by witness, Evelyn's journey from Otterburn to Belsay can be plotted using the statements which were sitting in the files all along. Miss McDonnell's story adds an element of circumstantial confirmation, because her evidence suggests that the car stopped suddenly, rather than executing a planned turn. A further point in favour of this evidence is that Bessie correctly described a grey car with particularly shiny door handles. (Joseph Foster and William Jennings confirmed that the car was 'sea green' – which would have appeared grey in the moonlight, and that the door handles were nickel plated.)[17] Unlike other witnesses who knew that Evelyn's car was on the road that night and therefore convinced themselves that a car they had seen was hers, Bessie McDonnell never claimed to have recognised a specific car, but simply described a car she had seen.

Piecing all this together suggests that the Hudson would have headed north again, from Belsay, at around 7.55. Having traced Evelyn all the way to Belsay, is it possible to identify her car anywhere on the final leg of its journey? If the scenario in which the Hudson turns on the edge of the village just minutes prior to the arrival of Tait's bus is correct, then the bus driver, Robert Harrison, should have seen the northbound car – but his testimony on this point is perfectly straightforward – he did not remember whether he had seen any vehicles or not.

The available evidence suggests that after 8 p.m. the roads were becoming quieter. Between 7.45 and 8.20, the Kirsopp-Reeds drove as far as Otterburn, apparently not encountering another car over a distance in excess of a dozen miles. They did see a large southbound lorry, but the driver was never traced, and, apart from this one vehicle, if the Kirsopp-Reeds were correct, there was a complete absence of southbound cars on the road.

Several local people came forward to say that they had made journeys which had taken them on and off the main road for short stretches, but when their stories are woven into the pattern of traffic movements, it is clear that only one of them would have been in the right place to have encountered a car travelling north at around 20–25 mph which had left Belsay at just before 8 p.m.

The driver in question was John Stott, who had been at a meeting in Capheaton until 8. Stott travelled south along the main road from the Capheaton turn until just before Belsay, where he took the lane which led to his farm, Bradford House. He recalled only one car passing him – a saloon, driving at 'moderate speed' – which he saw near West Shafto Gate, and it is possible that this was Evelyn's car.[18]

Establishing as accurately as possible what time the fire started was another key to understanding Evelyn's journey. It seems probable that the outward journey was undertaken at around 28–30 mph, but that the return journey was accomplished much more slowly. An average speed of 20mph would have brought the Hudson back to Wolf's Nick by around 8.35. With the exception of the possible sighting by John Stott, the police files provide no corroboration whatsoever for this northbound leg of the journey, and at this point Sir Claude's 'negative evidence' comes into play again.

Evelyn's own account of the journey tends to suggest that she did not meet many cars on her way back north and the evidence of the police files supports her. Essentially, just as had occurred during her brief sojourn in Otterburn, Evelyn and her assailant were 'invisible' on the drive north from Belsay to Wolf's Nick, for the simple reason that there was no one there to see them. This scarcity of cars or pedestrians offered no potential witnesses to a car being driven erratically, and gave Evelyn no opportunity of attracting attention to her plight. It may also have encouraged her passenger to become confident about the success of an attack.

Sydney Henderson, the shepherd, said that he first noticed the blaze at Wolf's Nick at about 8.45 and that it was already dying down by 9 p.m.[19] John Coulsdon, who lived at Blaxter Cottages, saw a car travelling north at about 9.15 while standing at his gate, and remembered it as a two-seater Morris which was travelling fast. He was among half-a-dozen other witnesses who also saw or heard a large saloon car going north 20 to 30 minutes later. [20] When Walter Beattie was asked to estimate what time he had arrived at Wolf's Nick and seen the car on fire, he guessed at somewhere around 9.50, but the car he was driving, a Morris two-seater, matches the description of the earlier car seen by Coulsdon, which means Beattie's car had probably passed Wolf's Nick at least 40 minutes earlier than he thought.[21]

Evelyn must have prayed for a passing vehicle while the car was stationary at Wolf's Nick, but nothing came along until the Hudson was alight, when she heard a vehicle stopping, accompanied by a screech of brakes and someone whistling.

Beattie denied that any of the sounds could have emanated from him or the vehicle he was driving, and in his determination to ridicule every aspect of Evelyn's story, Fullarton James was content to accept that Beattie's was the sole vehicle to pass Wolf's Nick between the firing of the car and the arrival of the bus. This represented yet another failure to retrieve and analyse the information collected by his own officers, for as we have seen there was evidence to suggest that Beattie was not the only motorist to have driven past the scene after the attack.

There is the large car seen and heard by several witnesses, which travelled past Blaxter Cottages about 20 to 30 minutes after Beattie's Morris had gone by. There is also evidence of a southbound car that pulled up outside Newhouses, about a mile south of Kirkwhelpington, at around 9.45, where Robert Beattie (no relation) had just gone out to the dog kennel at the back of his house. On hearing the car, Mr Beattie walked round the side of the house to investigate, and saw that the driver had stopped to urinate, after which he lit a cigarette, climbed back into the car and drove away.[22] The car, described as a black saloon, was never identified, but it may have passed the burning car on the moors. This same car or one very like it is mentioned in the statements provided by both Cecil Johnstone and Robert Harrison, who were respectively driving the last Foster's and Tait's northbound bus services of the evening. Both drivers independently recalled meeting an oncoming saloon car as they approached Harle Post Office at about 9.50.[23]

It is entirely feasible that either the southbound car or the northbound car paused, just as Walter Beattie had done, to get a better look at the blazing vehicle. Beattie's instinct was to drive on without investigating and it was an instinct which others may have shared.

CHAPTER 24

Are there other elements within the evidence that support Evelyn Foster's version of events? Fullarton James, when not theorising about an entirely imaginary 'local lover', seems to have believed that Evelyn either set fire to the car in order to scam the insurance company, or else set fire to it in order to gain some kind of notoriety for herself, with her death presumably arising as an accidental side effect, rather than a deliberate outcome. It is difficult to understand how the chief constable could persist with such a theory once he had visited the roadside and looked at the embankment where the Hudson descended onto the moor, because the nature of the place leaves little doubt that to deliberately drive a car off the road at that point would risk serious injury. His own expert, William Jennings, pointed out that only the intervention of the large boulders at the top of the embankment had prevented the car from turning turtle, and it seems hardly likely that Evelyn had made a careful calculation and determined that the boulders would save her. The paradox is perfectly summed up in the attitude of Mr Dodds, the coroner, who ridiculed the idea that the mystery man would have risked his neck, deliberately driving the car down the steep embankment, while apparently forgetting that in order to set fire to the car where it was found on the moor, Evelyn herself would have had to undertake this same suicidal course.

If Evelyn had merely intended to fake a car fire, there were better spots for the car to have been driven off the road – and why bother to go onto the moors at all? Evelyn's story of the attacker would have worked just as well if she had stayed on the road.

The chief constable appears to have accepted Jennings' proposition that someone had driven the car onto the moor before setting it on fire, but the position of the car actively argues against this. Why would Evelyn – or anyone – have waited for a ditch to stop their car, rather than using the brake? The very fact that the Hudson was found in gear, with the handbrake off, cries out in support of there being no one at the wheel. Again, Evelyn would have had to calculate the topography very well to have accurately anticipated this outcome of a journey across moonlit moorland.

As previously discussed, Jennings was also completely wrong in his assertion that the unscorched heather along the course of the car's route was another indicator that the fire had not been started until the car came to a halt. The coroner's theory that Evelyn had tossed petrol onto the back seat while standing on the running board and accidentally caught alight herself as a result – a theory that places Evelyn outside the vehicle for the duration of the fire, and in a standing position at the start – is not borne out by the injuries she sustained. There may also be something to be deduced from what remained of her clothing. Aside from the remnants left on her body, the majority of her burned clothing was found outside the car and would therefore support either Evelyn's account or the coroner's theory. Her coat was almost completely destroyed, but her scarf, which she must have shrugged off when removing her coat, was virtually undamaged. However, it is Evelyn's hat that's the most interesting clue. Logic would suggest that the hat would have either stayed on her head (and therefore like her hair been relatively unharmed), or else, like the scarf, the hat would have fallen off when she threw off the burning coat. If the hat had fallen off outside the car, there seems no reason why it should not have survived as well as the scarf did, but in fact Evelyn's hat was never found.

At this point a variety of possibilities suggest themselves. It was an icy, windless night, so there is no likelihood of the hat having blown away. There is always the remote chance that an early visitor to the scene arrived before the police and for reasons best known to themselves removed Evelyn's hat. It is possible that Evelyn's attacker took it as a souvenir, though this, too, seems unlikely. An alternative solution is that the hat was completely destroyed in the blaze, which consumed the rear passenger seat of the car and anything lying on it. For this to have happened, either Evelyn must have removed the hat herself prior to starting the fire – though it is not easy to see why she would do so on such a bitterly cold night – or else Evelyn's hat fell off while she was struggling with a third party in the back seat of the car. Though circumstantial, the missing hat is yet another small link in the chain of evidence supporting Evelyn's story.

Thanks to a much more recent tragedy, it is even possible to say that Evelyn's injuries are entirely consistent with an assailant having thrown flammable liquid at her and then set her alight, because a direct parallel exists in the tragic case of 35-year-old Stacey Mackie, who was murdered in January 2012. Stacey's assailant threw a bottle of white spirit at her and set her alight while she was in her Kendal flat. At the time, Stacey was wearing only a nightdress and had a duvet draped around her, which she had used as an impromptu dressing gown when getting up to answer the door. The duvet is roughly equivalent to Evelyn's layers of indoor and outdoor clothing, but it is notable that in spite of swiftly shrugging off the duvet – much as Evelyn rid herself of her blazing coat – Stacey suffered third-degree burns to her body, and her nightdress was almost completely destroyed. The police arrived within a few minutes of the attack and at that point Stacey was able to stand, walk a few steps and talk to them coherently. Until given sedation, she remained fully conscious and coherent in hospital and seemed aware that her injuries were fatal. Though she needed some pain relief, her agony was alleviated by the fact that, like Evelyn, her nerve endings had been destroyed in the worst affected areas of her body. The burns to her face were minimal, but her trunk, arms and legs had suffered fatal damage. In spite of the advances in medicine, with intravenous fluids available to Stacey within less than an hour of the attack, the prognosis was the same as it had been for Evelyn some 80 years earlier, and Stacey survived just 15 hours.[1]

One of the strongest arguments against there ever having been an assailant at Wolf's Nick was that the man remained invisible after the alleged attack, as he had done throughout the evening. How could this man have simply vanished from the scene of a crime described as 'in the middle of nowhere'?

Though the initial message received by the police was that, after the attack, the man had been picked up and carried away by another car, it seems extremely unlikely that a man who had just attacked a woman and set her car ablaze would have attempted to hitch another lift immediately. Having disposed of the young woman and her car, he would have found himself standing on a deserted moorland road, miles from anywhere, and though the woman herself was unlikely to give him any more trouble, the first passing motorist would surely associate him with the burning vehicle and probably stop with an offer of help. To complicate matters further, there had been a sensational murder associated with a burning car not three months previously, in which the perpetrator had been spotted leaving the scene.[2] Though there had been no passing vehicles for some time, the attacker was probably aware, however limited his local knowledge, that he was standing alongside a main route into Scotland, which meant that sooner or later someone was going to come along. What does he do next? Since it was far too risky to hitch a lift, it is a reasonable assumption that the attacker began to walk.

During the early days of the investigation, reports of strange men walking in the surrounding area flooded in. In many cases these sightings referred to men who failed to match the description provided by the victim, while others would have required him to have developed the power of jet-propelled flight. Some of these men were accosted while they were still on the road, others were eventually identified and eliminated from the enquiry. One bowler-hatted stranger created considerable interest in the Barrasford area, where his presence was noted by half-a-dozen separate witnesses. The chief constable noted on these statements that the man could be of interest and suggested that he be traced, but as the officers charged with handling the investigation had no clues whatsoever regarding the man's identity or whereabouts, they were unable to comply.[3]

The Barrasford man had been seen during the mid-afternoon of 7 January, and, though he could have been Evelyn's assailant, the odds against it seem high. Barrasford is less than 15 miles from the scene of the crime, so unless the man had been hiding somewhere and only began walking again after midday, he would have got well beyond Barrasford by then. It seems unlikely that the attacker would have taken refuge in a local barn, or outbuilding, as he must have realised that some sort of search would be organised as soon as the crime was discovered. Nor does the journey taken by the Barrasford suspect make much sense in the context of what little we know of Evelyn's attacker, because from Barrasford the man caught the ferry across the North Tyne River, then set off to walk in the direction of Chollerford, which in turn takes him towards Hexham. Though the events of the previous night could have wrought a radical change of plan, one of the few things we know about the mystery assailant is that he apparently did not want to go to Hexham, but rather to Newcastle.

According to Evelyn's story, her attacker forced her to turn the car around and even made an enigmatic remark about going to fetch his own car, but these were the actions of someone who had presumably made up his mind to convey his victim to a lonely spot and assault her, and cannot necessarily be viewed in the light of a genuine change of plan. At the outset of their encounter, the mystery man had wanted to get to Newcastle, and the balance of probabilities is that even having attacked his driver and set fire to her car, that particular imperative had not really changed.

His instinct must surely have been to put as much distance between himself and the blazing car as possible. A trek across unknown moorland is hardly an appetising prospect on a freezing winter night, while the road north to Otterburn would have taken him in the direction from whence someone was quite likely to come looking for the taxi girl. It is hardly rocket science, then, to assume that the man walked south, with a view to getting off the main road as soon as possible.

The first opportunity to leave the main road occurs less than a mile south of Wolf's Nick. It is a narrow lane serving farms called Catcherside and Chesters and it is possible that our man left the main road here. However, even today there is no signpost to suggest that it leads anywhere other than to an outlying farm, and the lane has every appearance of being a dead end. By now the mystery man had already travelled up and down this section of the Newcastle road twice, so he was probably aware that better opportunities would present themselves further down the road.

The next junction is the Knowesgate crossroads, just a mile along. Assuming that our man was young, fit and not exactly loitering, he could have reached this point in under 20 minutes. Though it is impossible to determine precisely to the minute when the fire started, when the attacker left the scene or when Walter Beattie drove by, it is perfectly feasible for the mystery man to have made it as far as Knowesgate junction before Beattie, the next known car to travel past the crime scene, would have reached the spot. It is equally fair to say that if he was still on the road when Beattie approached, the sound of the car engine would have prompted him to make himself less visible, and the car salesman from Scotland was probably going fast enough not to notice any but the most obvious of pedestrians.

At the Knowesgate crossroads, signposts offer a choice between Bellingham to the west and Cambo to the east. It is possible that neither meant anything to a stranger, but our man needed no more than a rudimentary knowledge of northern England to be aware that Newcastle lay south-east rather than south-west of Otterburn, and this tends to narrow the odds in favour of the road leading east.

The lane running east from Knowesgate is an easy level walk of two miles to the junction with the road running south to Cambo, where it is then less than a mile and downhill all the way to the village itself. (If he had taken the lane serving Catcherside and Chester, it would ultimately have brought him onto this same road.) In just under an hour, the attacker could have put five miles between himself and his victim.

If the man was a relative stranger to the area, he would have been relying on road signs to navigate towards Newcastle. As a smoker (and an arsonist), it can be assumed that he had either a cigarette lighter or matches, which would have enabled him to read the signs if the moonlight proved insufficient. However, in Cambo he would have faced a different kind of problem, because here the signs made no mention of Newcastle, but rather offered a choice between one road leading to Hexham and the other to Morpeth. Even assuming that the man had no local knowledge at all, we know that he had earlier turned down a ride to Hexham, so he would surely have perceived this as the wrong direction and chosen the road towards Morpeth instead.

A further mile-and-a-half of level walking in this direction would have taken him beyond the tiny settlement of Scot's Gap to a turn heading due south, signposted for

Middleton, Bolam and Belsay. He may have been led to choose this road by a good natural sense of direction, which made him realise that he needed to strike south, rather than east, in order to make his way to Newcastle. It is possible, too, that he recognised the name Belsay as one of the places on his earlier route to Ponteland.

If the attacker chose this road he would have found himself on another relatively level route, able to maintain a decent pace. If he left Wolf's Nick at approximately 8.50 and continued to walk briskly along the route suggested, it would, give or take ten minutes, have brought him to the tiny crossroads known as Bolam West Houses by around 10.30 that night – and that is where he was seen by George Jackson – the first and only witness to have glimpsed the killer as he made his getaway.

Jackson was a railway surfaceman who lived in Bolam. On 6 January he had been visiting someone at Bolam West Houses and was approaching the crossroads from the west when he saw a man pass in front of him, walking south in the direction of Belsay. He noticed that the man was walking briskly, with a 'smart gait', but on hearing Jackson's approach, though the man did not pause, he glanced in his direction. The railwayman could not see the stranger's features in the dark, but he took particular notice of him, because it was most unusual to see anyone at that time of night. The witness was convinced that had this been a local man, he would have recognised him.

Jackson himself was 5ft 6in and estimated the stranger to be about the same height. Without being able to see his face, it was obviously difficult to estimate his age, but by his walk and general appearance, Jackson put him at about 30 years old. The railwayman noticed that the stranger made little noise when he walked, which indicated shoes rather than workmanlike boots. He was wearing a dark overcoat that was smartly cut and had the collar turned up, dark gloves and a bowler hat.[4]

As the man was heading south and Jackson was heading east, the encounter was necessarily brief. The man passed across the junction in full view of Jackson, but in a matter of yards the slight bend below the crossroads took him out of sight.

George Jackson was an exceptionally observant witness, whose evidence had the advantage of being fresh in his mind, because he approached the police and gave a statement the very next day, arriving at the Otterburn Police Office at 6.40 in the evening on 7 January,[5] so there is no possibility of confusion as to which night this encounter had taken place. Aside from the possibility of deliberate fabrication (and there is no reason to suspect it), the story George Jackson told was compelling. He had seen a man who fitted the description provided by Evelyn Foster at a time and place where it was not only possible, but actively likely, that the man would have been.

It is also reasonable to ask, if this man was not Evelyn Foster's killer, who on earth was he and what was he doing at this out of the way spot, late at night? Men seen catching the ferry in the middle of the afternoon in Barrasford might well be going about their legitimate daily business, but relatively few people's legitimate business took them on long nocturnal walks through a backwater like Bolam West Houses. The road on which this encounter took place is no more than a lane linking a series of farms and hamlets. It is neither a direct route, nor a shortcut, to anywhere in particular. No wonder George Jackson took an interest in the man, who was rather smartly dressed to be travelling on foot and who, though he saw and heard George Jackson, ignored the rural courtesy of wishing him 'Good evening' in passing.

Though George Jackson's statement is probably one of the most significant in the investigation, there is nothing to suggest that the police placed any value on it at all. Jackson was not called at the inquest and his statement became buried among dozens of others; a forgotten witness who actually set eyes on the 'invisible' man.

In any fair and comprehensive assessment of the available evidence, it becomes obvious that the inquest jury was right and the chief constable was wrong. Someone had murdered Evelyn Foster – but who was it?

CHAPTER 25

The outcome of the inquest in the first days of February put the chief constable in a difficult position. He had presumably anticipated that the jury would bring in the verdict he had personally attempted to orchestrate – that Evelyn had met her death accidentally while attempting to set fire to her car – an outcome that would have signalled the end of the enquiry.

Even before the inquest, Fullarton James had already begun to wind up the police operation and this process continued in the following days. On 11 February, he wrote a letter of thanks to the various chief constables whose men had assisted in any way with the investigation into 'the death of the young woman at Otterburn'. It perhaps gives us some indication of his state of mind that he could not bring himself to write her name, though he did include without comment the information 'as you probably know, a verdict of wilful murder ... was recorded at the coroner's inquest'. The letter went out to 53 different police forces ranging from Aberdeen to Exeter[1] and many of his opposite numbers wrote back, thanking him for his thanks – gentlemanly courtesy was paramount among equals, if not always with the community one was appointed to serve.

Having earned the widespread scorn and revulsion

of the local community, Fullarton James seems to have developed a persecution complex, sending a memo to Shell on 8 February, advising him to warn officers in his district to 'walk warily' and 'stay silent'. 'There would appear to be a campaign of vituperation at the moment, and as we are not at liberty to express ourselves, better go carefully and keep our eyes and ears open.'[2] The 'campaign of vituperation' was presumably connected to the Foster family's campaign for justice. On learning of the uncomplimentary remarks questioning the verdict which had been attributed to the chief constable in some newspapers, Joseph Foster had announced his intention to contact his member of parliament, pointing out that it was up to the chief constable to accept the verdict of the inquest and continue the investigation into his daughter's death – something which the man in charge appeared in no hurry to do.[3]

Instead of focusing on the investigation into Evelyn Foster's demise, Fullarton James had realised that his handling of the enquiries might be called into question and began to busy himself with an exercise in self-justification, assembling notes on precisely when and how his various officers had been notified of the incident, what steps had been taken and by whom.[4] On 12 February, he circulated a memo headed 'Otterburn' stating that 'since the verdict of the coroner's jury, the above must be called "The 'O' Murder".'[5] The continuing reluctance to use Evelyn Foster's name, or even spell out the village where she had lived, is a disturbing reflection on the perverse and childish mindset of the man.

A few days later, Fullarton James sent yet another memo to Supt Shell, instructing that under no circumstances was any officer to use the telephone to speak to Otterburn in connection with the murder or on 'any other matter of a private nature'. The chief constable's reasons for assuming that some unauthorised person was listening in on the phone line to Otterburn are not revealed.[6]

Though the Fosters initially spoke of sending a complaint to their own member of parliament, it probably did not take them long to realise that this was a complete waste of effort. Colonel Douglas Clifton Brown's background – Eton and Cambridge, followed by the army, then election as a Unionist to the parliamentary constituency of Hexham in 1918, a constituency which was particularly handy for his country seat at Ruffside Hall – made him a natural buddy of the aristocratic Captain Fullarton James.[7] Indeed, when quizzed on the matter by reporters, Clifton Brown openly admitted that his friendship with the chief constable would place him in 'a difficult position' from which to take up the Fosters' complaint.[8]

Joseph Foster therefore wrote direct to the Home Secretary, J.R. Clynes, taking the precaution of releasing a copy of his letter to the press, so that its contents could not merely be buried.

The letter read as follows:

May I respectfully call your attention to the extraordinary and unprecedented position that exists following the coroner's inquiry into the death of my daughter, Evelyn Foster? You are in a position to examine the official documents yourself, but you are probably already aware from newspaper reports that my daughter was found lying seriously injured near her burned out car at Wolf's Nick, a few miles from her home.

My poor suffering girl cried 'Oh that awful man!' when she was discovered lying in terrible agony on the lonely moorland. When she was brought home and placed in bed she made a lucid statement which explained that she had been attacked by a fare in her car and that this man had poured some liquid over her and set her car on fire.

The coroner for the district very properly ordered an inquest and the jury returned a verdict that my daughter was murdered by some person or persons unknown. Many painful and scandalous innuendoes against my daughter's character were made during the inquest. It was even suggested that she had fired the car herself to obtain the insurance money, although no one pointed out that insurance companies settle a claim on the market value of the car and not on the sum for which it is insured. It was also suggested that my daughter may have set fire to the car to gain notoriety for herself. There was not a tittle of evidence to support these shameful theories, but I recognise that they were perhaps inevitable, distressing though they were to my family. The jury's verdict vindicated my girl's integrity and good faith.

I pray you will devote your attention to the following questions: Was my daughter's burned car left unprotected for hours, so that finger prints could not be taken? Is it also a fact that the police made no attempt to check footprints on the scene of the tragedy until the ground had been tramped over by curious sightseers? Why was the skill and experience of Scotland Yard ignored by the Northumberland

Police?

We have suffered a great bereavement and terrible shock that will remain with us to the end of our days. All I can do now is to defend my daughter's honour along the lines which may protect other parents from the painful procedure to which Mrs Foster and I have been subjected.[9]

On 24 February, the Fosters informed the press that they had received a reply from the Home Secretary stating that if they had a complaint, it should be made to the local standing committee.[10] In spite of appearing to fob off the Fosters, representatives of the Home Secretary did write to the chief constable, asking him whether he wished to comment on a whole variety of issues, including the police's failure to obtain a statement from the victim. Fullarton James replied that the police had been unable to speak with Miss Foster any sooner than they did owing to her being attended by a nurse and then by two doctors.[11]

In respect of the allegations about the car being left unguarded, and this having prevented fingerprints or footprints being taken, Fullarton James responded at some length, explaining that it was the fire and frost that had destroyed any fingerprint evidence, while the nature of the terrain and sub-zero temperatures had precluded there being any footprint evidence.[12]

It was somewhat unfortunate that the Fosters had latched on to these two particular 'failings'. There were a variety of relevant criticisms that could have been levelled directly at the chief constable, from the woeful shortage of manpower made available at the outset to his own general mismanagement of the case, whereas his defence regarding a lack of fingerprints and footprints was perfectly sound, with fingerprint evidence in any case hardly ever of use where the vehicle involved is a hire car, which necessarily comes into contact with numerous hands and fingers.

However, the Home Secretary was evidently not satisfied with these initial responses and wrote again, posing further questions about the handling of the case.[13] Fullarton James replied by enclosing a large package of statements detailing the involvement of every officer on the night of the attack, and in his accompanying missive protested about the difficulties of getting manpower to isolated spots in a constabulary that covered an enormous geographical area.[14] In yet another letter, Fullarton James further defended himself regarding the 'failure' to call in Scotland Yard, pointing out that whenever a police force was engaged in a serious enquiry, the 'parrot cry of "Call in the Yard"' went up immediately, adding that his enquiries had been actively hampered by the 'demands' of the press and the fact that they had tied up all the telephone lines.[15] The sheer quantity of material sent to the Home Office suggests that, as February moved into March, the major focus of the enquiry had shifted from investigating a death to defending the investigation into it.

Ultimately, the Home Office appears to have been satisfied with the chief constable's explanations, because on 30 March they wrote to him in conciliatory terms, sympathising with his mauling at the hands of the press, but adding that there was very little they could do to control its excesses.[16]

Having made his defence to the Home Office, Fullarton James then had to report to the local police standing committee. This probably gave him rather less cause for concern, since the local politicians and members of the Watch Committee who sat on it would all have been well known to him personally. Nevertheless, it must have irked him to be quizzed in this way and to have his competence questioned. Small wonder that his loathing of the Fosters and their daughter intensified the longer the affair went on.

It can have come as no surprise to anyone when the standing committee found in the chief constable's favour, stating they were satisfied that, in the emergency and unusual circumstances, the police had conducted their investigation in the proper manner. They further agreed that it had not been necessary to call in Scotland Yard and dismissed the Fosters' complaint regarding the remarks attributed to Fullarton James after the inquest, as they accepted the chief constable's contention that he had made no statement to the press regarding the verdict of the coroner's jury. Captain James 'had had what he considered a confidential conversation with a reporter about two hours before the jury reached their verdict. He had no idea the conversation would be published and had complained to the newspaper concerned, immediately he saw the paragraph claiming to set out a summary of the conversation'.[17]

While stopping short of instigating a chorus of 'For He's a Jolly Good Fellow', the standing committee had rolled over.

CHAPTER 26

In the meantime, despairing of appropriate action from their local police force, the Foster family turned detective themselves. As early as 9 February, the Evening Chronicle reported that Mr Foster had 'brought in his own expert', who shared his opinion that there was no one at the wheel of the car when it went off the road.[1]

During this same interview, Joseph Foster told the press that he would do everything in his power to bring the murderer to justice. It was said that Mr Foster, his family and friends, were working 'night and day' on their own lines of enquiry, following up new clues. Alas, the Fosters were not familiar with the wiles of newspapermen and unaware that the media were as interested in manipulating events to get a good headline as they were in obtaining justice for Evelyn. The family unwittingly played into the hands of reporters whom they believed to be their allies and friends, which facilitated yet another rash of supposedly suspicious incidents finding their way into the papers, with considerable prominence given to those unreliable young men Bell and Wallace, and their cycle ride from West Woodburn to Rochester, and to stories like those of Mary Ferry and Annie Carruthers, which bore only passing resemblance to the statements they had made to the police a few weeks earlier.[2]

Suggestions also began to appear in the press that the murder had a local link. On 12 February, the Evening Chronicle told its readers that new facts had been disclosed, which suggested that the Hexham road, rather than the Newcastle road, 'holds the secret'. By 19 February, a Chronicle reporter had taken it upon himself to do a bit of detective work of his own, noting that though no one along the road to Elishaw had reported hearing any cars when questioned by the police, he thought he 'might find someone at Troughend Hall who had seen or heard a car', but though he had called there, his enquiries were fruitless.[3]

Anyone looking at a map of the area might have wondered why the reporter would imagine that anyone at Troughend Hall, a huge crumbling pile standing well back from the road, was particularly likely to have seen or heard anything, but there was rather more to the reporter's interest in Troughend Hall than initially meets the eye.

It appears that, in their desire to get at the truth, the Fosters were prepared to believe almost anything, and one particularly unfortunate piece of gossip reached their ears, which related to the Clarks of Troughend Hall. The alleged involvement of Mrs Charlotte Clark in Evelyn Foster's murder – though entirely false – has been handed down the generations. Jonathan Goodman included a version of the story, coupled with a character assassination of Mrs Clark, in The Burning of Evelyn Foster.

For reasons best known to himself, Goodman referred to the late Mrs Clark as 'Mrs X', but provided sufficient information about her and about where she had lived, that even the most amateur sleuth could have worked out her identity.[4]

By the time Goodman wrote his book, Charlotte Clark was dead and her one-time home, Troughend Hall, had long since been demolished. Her father, William Thompson Hall, had purchased Troughend Hall in 1861. Charlotte, the fourth of five children, had grown up in this large Georgian house, enjoying a privileged Victorian country childhood of servants, governesses, dogs and horses. By 1931 the household was considerably reduced in both wealth and numbers. William Thompson Hall had died in 1906 and his youngest son had been a casualty of the Great War. His elder daughter and two remaining sons had both married and moved away, leaving his widow Hannah, by then in her eighty-third year, living with the youngest daughter Charlotte and her husband John Clark, a Glaswegian businessman and member of the family who owned Coats & Clark, the thread manufacturers. By the time of the Foster murder Charlotte was 42. She and her husband managed the farm with the help of some staff and she took care of her mother.[5]

At some point well before the death of Evelyn, Mr and Mrs Clark had fallen out with the Fosters regarding an unsatisfactory business transaction to do with the hire of a lorry. After this, the Clarks had patronised Reed's Garage in Otterburn for their petrol and used the services of Anderson's in Rochester if they needed to transport any livestock. Feelings were further ruffled when Mrs Clark failed to call on Mrs Foster in the wake of Evelyn's death.[6]

In spite of this rift between the two households, Mrs Clark, respectable, middle class and approaching middle age, seemed an unlikely person to have become involved in murder, but unfortunately when amateur detectives and local vigilantes start putting two and two together, even the most unlikely propositions can appear to make sense. The well-publicised claim by Wallace and Bell that they had encountered no cars on their ride between Woodburn and Rochester had been coupled with the sighting of the fast-moving car seen at Elishaw Bridge by Beach and Oliver. Surely, the theory ran, the only way for the car to have 'disappeared' from the road was if it had belonged to a local person who had turned into their property before the cyclists reached that point on the road?

Given that this supposed local person had not come forward, the 'obvious' inference was that they knew something about the murder, and coupled with this came an even more tantalising story, for it was being said that Alfred Johnstone, one-time employee of the Clarks, had been sacked for saying that Mrs Clark had been out in the car on the night that Evelyn was attacked.[7]

The police were first alerted to this theory when Mrs Foster wrote to them, enquiring whether they could follow Mrs Clark when she took the bus into Newcastle. The police visited the Fosters and listened to their suspicions regarding Mrs Clark. They then followed up the story about the sacking of Johnstone, tracking him to his new employers at Chirdon, an out-of-the-way spot half-a-dozen miles west of Bellingham, where the young man assured them that the story of his being sacked was completely false. He had left Troughend of his own accord, he said, because he did not get on well with his fellow farm workers there. He had no idea how the rumour of his being sacked had started, and far from incriminating Mrs Clark in any way, he was able to provide her with an alibi for the entire evening of the murder.

The police also visited Troughend, where they spoke with Mrs Clark, who was equally amazed by the story of Johnstone being sacked. She reiterated that she had been at home throughout the night of the murder, and when asked by the police whether it was possible for anyone else to have taken take the car out, she said she did not believe anyone could have done so without being heard by herself or her husband, but that in any case she knew for a fact that the car had not been out between 6 and 7 p.m. on 6 January as she had been doing something out in the garage, with the car in view the whole time. Both Mr and Mrs Clark, together with her mother and several of their employees, had all been at home on 6 January and could collectively attest to Charlotte Clark's complete innocence in the matter of Evelyn Foster's death. In spite of this, the rumours of Mrs Clark's involvement continued to buzz around Otterburn for many years.[8]

In The Burning of Evelyn Foster, Goodman links 'Mrs X' to a mysterious pair of brothers – bad lots who were supposedly involved in her misdeeds. This, too, was a rumour that appears to have resulted from the Foster family's amateur detective activities. The brothers are named in police files as the Lawsons of Noreheugh Farm, and the police made some checks on their whereabouts, but it eventually transpired that the only evidence against them amounted to the fact that a clairvoyant had contacted the Fosters and told them that Evelyn's murderer was named Lawson.[9]

Evelyn's mother, in particular, appears to have set considerable store by clairvoyants, frequently forwarding suggestions obtained from them, together with a smattering of leads provided by astrologers and spiritualists. It is to the credit of the officers who remained involved in the case that they attempted to follow up these 'clues' wherever humanly possible.

The Clark affair, however, was in a different league, and having followed up the allegations concerning Mrs Clark, Supt Shell visited Mr and Mrs Foster and had a long chat with them. He explained that recent letters forwarded to the police suggesting that a whole variety of people were responsible for the crime had been investigated and had proved to be without foundation in every case.[10] He pointed out that a great deal of nonsense was being told to them by people whose motives were not always of the best, and that a lot of police time was being wasted following up 'these futile and very obviously untrue statements'. Finally, he warned them that if they continued to pursue things in this way, it would probably end up in a case of libel.

During the course of his visit to the Fosters, Shell learned that Alfred Johnstone had already been summoned to The Kennels, and had told Mr Foster in person that there was no truth in the story of his being sacked, or of his saying that his employer had been out in her car that night, in spite of which Mrs Foster was still pursuing the idea.[11] While the family's grief and frustration was understandable, it is hardly to their credit that they allowed rumours against the wholly innocent Mrs Clark to continue among their friends and associates in the village.

After the Clark affair, the police decided to be more circumspect regarding information received from the Fosters – 'genuine clues' would continue to be followed up, Shell wrote,[12] but there would be no more wild goose chases. In spite of this, as late as January 1932, following the receipt of yet another communication from The Kennels, the faithful PC John Eckford accompanied Joseph Foster to the Armstrong Bridge in Newcastle, where Mr Foster stood waiting for an hour while the policeman remained concealed nearby, but the anonymous letter, promising that someone would bring valuable information concerning the death of his daughter, proved to be another in a long line of hoaxes.[13]

Essentially the clues had run out. Or had they?

CHAPTER 27

Plenty of names had been suggested to the police in the early days of the enquiry, both by members of the public and other police forces. The whereabouts of several known sex offenders were followed up and the men concerned subsequently ruled out, as were some people who had committed no other crime than to be thought a bit odd by their neighbours.

Cumberland and Westmorland Police drew their Northumberland counterparts' attention to a man called Robert Irving, who had been convicted of fraud in September 1930.[1] Irving was in the habit of engaging taxis that he couldn't pay for, and had committed various petty offences, but there was nothing in his history to suggest offences of a particularly violent or sexual nature, and perhaps the strongest argument against his involvement was the fact that he did not fit the description, as he stood 6ft 1in tall. This was considered fairly exceptional at a time when the average for a man was 5ft 6in and Evelyn said she had used her brother as a yardstick by which to gauge the height of her attacker, so she is unlikely to have been a good five or six inches out.

Many criminals exhibit patterns of offending, but the offence in this case was unusual – a sexual assault that had stopped short of physical penetration, followed by an attempt to burn the victim alive – and there was no directly comparable attack on record. Though there had been another 'burning car murder' in 1930, the Rouse case had been a very different scenario with an entirely different motive.[2] Not quite three years later, however, there would be another murder which involved a body in a burning car, and while there is no evidence that Northumberland Police spotted a possible link, it has subsequently been suggested that the man convicted in that case, Ernest Brown, may also have been responsible for the murder of Evelyn Foster.

Ernest Brown was convicted of the murder of Frederick Morton in December 1933.[3] Brown had been enjoying the sexual attentions of Morton's wife, Dorothy, but the relationship had soured and this was believed to have culminated in the murder of Morton, who was shot before being left in his car, which was then burned inside the garage of his Yorkshire home in a failed attempt to destroy the evidence.

Apart from sharing the common feature of a burned-out car, the main reason for suggesting that Brown may have been responsible for the Foster murder is the story repeated by Jonathan Goodman, that in the seconds before he was executed, Brown uttered either the words 'ought to burn' or possibly the single word 'Otterburn'.[4] There does not appear to be any reliable, first-hand confirmation as to whether Brown said anything at all on the scaffold, and, since Goodman provides no indication of his source for this tale, I have found it impossible to verify.

Irrespective of whether or not Brown issued this tantalising confession, the superficial similarities between the two cases render Brown a suspect worthy of further investigation. In both cases the intention appears to have been to disguise a murder as an accidental death. Staging a fire for this purpose is not a particularly original idea, and on its own would offer very little connection with the death of Evelyn Foster, but the Brown case is usually reported as involving an element of sexual assault against Mrs Morton, which takes a possible connection with the Foster case a step closer – or it would, were not the apparent similarity misleading.

There is no dispute regarding the fact that Ernest Brown, a groom employed by Frederick Morton, had been engaged in a lengthy affair with Mrs Dorothy Morton. What is far less certain is the truth of Mrs Morton's claim that, when she tried to end their liaison, Brown forced her to have intercourse with him. Brown strenuously denied that his relationship with Dorothy Morton had ever involved any violence or coercion on his part, and it emerged during the police investigation that Mrs Morton had a lively sexual history and appeared to have pursued her relationship with Brown enthusiastically. Though she attempted to play down her various sexual adventures in court, there is significant evidence within the case papers in support of Brown's contention that, far from forcing Dorothy Morton to maintain relations with him, Brown had actually attempted to leave the household, and only returned as a result of his mistress's pleading with him to do so. The court gave the tragic, upper-middle-class widow a very easy ride, but it is clear that neither prosecution, defence nor the general public found Mrs Morton's story of coercion particularly believable.[5]

The issue before the jurors, however, was not whether Ernest Brown had forced himself on Mrs Morton, but whether or not he had murdered her husband Frederick. Since the accuracy or otherwise of Dorothy Morton's version of their affair was not the main point in question, her allegations regarding Brown are often accepted at face value by anyone with a superficial knowledge of the Morton case, leading to the belief that Brown was a sexual predator. However, if it is the case that Mrs Morton got away with distorting the details of her relationship with Brown in order to salvage something of her own reputation, then Brown's character undergoes a significant change, and he is transformed from a violent sex offender who was convicted of murder into a mere adulterer convicted of murder.

It is generally accepted that sexual offenders tend to rack up a catalogue of similar offences, but Ernest Brown had no such history. Aside from his time in the army, Brown had lived in the same area of Yorkshire all his life and was well known to the local police, but not for offences against women. By the time of his arrest for the murder of Frederick Morton, he had acquired a police record that began with a couple of petty juvenile thefts and moved on to half-a-dozen arrests for drunk and disorderly, but there

is absolutely nothing to indicate that Brown had ever offered violence to a woman, and no suggestion that he had
ever been suspected of, or implicated in, any crimes of
a sexual nature. The supposition that Brown was a man
with a tendency to assault women was flawed – the fact
is that the murder of Frederick Morton was a domestic
affair, involving a man who was having an affair with
another man's wife. This is an entirely different kind of
crime to that in which a man sexually assaults and then
murders a complete stranger.

It has further been suggested that the description of
Evelyn Foster's attacker fitted Ernest Brown, but this is
true only inasmuch that the physical description fitted
half the population of the north of England. Since
Brown worked as a groom, Goodman seized on the fact
that grooms often wore bowler hats, but this is another
misleading simplification. Some grooms working for
high-status households wore bowler hats, but there is no
evidence that Brown ever did so. Following his arrest, a
number of different photographs of Ernest Brown were
reproduced in newspapers, in which he is always shown
wearing a hat. In some of these pictures he is riding, or
showing horses, but in no case does he appear wearing a
bowler hat. On the contrary, the headgear favoured by
Brown was a very broad, flat cap, of a type which was
extremely fashionable in the late 1920s and early 1930s.[6]

Evelyn described her attacker as being a bit of a
'knut', whereas Brown, who as a mere groom was not
exceptionally well paid, does not appear to have been a

particularly natty dresser. There is no evidence that he owned a smart, dark overcoat like the one that made such a favourable impression on the young woman from Otterburn. When he appeared in court, Brown wore a brown suit, and when travelling down to London from Leeds for his high court appeal in December, a reporter observed that he was wearing this same suit. Although it was a cold January day, there was no mention of any overcoat and it is possible that Brown did not possess one.[7]

Finally, we have the claim made by Jonathan Goodman that Ernest Brown sometimes travelled into Scotland in order to attend markets and purchase animals on behalf of his employer, who was a cattle dealer. This assumption is probably based on the information available in newspapers at the time of the Morton murder, linking Frederick Morton to the purchase of cattle in Scotland in the same week that he died. It is true that Mr Morton's business interests regularly extended north of the border, but the witness statements of both Brown and his fellow employees make it absolutely clear that neither Brown nor any other employee ever purchased animals on behalf of Frederick Morton, who attended the markets and did all the bidding and buying himself.

In 1931, Brown had nothing whatever to do with the buying and selling of stock. His role was entirely devoted to caring for the Mortons' horses, and he was based at the Mortons' Yorkshire home. During the final few months of his employment, his duties did change to encompass the delivery of cattle to various local farms, and this entailed Brown's driving the farm's horsebox, but there appear to be no conceivable circumstances at any stage in his employment when he would have been travelling long distances by bus or train while engaged in some errand on behalf of his master, and given that he only enjoyed one day off a week, it is somewhat unlikely that he would have taken it into his head to travel up to Scotland in the middle of the working week and become stranded in Jedburgh.

Essentially, every apparent link between Ernest Brown and Evelyn Foster is a false lead. Brown was not a sexual offender, did not have a history of violence against women, had no known history of travelling to Northumberland or Scotland, and no apparent reason to be travelling through Otterburn in January 1931. The Northumberland Police rightly took no interest in Brown, though by the time of his conviction they had made some enquires about an entirely different – and much more likely – suspect.

CHAPTER 28

In January 1932, Northumberland Police received some interesting information from their opposite numbers in Kircudbright.[1] A 41-year-old man named George Maxwell had been receiving hospital treatment for an infected foot and, in the course of a conversation with the matron regarding the recent arrest of a local man called Alexander Kirkpatrick, Maxwell had remarked that he always believed Kirkpatrick to have known something about the 'Otterburn affair'. The matron had passed these remarks on to the doctor, and, feeling that there could be something in it, the doctor had called in the police.

On interviewing Maxwell, they discovered that he was himself an ex-policeman, who had served for 11 years in the Northumberland force, though for the last six years he had returned to agricultural work. Maxwell told the officer despatched by Kirkcudbright Constabulary that in January 1931 he had been working on Lochill Farm at Ringford near Kirkcudbright, where the dairyman had been a man called James Kirkpatrick. About a week after the Foster murder, James Kirkpatrick's brother, Alexander, had come to stay with him.

Maxwell had evidently formed an extremely

unfavourable impression of this man, who was on a month's leave from the army at the time. According to Maxwell, Alexander Kirkpatrick's conversation was mainly about girls and the escapades he'd had with them. The young man was in the habit of going out in the evening dressed in a dark blue suit, dark overcoat, kid gloves and a bowler hat – an exceptionally smart outfit by the standards of a working man or an off-duty soldier from the lower ranks – and during the course of the visit, Kirkpatrick had told Maxwell various stories about his romantic adventures, including one about picking up a girl at a ball by pretending to be a chauffeur.

Alexander Kirkpatrick had then been serving with the King's Own Scottish Borderers, stationed at Berwick-upon-Tweed, but his leave had begun a few days before the Evelyn Foster murder. According to what he told his brother and Maxwell, he had spent the first week of it 'joyriding [scamming lifts from unsuspecting motorists] all over the place'. After this he had stayed two days with his mother (who also lived in Dumfriesshire) before arriving at the farm in Ringford.

The Foster case would have been all over the papers during this time and no doubt formed a natural source of conversation and comment. Maxwell recalled that when he had remarked in Alexander Kirkpatrick's presence that it was 'a bad affair down in Otterburn', the young soldier had responded that 'it was what a few more of them needed'.

While George Maxwell evidently did not take to the

young man during this visit, nor did he find anything sufficiently suspicious in what he had said to report it to the police. However, matters had recently taken a more sinister turn when Alexander Kirkpatrick was arrested and charged with attempting to rape a six-year-old girl, and it was this that had prompted Maxwell's conversation with the nurse.

Appraised of this possible lead, Fullarton James instructed Superintendent Cunningham in Berwick-upon-Tweed to contact Kirkpatrick's regiment, but the contact provoked a somewhat surprising response. According to the army, Lance Corporal Kirkpatrick was a model soldier, very popular with his comrades and a man of 'sober, steady habits', whose conduct had never given the slightest rise for complaint. So far as the current charges were concerned, he had 'never given reason to think there was any tendency in that direction'.

The King's Own Scottish Borderers' records showed that Alexander Kirkpatrick had enlisted in September 1929 and had been on leave from 30 December 1930 until 26 January 1931, and again from 28 December 1931 to 24 January 1932, during which the alleged sexual offence against the little girl had occurred.[2]

Presumably, the Northumberland officers could have requested an interview with Kirkpatrick while he was being detained, awaiting trial, but instead Captain James merely asked the Kirkcudbright police to keep him informed of the outcome of the trial.[3] In April 1932 the suspect was found guilty of assault and attempting to 'ravish' a six-year-old girl and sentenced to four years' penal servitude. It also emerged at the conclusion of the trial that Kirkpatrick had previously been found guilty of the same offence, again involving a six-year-old girl, in August 1919, after which he had been sentenced to 18 months in prison.[4]

Here, then, was a man who was 27 years old in 1931, stood 5ft 8½in tall[5] and had a criminal record for two sexual assaults, which in each case had stopped short of actual rape. He had been on leave when he committed the most recent assault and had similarly been on leave when the attack on Evelyn Foster took place. He was allegedly in the habit of dressing like a gentleman and affecting a knowledge of motor cars in order to impress women. On his own admission, he had spent part of his January 1931 leave 'joyriding'. If he was able to impersonate a gentleman, then he could probably have managed to disguise his accent sufficiently that Evelyn couldn't place it, and, if George Maxwell was to be believed, he had shown no sympathy for Evelyn Foster's fate, believing that she had 'deserved it' – a not untypical view of sexual attackers in respect of their victims.

Though entirely circumstantial, this was a compelling set of clues. Now that the man had been found guilty, Fullarton James belatedly set in train some enquiries as to where Alexander Kirkpatrick had spent his leave in January 1931. Dumfriesshire police were asked to call on the man's 68-year-old mother, who told them that she could not remember whether he had spent the whole of his leave with her in 1931, but thought that part of it had been spent with his brother Andrew. Whether a genuine lapse of memory or a disingenuous answer, we will never know. Kirkcudbright Constabulary did no better with Andrew Kirkpatrick, who agreed that his brother had probably spent some of his leave with him, but was 'now vague about the dates'.[6]

At this point, the officers charged with questioning the Kirkpatrick family were guilty of a glaring error, for the original story had not entailed a stay with Alexander Kirkpatrick's younger brother Andrew, who in 1931 was working as a dairyman in Kelton, near Caerlaverock, but with one of his older brothers, James, who had been the dairyman at Ringford, a good 30 miles along the coast. In line with the sort of dire coincidences littering the Foster case, James Kirkpatrick had since moved from Lochill Farm to Townfoot, near Kirkcudbright, while Andrew Kirkpatrick had moved to take up a post as a dairyman at another farm near Kirkcudbright, all of which undoubtedly increased the possibilities for an accidental misunderstanding about which brother they needed to question.[7]

There is no suggestion within the files that Northumberland Police tried to dig any more deeply into Alexander Kirkpatrick's history, but they would have been well advised to have done so. Kirkpatrick's first conviction had occurred when he was 15 years old. He had come before the courts accused of sexually assaulting a six-year-old girl, having done so in such a way that the child's genitals were inflamed and swollen, though penetration had not occurred. Contact had however been of sufficient intimacy that he had infected the child with the gonorrhoea, from which he was then suffering.[8] The comparison with Evelyn's own injuries and allegations is striking.

To describe the police response on learning of this suspect as a half-hearted effort would be a generous reckoning. Having failed to notice that the Dumfriesshire police had questioned the wrong brother, the desultory 'investigation', if it could be dignified with such a term, was allowed to rest. There were so many questions that could have been asked. Was Alexander Kirkpatrick a smoker? Could he drive? None of these questions were put to his family. It is true that the chances of obtaining a conviction would have been small, because there was nothing but circumstantial evidence to link Kirkpatrick to the crime. Even so, the issue was hardly pursued with enthusiasm.

What went through Fullarton James's mind as he read these reports? Did he ever once pause to question whether Evelyn might have been telling the truth all along?

CHAPTER 29

No one can say with certainty what happened at Wolf's Nick on 6 January 1931, but having had the opportunity of seeing all the original evidence, I have formed my own theory, for what it's worth. Alexander Kirkpatrick may be completely innocent of Evelyn Foster's murder, but he is undoubtedly a suspect who should have been the subject of much closer investigation. Kirkpatrick spent his leave 'joyriding', which means that he was in the habit of conning motorists into giving him lifts. The young soldier had evidently perfected an act that entailed dressing and acting the gent, adapting both his accent and his appearance to the part. He was also a sex offender who preyed on females much smaller and weaker than himself.

I strongly suspect that at some point on 6 January, Kirkpatrick had fallen in with a couple of people who were travelling south, perhaps latching on to them in a similar way to that in which he initially encountered Evelyn, moving seamlessly from one set of good Samaritans to the next. No doubt he was ready with some plausible story of a mishap that had resulted in his needing a lift. Sometimes the sympathetic suckers he had chosen not only gave him a lift, but stood him a meal – as had perhaps happened on 6 January – possibly not afternoon tea, as interpreted by the English, but high tea as understood by the Scots – a proper meal in a hostelry somewhere. Though their journey had taken them through Jedburgh, the meal need not necessarily have been partaken there and this may explain why no one recalled the group, particularly since enquiries never seem to have extended to catering establishments beyond the confines of Jedburgh itself and Hawick. When the motorists stopped for their refreshments, it's easy to imagine Kirkpatrick being invited to join the driver and her companion(s) for a meal, no doubt protesting that they were being too, too kind.

It is highly unlikely that Kirkpatrick ever asked around in Jedburgh for a bus, because his objective would have been to move seamlessly from one free lift to another, with who knew what generous hospitality tacked on. In the same vein, being dropped at Elishaw, the point where the Newcastle and Hexham roads diverged (effectively 'the middle of nowhere') would have suited him far better than being taken right into Otterburn where there might very well be a bus bound for Newcastle, which would ruin his excuse for needing a lift. There was far more likelihood of scamming another free ride if he was seen to be getting out of a private car, as this added a veneer of safety and respectability to him. It is easy to imagine him assuring his previous helpers that they must not go out of their way to drop him in Otterburn – they had already 'done more than enough'.

Kirkpatrick must have thought that there were strong odds that the next southbound car would be going as far as Newcastle and that a good number of motorists would wave away the suggestion of him getting out at Otterburn for the bus: 'my dear fellow, I am going to Newcastle myself, you may as well come with me, it's not out of my way...'[1]

One of the cars that had immediately preceded Evelyn was driven by Alastair Bull, who would undoubtedly have taken that line. He was already carrying two hitch-hikers – the more the merrier. Fullarton James himself queried the odds of the man encountering the one hire car that happened to be out and about in the district, and this must surely have been Kirkpatrick's own reaction. Here was the one person who would indeed take him to Ponteland or Newcastle – but would want payment in exchange.

It was an awkward situation. Kirkpatrick could hardly decline Evelyn's offer of a ride as far as Otterburn, because that would appear strange to the people who had brought him this far. It would be better to continue to Otterburn and see how the situation developed. Evelyn must have explained that she would need to fill up the tank, and this temporary hiatus opened up the possibility of another free ride appearing. When they arrived in the village, Kirkpatrick said that he would walk down to the inn and ask for a lift – something that, for whatever reason, he didn't do – while Evelyn went inside to check the fare and fill up the car with petrol. While it is unlikely that he had decided to attack Evelyn by that stage, he needed to avoid an encounter with any troublesome busybodies who might suggest payment up front, and perhaps he hoped that while she was engaged in preparing the car at the northern end of the village, he might pick up another lift from a passing motorist going south, but as the evidence shows, there were no other cars passing through the village at this time, so after standing on the bridge for a few minutes, Kirkpatrick would have seen Evelyn's car approach and slow to a halt. He stepped forward and climbed inside.

As the car headed south they conversed a little. Scant reliable information has survived about Evelyn's character, but in common with the majority of hire car drivers she seems to have enjoyed chatting to her passengers. Her fare that night appears to have been a reticent sort of chap, providing her with very little information about himself, the reason for his journey or his ultimate destination, speaking in the vaguest of terms about his connections with 'the Midlands' and sticking with general topics such as cars and driving. Kirkpatrick – if it was he – smoked numerous cigarettes, perhaps an indication that he was becoming strung up and nervous, because now he was in the car, how was he going to manage things? In some people, anxiety and uncertainty can easily transform into aggression. No doubt Kirkpatrick was somewhat annoyed by his bad luck in flagging down a hire car rather than a private motorist, and only too ready to take it out on the person he perceived as the architect of this misfortune – the young woman who expected payment for something he was accustomed to getting for free.

As the car ate up the miles, his mood and intentions darkened until the moment when the car entered Belsay and he ordered Evelyn to turn back, refusing to explain why. When she protested, he struck her, and, when it looked as if she might refuse to co-operate, he took the wheel himself. From now on he had reached a point of no return. He had attacked this young woman and there was no way that he could stop the car anywhere that she might be able to obtain help.

Sexual assault and rape are often less about sexual gratification than about power, anger and taking revenge on women, specifically and generally. Kirkpatrick would have been very angry – his scheme for free transport had come badly awry and it was all down to this wretched young woman with her demands for money. He must have known that Evelyn was terrified by this time, and when he finally halted the car at Wolf's Nick – one of the most desolate spots on the route – perhaps he enjoyed some teasing talk, remarking about what an independent young woman she was, offering her a cigarette, pinching her arms, probably making suggestions that Evelyn had not cared to repeat.

When she decided to put some space between them by getting out of the car, Kirkpatrick swiftly followed, opened the rear passenger door and shoved her into the back, where a struggle took place and he sexually assaulted her. Evelyn said she 'fought for her life' but she can have been no match for a much larger, stronger assailant.

It is possible that he was enraged by the discovery that Evelyn was menstruating, because menstruation was then widely perceived as dirty and disgusting. This vile woman had been a thorn in his side ever since she turned up at Elishaw – thwarting his plans for a free lift, resisting his advances and now turning out to be unclean into the bargain. At some point, Kirkpatrick may have lost control completely and dealt Evelyn the blow that knocked her senseless. Was he so furious and disgusted with his victim that he decided she had to die, or did he see her lying insensible on the back seat and panic – what if he had killed her? Could it be made to appear like an accident?

There were no all-night garages in rural Britain then, and like everyone else Kirkpatrick would have known that nine out of ten regular motorists carried a spare can of petrol. It would have taken only seconds for him to climb out onto the road, open the clips securing the lid of the luggage box, grab the petrol tin and throw some of the contents onto the woman in the back seat. Natural instinct was to put the can back into the still-open luggage box. To Evelyn, barely conscious in the back of the car, the dark shadow at the door appeared to 'take something from his pocket and throw it on her'. It would be easy enough during these terrifying seconds to confuse precisely what the man was doing and in what order, and though the petrol had not come from his pocket, the matches or cigarette lighter which he used to ignite it presumably did.

Evelyn's burns are entirely consistent with having petrol

thrown on her as she sat partially collapsed in the back seat of the car. The petrol would have naturally pooled in her lap and drained down onto the seat, initially concentrating the blaze in those areas. As the fuel was thrown at her, small amounts would have splashed up onto her clothes, across her right arm and down onto her right leg, whereas her left arm and leg would have been furthest from the open door and partly shielded by her trunk and right leg, all of which is reflected in the pattern of her injuries. Evelyn's hands and face would have suffered considerable damage as she instinctively looked down and attempted to bat out the flames.

Having set the girl ablaze and slammed the rear door on her, it is likely that Kirkpatrick would have reached in through the driver's door (which may have still been open after Evelyn's earlier attempt to escape), taken off the hand brake, put the car in gear and sent it on its way, pulling the steering into the right-hand lock, which would take the car across the road and over the embankment, then jumping clear without bothering to close the driver's door. He may have expected the car to overturn, but it didn't – instead it careered crazily down the embankment and continued for some distance across the moor, glowing eerily as the fire blazed in the rear.

It is unlikely that the petrol tin remained in an upright position during this exercise and it was probably lying on its side when the car came to rest, but was picked up by one of the men who initially visited Wolf's Nick to view the car, who then replaced it in an upright position – an instinctive act of tidiness, with no thought to the importance of maintaining a crime scene intact. (The fact that the neck of the tin was found several inches away from the tin itself proves that the upright tin seen by Inspector Russell was not in its original position, because if the tin had been upright when the solder melted, the neck would have simply dropped onto the top of the tin.)

Kirkpatrick must have known that another vehicle would come along at some point, and that once the burning car was discovered, anyone seen plodding along the main road or looking for a lift was going to be a suspect. The answer was to get off the main road as soon as possible and head south-east, towards the anonymous bustle of Newcastle. There was very little risk of being seen along the deserted country lanes and Kirkpatrick remained invisible until he was seen passing the crossroads by George Jackson. From the crossroads, it was a walk of at least another 15 miles to the centre of Newcastle itself, but a hike of this length hardly represented an insurmountable distance for a fit young soldier.

The Newcastle Police confirmed that, during the early hours of 7 January, just six tickets were sold for travel from the Central railway station. Four were for trains departing for Liverpool at 1.31 and 1.50, one was for the Aberdeen train which left at 1.17, and one was for travel to Glasgow. Three services left Newcastle for Glasgow that night, at 1.17, 3.17 or 4.30 respectively. A man travelling on foot from Bolam crossroads could not have arrived in Newcastle in time to catch the Liverpool or Aberdeen trains, but he could have made one of the later Glasgow services. It is extremely speculative to suggest that the Glasgow ticket sold that night was purchased by the killer of Evelyn Foster, but taking the train would have been an expedient way of putting many miles between himself and the crime.

Then again, he perhaps realised that there was no need to draw attention to himself by entering a virtually deserted station in the early hours of the morning. It may have made more sense for Kirkpatrick to dawdle on the outskirts of the city until a later hour, melt into the crowd, then catch a later train home to Dumfriesshire... and get away with murder.

Afterword

Evelyn Foster was not just a victim of murder, but of the times in which she lived. Today, no 30-year-old woman in England would have been so ignorant of sexual matters that she was unable to articulate what had happened to her. Her final hours would have been spent in hospital, where properly trained police officers would have interviewed her in a far more effective way. It is even possible that her assailant would have been apprehended while he was still on the road, thanks to fast-response police cars equipped with radios.

The conduct of the investigation would not have been left in the hands of a lone, untrained maverick, and it is unthinkable that when Kirkpatrick's name came to the attention of the enquiry, he would not at the very least have been interviewed and asked to account thoroughly for his movements in the early part of January 1931. There is even a faint possibility that some DNA evidence might have survived the fire, which would have enabled the police to eliminate him or bring in a conviction. The arduous process of logging and comparing witness statements to produce a coherent timeline could have been accomplished much more quickly by means of a computer programme. (Though pen and paper can be an equally effective medium in the right hands.)

Even if Evelyn's killer, whether he was Alexander Kirkpatrick or some other man, had escaped justice, the Fosters would not have been subjected to the awful ordeal of having their daughter portrayed as deranged, a liar or a combination of both. Mrs Clark would not have been forced to endure the ludicrous gossip perpetrated by her neighbours, not only during her lifetime, but long after her death.

It is, however, unfair to judge any investigation by present-day standards. In the context of the time, many rural forces in Britain would have struggled with the demands of a full-scale murder enquiry of this complexity. Several of the officers involved, in particular PC John Eckford of the Newcastle Police were conscientious in the extreme, but Evelyn Foster was the victim of a series of circumstances that together proved disastrous.

The perpetrator of the crime was incredibly fortunate in that he not only went unseen for the greater part of his adventures, but also because whoever had given him a lift from Scotland that day either failed to appreciate the significance of the subsequent police appeal or elected to stay silent rather than become involved in a particularly sordid crime. Evelyn's own story appeared to diverge from the facts when it came to the method used for setting the car alight, and the waters were muddied further by a crime scene that was tampered with by just about everyone who came into contact with it prior to the investigation getting properly underway.

The relatively young and inexperienced Dr McEachran signally failed to understand the importance of obtaining a proper statement from Evelyn — a rather shocking indictment of a presumably intelligent man. Sergeant Shanks failed to take charge of the situation and insist on a proper interview, though in his defence, he probably did not know that this was his one chance, because Evelyn was dying. Both men lacked the common sense or strength of personality to clear all extraneous persons from the room and get to the bottom of exactly what the man had done to Evelyn.

Captain James, who was by no stretch of the imagination competent to head a serious investigation, having learned on the second day of the investigation that there was no evidence of Evelyn's being raped, never stopped to consider alternative possibilities, but instead began to work to a particular conclusion with a closed mind. While the greatest personal blame for the misdirection of the enquiry undoubtedly lies with Fullarton James, there is considerable culpability among the so-called 'experts'. These include William Jennings, whose evidence regarding the progress of the car across the moor was clearly based not on his own knowledge or observation, but simply on his personal assumptions, and though such behaviour was common among 'experts' in 1931, there is still no excusing it. Jennings clearly did not know what would happen if a driverless car was set on fire and sent down an embankment, and that is what he should have told the police when asked.

Professor McDonald's behaviour was even worse, for he ignored some of his own findings, deliberately playing down the injuries to Evelyn's face in a shameless attempt to fall in with the chief constable's theory that there had been no attack at all.

It was a mischance, too, that the inquest proceedings came within the jurisdiction of Philip Dodds, who was lamentably willing to accept as factual evidence that did not logically hang together, and to assume the worst of a young woman who was not there to defend herself. Faced with a set of circumstances well outside his normal experience, Mr Dodds failed to bring an independent, open mind to the question of how Evelyn Foster had met her death. It is difficult to imagine his direct contemporary, the coroner for Croydon, Dr Henry Jackson,[1] conducting an inquest so biased and lacking in competence as that presided over in Otterburn by Mr Dodds.

It is often wrongly suggested that long-closed police files contain the solutions to historic murders, but in the case of Evelyn Foster this has proved to be at least partially true. Using the witness statements obtained by the police, it is not only possible to show that the vast majority of the victim's story was true, but also to conclude that her murderer probably left the scene of the crime on foot, heading towards Newcastle, and managing to put several miles between himself and the crime scene before an initial telephone call had even alerted the local police. The files even offer us the name of a credible suspect.

The Otterburn case has often been described as unique, inasmuch that in spite of the official verdict of the inquest, significant doubts have remained as to whether Evelyn Foster was the victim of murder at all. It may be unique in a second and unexpected way, because the initial thoroughness with which the police collected statements provides a window on an entire community, offering a snapshot of the way dozens of people spent an ordinary winter evening. The files could almost be subtitled 'A Night in the Life of a Village', though even this would not encompass the scope of the records, which extend to the activities of many people who lived miles beyond Otterburn itself.

From these statements it emerges, for example, that Betsy Dickson, housekeeper to Mr Brodie at Monkridge Hall, having spent the day in Newcastle, later joined a carload of friends heading off for a dance held in Thropton Village Hall; that Charles Trevelyan and two of his cousins from Wallington, accompanied by four of Sir Claude Morrison-Bell's offspring, stayed out ice-skating on a moonlit frozen reservoir until after midnight; that the committee of Rochester Football Club, Joseph Anderson, Robert Wilson, George Leighton and William Corbett, spent the early part of the evening picking a side to play against Colwell on the coming Saturday; while young bloods John Mowitt, Andrew Goodfellow and John Anderson attended a party at Woolaw Farm. It is possible to determine who habitually bought their newspapers from Lukes' shop, and which local men invariably partook of a nightly pint in the Percy Arms; who sang a song in the Redesdale Arms that night, and how a Mrs Coxon of Newcastle had played the piano for the entertainment of patrons there that afternoon.

The statements reveal the numerous long walks routinely undertaken in order to get to and from shops, markets and places of worship, or simply to visit friends and family. We see also the acute poverty of people 'on the tramp' juxtaposed with the kindness displayed by Reverend Winter to the unfortunate Cuthbert Stappard, and the generosity of Alastair Bull to Thomas Connor and John Reed, the young men from Scotland who were on the road, looking for work. Small acts of neighbourliness and generosity are frequent, with Robert Ormison, pausing on his drive home to pick up any local people who happened to be walking that way (which on 6 January 1931 included Mr and Mrs Ord of Crosshouses, and Edric Hedley of Overacres); and Cecil Familton of Checkgate Farm going to considerable trouble to help young John Armstrong of Raylees, whose car had broken down en route to the dance in Thropton.

The inhabitants of rural Northumberland in 1931 come to life in these bald accounts of everyday life, illuminating people who were for the most part hardworking, fun-loving and overwhelmingly cheerful. A dreadful tragedy overtook one of their number that night and overshadowed their communities for years to come. It was a tragedy made all the more terrible by its lack of resolution, the insensitivity of the most senior police officer involved, and the false rumours that inevitably followed. It is my sincere hope that this book will help to finally set the record straight.

References

The following frequently used references will be found in abbreviated form in the notes below:
Evelyn Foster case files, Northumberland Police Archives – appears as NPA.
'Inquest Report into the Death of Evelyn Foster' COS/3/54/1,
Northumberland County Record Office – appears as COS/3/54/1.

CHAPTER 1
1. The time of bus services and all other details have been taken from the witness statements provided, with particular reference to those of John Joseph Foster, Margaret Foster, John Gordon Foster and Dorothy Foster found in NPA.
2. Isabel Rutherford was the woman who watched the luggage. Statement of Isabel Rutherford, 14 January 1931, NPA.

CHAPTER 2
1. In 2012, Les Pringle, born in 1928 and a lifelong resident of Otterburn, vividly described the social life which revolved around The Institute for my benefit. 'People got out and about more,' he said, 'because there was no TV.'
2. It has been suggested elsewhere that John Joseph Foster had lived in Otterburn all his life and that his business dated from much earlier, a misunderstanding based in part on a brief memoir he wrote himself, which was published in Otterburn Parish Magazine in 1957, a copy of which can be found in the Northumberland County Record Office. However, official records of the births of his elder children and the 1901 census return prove, without doubt, that in 1901 John Joseph Foster was living in nearby Rochester and working as a plate layer, probably at the local colliery.
3. The account of Evelyn Foster's day is taken from the statements of John Joseph Foster, 10 January 1931, Margaret Foster, undated and 10 January 1931, and John Gordon Foster, 10 January 1931, NPA. John Joseph Foster was always known as Joseph and his son, John Gordon Foster, was always known as Gordon.
4. The account of the journey north from Otterburn to Birdhopecraig Farm relies on the statements of John Gordon Foster, 10 January 1931, Mary Murray, 7, 9 and 11 January 1931, Robert Dunn Wilson, 7 and 9 January 1931, Hedley Anderson, 7 January 1931 and William Glendinning 7 and 11 January 1931, NPA.
5. Though not explicitly stated anywhere, it is evident that the calves had been delivered to Horsley earlier by one of the Fosters' cattle wagons.

Continues overleaf

REFERENCES

CHAPTER 3

1. The account of Evelyn's arrival home relies on the statements of Margaret Foster, undated and 10 January 1931, and John Joseph Foster, undated, 7 and 10 January 1931, NPA and COS/3/54/1.

2. Jonathan Goodman, The Burning of Evelyn Foster (Newton Abbott, David and Charles Ltd, 1977).

3. For many years, The Burning of Evelyn Foster has been regarded as the definitive account of the Evelyn Foster case, with its author implying that much of his information derived directly from conversations with witnesses to the events in question. However, when comparing contemporary witness statements with what was printed at the time in the newspapers, it is apparent that when writing his book Jonathan Goodman relied on newspaper archives to a significant degree, and even information which Goodman supposedly derived direct from the Foster family turns out to contain some very basic errors. The situation is exacerbated by the fact that the newspaper coverage of the Foster case was particularly prone to errors and fabrications, which has led to a great deal of misinformation about the case entering the public domain. It must also be said that relying on people's memories of events which took place more than 30 years ago is an inherently unreliable method of establishing the truth of what occurred.

This book cannot possibly seek to highlight or correct every single error in the Goodman account – however, the example of George Phillipson is a useful one in establishing the extent to which The Burning of Evelyn Foster can mislead and misinform in respect of even minor details. According to Jonathan Goodman, Evelyn Foster broke off her engagement to a young man named Ernest Primrose, who then went back to Scotland, having left her father's employment due to the considerable awkwardness which now existed between them, not least because his shifts had been changed so that he and Evelyn would never encounter one another. In fact, as statements made to the police by Primrose himself and others make clear, he and Evelyn were still engaged to be married when he took up the offer of a job in Craster in December 1927, and their engagement was not called off until early in 1928. The couple then remained on good terms and had seen one another as recently as August 1930, when Ernest had visited Evelyn while she was in hospital, being treated for an infected thumb. In January 1931, Ernest Primrose was still living in Craster and did not return to Scotland. Goodman also suggested that Evelyn's reluctance to call for George Phillipson was due to her not wishing to call for him at an apparently disreputable, all-male lodging, owned by her father and known as 'the bothie', but according to George Phillipson's witness statement, he had been lodging with a family, at a private home in the village, since his arrival in Otterburn in December 1930. In 1974, the police revisited the case as a result of a 'tip-off' from a somewhat confused, elderly man, who suggested that Ernest Primrose had been responsible for Evelyn's death. Dorothy Foster confirmed that Ernest had remained friendly with Evelyn until her death, had not returned to

REFERENCES

Scotland, etc., all of which suggests that wherever Jonathan Goodman got his information about this, it was not from the surviving members of the Foster family.

4. The torch was found next day under the driver's seat of the burned-out vehicle.

CHAPTER 4

1. The account of the wait for Evelyn and her eventual return home derives from statements of Margaret Elizabeth Foster, 13 Jan 1931, Margaret Foster, undated, 10 and 12 January 1931, John Joseph Foster, undated, Thomas Bowes Vasey, 13 January 1931, Thomas Rutherford, undated, and Cecil Johnstone, undated, NPA and COS/3/54/1.

2. The description of Evelyn's injuries is taken from the post-mortem report of Stuart McDonald, 21 January 1931, and statement of Duncan McEachran, undated, NPA.

3. Statement of Adeline Jennings, 27 January 1931, NPA.

CHAPTER 5

1. Jonathan Goodman, op. cit.

2. Jonathan Goodman's detailed account of the policemen's inaction on arrival in Otterburn bears little or no relationship to actual events described by independent witnesses who were there at the time.

3. Telephone message, 6 January 1931, NPA.

4. The description of events which follow in this chapter derives from statements provided by Margaret Foster, undated, 10 and 12 January 1931, Dorothy Foster, 13 January 1931, Margaret Elizabeth Foster, 13 January 1931, Adeline Jennings, 27 January 1931, Wilhelmina Lawson, 15 January 1931, Duncan McEachran, undated, James Graham Miller, 15 January 1931, report of Robert Shanks, 12 January 1931, and notes of Andrew Alan Ferguson, 7 January 1931, unless specifically stated otherwise, NPA.

5. Kelly's Directory of Northumberland confirms that Otterburn was served by Dr Kirk, who held a weekly surgery there, every Friday. Until his retirement in 1930, the village had also benefitted from a weekly surgery on Tuesdays, provided by Dr Miller. Dr Duncan McEachran qualified in Edinburgh in 1926 and would eventually return to general practice in that city, but in January 1931 he was still working as a junior doctor at a hospital in Newcastle-upon-Tyne.

6. It is possible that Gordon Foster's wife, Mary, also assisted in the initial stages of nursing Evelyn. This is suggested in the Goodman account, and the involvement of this family member would appear a logical step. Against this is the fact that not one witness statement or report mentions her being there, and the police never took a statement from her – a singular omission since they appear to have questioned every other person who came into contact with Evelyn, however briefly, from the moment she returned to Otterburn until her death.

7. It has been suggested that, shortly before she died, Evelyn Foster regained consciousness and uttered the words: 'I have been murdered.' This dramatic tale was reported in several 1931 newspapers, and was repeated by Jonathan Goodman, but it has no foundation in fact. Jonathan Goodman, op. cit., p49. All contemporaneous witness statements make it clear that Evelyn Foster died without regaining consciousness.

8. The principle of double effect made it permissible to administer a fatal dose of pain killing drugs to a patient who was terminally ill, on the basis that the primary intention was to relieve pain, rather than to bring about death.

CHAPTER 6

1. The account of the attack has been pieced together using the statements of Margaret Foster, undated, 10 and 12 January, Andrew Alan Ferguson, undated, Duncan McEachran, undated, Adeline Jennings, 27 January 1931, Dorothy Foster, 13 January 1931, James Graham Miller, 15 January 1931, Wilhelmina Lawson, 15 January 1931, Margaret Elizabeth Foster, 13 January 1931, notes of Andrew Alan Ferguson, 7 January 1931, and report of Robert Shanks, 12 January 1931, NPA and COS/3/54/1.

CHAPTER 7

1. Report of Edward Russell, undated, NPA.

2. Thomas Shell, report detailing progress of police enquiry, 2 March 1931, NPA.

3. Report detailing progress of the enquiry, undated, NPA.

4. Statement of Henry Coulsdon Proud, 8 January 1931, COS/3/54/1.

5. The men's actions at the scene have been pieced together with reference to reports of Henry Coulsdon Proud, 8 January 1931, Andrew Alan Ferguson, undated, Robert Shanks, 12 January 1931, and statements of Cecil Johnstone, undated, 14 and 20 January, and Thomas Bowes Vasey, 13 January 1931, NPA.

6. Cecil Johnstone was questioned about this on a number of occasions, but he always stuck to his original story regarding the car doors.

CHAPTER 8

1. Report and statement of Edward Russell, both undated, NPA and COS/3/54/1.

2. Report of William Turnbull, undated, NPA.

3. Telephone message received by Hexham Police Station from Jack Jerome, 9 January 1931, NPA.

4. Telephone messages received by Hexham Police Station from Edward Russell, 7 January 1931, NPA.

5. Ditto.

6. Telephone message to unidentified officer, 7 January 1931, NPA.

7. Statement of Alfred George Anderson, 7 January 1931, NPA.

8. Statement of Benjamin Prior, 7 January 1931, NPA.

9. Note by Fullarton James, 9 January 1931, NPA.

REFERENCES

10. Statements of Cuthbert Stappard, 7 January 1931, and Charles Henry Winter, 7 January 1931, NPA.

11. Report of Edward Russell, 6 July 1931, with attached newspaper clippings, NPA.

12. Many of the statements taken by the police include the time and place where the witness was interviewed, and identify the interviewing officer or officers present. It is therefore possible to a certain extent to work out which officers were engaged in the investigation, where and what they were doing.

13. Telephone messages from Philip Dodds, 7 January 1931, NPA.

14. For example when a major railway accident occurred at Charfield, Gloucestershire on 13 October 1928, the local general practitioner, Dr Horace Welshman Ward, performed all the medical examinations and gave evidence at the inquest – a situation which was far from unusual.

15. Telephone messages and memos dated 7 January 1931, NPA.

16. Ditto.

17. The full text of both messages can be found in NPA.

CHAPTER 9

1. Fullarton James's annotations appear on numerous copy statements including that of Mary Murray, NPA.

2. Telephone message, 7 January 1931, NPA.

3. Statement of Edward James Russell, undated, NPA.

4. Statement of William Jennings, undated, NPA.

5. Telephone message from Roxburghshire Constabulary, 8 January 1931, NPA.

CHAPTER 10

1. Evening Chronicle (Newcastle), 7 January 1931.

2. The statement of Annie Usher Carruthers, 8 January 1931, NPA, directly contradicts the material published in the Evening Chronicle (Newcastle), 8 January 1931, and provides one of many instances of journalistic misinformation.

3. Dozens of such reports can be found in NPA.

4. Statement of Alastair Maitland Bull, 8 January 1931, NPA.

5. Charles Chambers, who was driving south from Jedburgh, stopped to see if he could offer them assistance about three miles south of Otterburn. They told him that they had tramped from Yorkshire to Oban in July and were now making the return journey. Their baby was five weeks old. It was then about 5 p.m. and the temperatures were falling. Chambers and his companions, Thomas Nesbit and Sidney Steckles, gave the couple eight shillings. By 7 p.m. that night the couple had reached Kirkwhelpington, where they seem to have found somewhere to stop for the night. Statements of Charles Chambers, 7 January 1931, and Wilfred Burns Taylor, 12 January 1931, NPA.

6. Statements of Thomas Connor, 8 January 1931, and John Reid, 8 January 1931, NPA.

REFERENCES

7. Statement of Walter Smith Beattie, 8 January 1931, NPA.

8. Report from Scotland Yard, 8 January 1931, and statement of Thirumalalai Iyengar, 8 January 1931, NPA.

9. F.W. Memory had a reputation as one of the top investigative reporters of his day. Assertive and aggressive in pursuit of a story, he was not above concocting supposed exclusive interviews, perfectly capable of active distortion, and proved to be a complete pest in respect of several murder enquiries. See Diane Janes, The Case of the Poison Partridge (Stroud, The History Press, 2013) pp100–1.

10. References to individual publications become superfluous at this point, as just about every national and regional daily paper included this kind of coverage of the Foster case.

11. It was a difficult period for police–press relations. On 7 January 1931, the Yorkshire Post sounded a typical note when it carried an article which complained that the numbers of unsolved murders were increasing. The Post stated that whereas there had been just one unresolved case in 1928, this had jumped to five in 1929 and eight in 1930. During the investigation into Lieutenant Hubert Chevis's death in summer 1931, it would be the turn of the Surrey Constabulary to be on the end of a barrage of criticism over their decision not to call in Scotland Yard. See Diane Janes, The Case of the Poison Partridge, op. cit..

12. Evening World, 5 January 1931.

CHAPTER 11

1. The Scotsman, 10 January 1931.

2. Report of Francis Douglas, 10 January 1931, NPA.

3. Statement of Bessie McDonnell, 10 January 1931, NPA.

4. Ditto.

5. Memo from Thomas Shell to Fullarton James, 9 January 1931, NPA.

6. Text is in NPA and was also reproduced in some newspapers.

7. Letter from Fullarton James, 9 January 1931, NPA.

8. Dozens of memos from Fullarton James in this tenor are preserved in the case files. The specific memo cited is dated 9 January 1931 and Shell's response is dated 11 January 1931, NPA.

9. Statements of Ernest Primrose, 7 January 1931, Ena Elizabeth Scott, 9 January 1931, and Jane Spears, 10 January 1931, NPA.

10. Memo from Fullarton James, 18 January 1931, NPA.

11. Memo from Fullarton James to Thomas Shell, 10 January 1931, NPA.

12. Memo from Fullarton James, 11 January 1931, NPA.

13. Report of Edward Russell, 9 January 1931, NPA.

14. In Russell's report to Shell dated 11 January, he mentions the chief constable's instructions regarding the statements and explains that he has sent Sergeant Archie Robson to fulfil this task. The irony of Robson's being one of the two extra officers who had been sent to assist with the investigation in response to Russell's plea for more manpower was probably not lost on either man, NPA.

REFERENCES

15. Sunday Sun, 11 January 1931.

16. The memo which specifically mentions the oil heater is from Fullarton James to Thomas Shell, 17 January 1931, NPA.

17. Memo from Fullarton James, 10 January 1931, NPA.

18. Dozens of statements, letters and telephone messages were received during 7–10 January 1931 and are preserved in NPA.

19. Sunday Sun, 11 January 1931.

CHAPTER 12

1. Evening Chronicle, 9 January 1931, is among those reporting the raison d'être for holding the funeral on a Sunday. The Newcastle Journal, 12 January 1931 provides a particularly good description of the funeral. The arrangements for the funeral tend to give lie to the idea that there was a significant level of discord between the Foster family and their employees at this time.

2. Though not every statement contained a note of the officer to whom it was made, there is sufficient information to demonstrate which officers were regularly working on the case and when.

3. Note from Fullarton James, 11 January 1931, NPA.

4. Ditto.

5. Report of Edward Russell, 12 January 1931, NPA.

6. The 10 January edition of the Yorkshire Post was typical, including in a single article, sightings of 'a man' seen by road-workers on Watling Street and a lorry driver near the Ottercops, a blacksmith who had seen a man with an oddly stained overcoat, the Elsdon schoolmistress, who had been 'insulted by a man' and Mr Reed of Otterburn, who had seen a man 'within ten miles of the village'. Their comment that 'the area is full of rumours', appears to have been something of an understatement.

7. Yorkshire Post and Leeds Intelligencer, 10 January 1931.

8. Evening World, 8 January 1931.

9. For a discussion on the subject of hitchhiking in 1931, the dangers and the accepted norms, see The Scotsman, 10 January 1931.

10. Statements of Albert Beach, 9 January 1931, and John Oliver, 9 January 1931, NPA.

11. Statement of Robert Gibson Towns, 10 January 1931, NPA.

12. Statement of William Frederick Blackham, 12 January 1931, NPA.

13. Statements of Edith Maughan, 12 January 1931, and George Maughan, 11 January 1931, NPA.

14. Statement of Robert Luke, 12 January 1931. Northumberland Police Archives.

15. Statement of John Thompson, 14 January 1931, NPA.

16. Initially the only officers available to assist Russell in taking statements were Sergeant F.J. Armstrong, and three local village constables, Andrew Ferguson, Francis Sinton and William Turnbull. Sergeant Shanks from Bellingham helped out in the first 24 hours, but then returned to normal duties. PC John Eckford appears to have been loaned to the investigation by

REFERENCES

Newcastle City Police from 8 January onwards. On 11 January, their numbers were supplemented by Sergeants William Burns and Archie Robson, but this remained a pitifully small team to conduct an enquiry which called for interviews with dozens of witnesses, scattered over a wide geographical area. From statements which bear the date, time and location of interviews, it is possible to determine that the men were working in excess of 12 hour days, frequently spending hours on the road, travelling to remote farms and hamlets by pedal or motor cycle, often in atrocious weather conditions. On 12 January, Sergeant Burns interviewed at least ten witnesses, spread over a wide area of north Northumberland. On the same day, PC Eckford commenced taking statements mid-morning and concluded his interview with William Kirsopp-Reed at Old Town at 10.45 p.m. From 14 January onwards, the village constables appear to have played less of a part in the enquiry, with Armstrong, Eckford, Burns and Robson taking virtually all the witness statements. As well as working extremely long hours, the men had few days off. Dated statements prove that William Burns and John Eckford both worked at least seven days at a stretch, which suggests that their colleagues probably did too.

17. Statements of William Kirsopp-Reed, 12 and 13 January 1931, NPA.
18. Statement of Margaret Kirsopp-Reed, 15 January 1931, NPA.
19. Statements of Robert Edwin Harrison, 10 and 13 January 1931, NPA.
20. Statement of John Scott, 13 January 1931, NPA.
21. Statement of Gladys Tatham, 13 January 1931, NPA.
22. Statement of John Robson, undated, NPA.
23. Statement of Oswald Young, 13 January 1931, NPA.
24. Statement of Sydney Henderson, undated, NPA.

CHAPTER 13
1. Report of Superintendent Taylor, 13 January 1931, NPA.
2. Telegrams timed at 8.18 and 10.35, 13 January 1931, NPA.
3. The conference is reported in the majority of newspapers which were covering the story.
4. Daily Express, 14 January 1931, not only reported this, but also tried to claim credit as the originators of the theory.
5. Daily Mail, 13 January 1931.
6. Statements of James Graham Miller, 15 January 1931, Wilhelmina Lawson, 15 January 1931, and Adeline Jennings, 27 January 1931, NPA.
7. PC Eckford initially heard about the attack on 18 January and reported it to Superintendent Shell. By 20 January, Shell was able to report to the chief constable that the girl had been traced and interviewed and the soldier eliminated. Statement of John Gordon Foster, 16 January 1931, and unattributed reports dated 18 and 20 January 1931, NPA. The men who ran to the girl's rescue were Oswald Young and Edward Hay.
8. Unattributed report, 13 January 1931, NPA.
9. The novel was The W Plan by Graham Seton, which had been made into a film in 1930. The long-suffering PC Eckford confirmed that Otterburn

REFERENCES

Public Library did not hold a copy. The book had also been suggested as the inspiration for the Rouse 'burning car' murder in 1930.

10. This communication was received on 22 January and is typical of many which survive, NPA.

11. Statements of Jack Mackenzie, 16 January 1931, Helen Wood, 16 January 1931, and Thomas Hughes, 16 January 1931, NPA.

12. Report from Roxburghshire Constabulary, 22 January 1931, NPA.

13. While in Jedburgh, Armstrong and Eckford took the opportunity of visiting other hotels and businesses with largely negative results, though they did find one shopkeeper who had been approached by a man and woman driving south, who wished to purchase a bottle of whisky, but had no obvious connection with the enquiry.

14. Statement of John Kennedy, 17 January 1931, NPA. There is some uncertainty about the nature of the gathering at the chapel, with some witnesses who attended referring to it as a service and others as choir practice. Doubt also exists regarding the precise details of the registration number as reported by Kennedy. Some copies of Kennedy's statement give the order of the numbers in the registration mark, but others are annotated to the effect that he was uncertain of the order.

15. Note from Fullarton James, undated, NPA.

16. Statement of Dennis Herdman, undated, NPA.

17. There are reports of house-to-house enquiries in Hexham, Prudhoe, Haltwhistle, Knowesgate, Harnham, Kirkwhelpington, Ridsdale, West Woodburn and the Rochester, Bellingham and Bavington areas and along Watling Street (with negative results), 18 and 19 January 1931, NPA.

18. Newcastle Journal, 16 January 1931.

19. Daily Express, 14 January 1931.

20. Daily Mail, 14 January 1931.

21. Letter from John Eckford. The letter is undated, but from the contents it can be reasonably construed to date from between 15–20 January 1931, NPA.

CHAPTER 14

1. Memoranda from Fullarton James, 14, 15, 19 January 1931 and undated, NPA.

2. Fullarton James's original letter to Wright has not survived, but the contents can be conjectured from the reply, letter of A.J. Wright, 17 January 1931, NPA.

3. Letter and document from Fullarton James, 28 January 1931, NPA.

4. Letter from Philip M. Dodds, 29 January 1931, NPA.

5. Letter from Fullarton James, 30 January 1931, NPA.

6. Evening Chronicle, 21 and 22 January 1931.

7. Statement of Edward James Russell, undated, NPA and COS/3/54/1.

8. Ditto. 9. Ditto.

10. Report of D.T. Dunn, 15 January 1931, COS/3/54/1.

11. Report of Stuart McDonald, countersigned by Duncan McEachran and Stuart McDonald Jnr., 21 January 1931, NPA.

REFERENCES

12. For a fuller discussion on these practices, readers are recommended to Diane Janes, Poisonous Lies: The Croydon Arsenic Mystery (Stroud, The History Press, 2010), pp145–52. Sir Bernard Spilsbury, revered in his heyday as a 'modern Sherlock Holmes', was a particularly dangerous witness, responsible for several miscarriages of justice.

13. Report of D.T. Dunn, 15 January 1931, COS/3/54/1.

14. Report of Stuart McDonald, 21 January 1931, COS/3/54/1.

15. Report of Stuart McDonald, 26 January 1931, COS/3/54/1.

CHAPTER 15

1. Some of these letters survive in the police files, together with multiple references to other deeply unpleasant letters received by the Foster family during this period.

2. Unless otherwise stated, the account of proceedings in this chapter is drawn from the statements and notes found in COS/3/54/1, supplemented by newspaper accounts of the proceedings, specifically, but not exclusively The Times, 3 and 4 February 1931.

3. The suggestion that women were less rational and more inclined toward criminality at particular times in their menstrual cycles had first been suggested during the Victorian age. By 1931, a number of studies had been undertaken into the question, but the parameters and methodology used often rendered the results suspect. Many researchers failed to allow for the fact that at any given time, between 25 and 50 per cent of women of reproductive age can be categorised as either premenstrual or menstruating, which gives an inbuilt bias to the results. Readers looking for further enlightenment of the subject are recommended to Julie Horney, 'Menstrual Cycles and Criminal Responsibility', Law and Human Behaviour, Vol. 2, No. 1, 1978.

4. Women's knowledge, or lack of it, regarding sexual intercourse is necessarily a difficult subject to research, but biographies and memoirs of Evelyn's contemporaries mostly underline that ignorance was the norm. Angela du Maurier, born two years later than Evelyn Foster, provides an excellent example, recalling how, at the age of 18, she was afraid that a kiss at a house party might have made her pregnant. This is all the more surprising because, when Angela was 12 years old, a school friend had undertaken to inform her with a reasonable level of accuracy about where babies came from, but Angela had dismissed this as such an unlikely and horrible suggestion as to be completely untrue. When Angela's mother learned that she had been discussing this forbidden topic with a friend, she became well-nigh hysterical, declaring that she could never trust Angela again, but offering no elucidation on the question of human reproduction. Jane Dunn, Daphne du Maurier and Her Sisters (London, William Collins, 2013) p10 and p73.

5. The expression 'interfered with' was still being used as recently as the 1970s. My own conversations with women born at various times during the first 50 years of the twentieth century suggest that it has never been universally understood to mean rape, and that when heard by someone who is not

knowledgeable about sexual matters, is as likely to imply 'something nasty, like putting a hand up your knickers', as it is to mean full scale sexual assault.
6. The Metropolitan Police guidelines on sexual assault in 2015 includes in its list defining what constitutes sexual assault: 'someone being touched in a sexual way that makes him or her feel uncomfortable or frightened (this could be through their clothes – like bottom pinching)'. www.safe.met.police.uk. Elsewhere, the same force's website stated: 'a person commits sexual assault if they intentionally touch another person, the touching is sexual and the person does not consent.'

CHAPTER 16
1. The account of proceedings given in this chapter is drawn from the witness statements in COS/3/54/1 unless otherwise stated. As far as possible, I have not relied on newspaper accounts covering the question and answer sessions, because the same exchanges vary widely between different reports and have helped to fuel confusion ever since. Where spoken words are quoted, they have come from The Times, whose coverage seems to have agreed with both the contents of the witness statements and makes sense when compared to other contemporary accounts.
2. The block policy covered vehicles much larger than the Hudson and the sum assured represented a maximum, rather than a minimum settlement. There was nothing unusual or irregular in the terms of the policy or the insurance arrangements.
3. Memo to Philip Dodds from Thomas Shell, 1 February 1931, NPA.
4. It is always difficult to translate the value of historic money into current day terms, but Evelyn's savings represented a large sum, sufficient for her to have purchased a small house outright, if she had wished to do so. Her estate eventually came to considerably more than the figure quoted at the inquest – £1,442.
5. Statements of Albert Beach, 9 and 10 January 1931, and John Oliver, 9 and 10 January, 1931, NPA.

CHAPTER 17
1. Details of the inquest derive from COS/3/54/1 and The Times, 6 February 1931, unless otherwise stated.
2. Various witness statements within the police files made by staff and guests strongly suggest that there would have been cars parked outside the inn throughout the early evening.
3. Empire News, 8 February 1931.
4. Daily Express, 6 February 1931, quotes the chief constable, but other papers reported that he left the inquest, refusing to make a comment. Fullarton James himself would later deny that he had made the statement quoted in the Daily Express.
5. News Chronicle, 7 February 1931.
6. Empire News, 8 February 1931.

REFERENCES

7. Ditto.
8. Ditto.

CHAPTER 18

1. Jonathan Goodman, The Burning of Evelyn Foster, op. cit.
2. Statement of Annie Carruthers, 8 January 1931, and report of John Eckford, 9 January 1931, NPA.
3. Jonathan Goodman, The Burning of Evelyn Foster, op. cit., pp138–9.
4. Statements of Mary Ferry, 7 and 8 January 1931, NPA.
5. Statements of George Sinclair, 11 January 1931, and John Murray, 22 January 1931, NPA.
6. Statements were taken from Gladys Tatham regarding the numbers of overnight guests, most of whom were interviewed in their own right, as were those who had visited the inn for a drink, including the personalities listed here.
7. The evidence of witnesses in the murder of Julia Wallace which also took place in 1931 provides a useful illustration, with at least one witness who claimed to be 'confident' about the time placing a meeting between himself and the suspect at an hour which cannot possibly have been correct.
8. Statements John Robson, undated, and Oswald Young, 13 January 1931, NPA.
9. Letter from Claude Morrison-Bell, undated, NPA.

CHAPTER 19

1. This chapter is based on the statements of George Maughan, undated and 11 January 1931, Edith Maughan, 12 January 1931, John Thompson, undated and 14 January 1931, William Frederick Blackham, 12 January 1931, Robert Luke, 12 January 1931, Thomas Vasey, 13 January 1931, and Eleanor Wilson, 22 January 1931, NPA.
2. The men who confirmed Luke's comment regarding hearing the clock strike seven included Gordon Foster.
3. Jonathan Goodman further speculated that the person Thompson observed wearing leggings was Dorothy Foster, who he claims had been serving petrol to customers. Suffice it to say that Dorothy was not serving petrol at any point during the evening, and that Goodman's theories on this point are entirely disproved by the original witness statements, except inasmuch that Thompson had indeed mistaken a woman in leggings for a young man – but the woman in question was Edith Maughan, not Dorothy Foster (in fairness to Thompson, the Maughans were walking quickly along the opposite side of an unlit road). Jonathan Goodman, The Burning of Evelyn Foster, op. cit., pp136–7, and statement of Dorothy Foster, 13 January 1931, NPA..

CHAPTER 20

1. The movements of witnesses given in this chapter derive from the statements of Leslie McClure, undated, Gladys Tatham, 13 January 1931, John Murray, 20 January 1931, John Geddes, 20 January 1931, William Thompson, 12

REFERENCES

January 1931, Annie Brown, 20 January 1931, Edric Hedley, 20 January 1931, Catherine O'Brien, 19 January 1931, George McDougal, 19 January 1931, George Lancelot Phillipson, undated, John Jackson, 23 January 1931, John Ormison, 13 January 1931, Thomas William Athey Gledson, 13 January 1931, Robert Drummond, 13 January 1931, Robert Hall, 13 January 1931, John Donaldson, 13 January 1931, and telephone message received by Andrew Alan Ferguson, 6 January 1931, NPA.

CHAPTER 21
1. Fullarton James made numerous lists of vehicles, not one of which is a comprehensive list of every vehicle reported.
2. Telephone call from Lancelot Robson, 8 January 1931, NPA.
3. Statements Alistair Maitland Hamilton Bull, undated, William Frederick Blackham, 12 January 1931, and John Geddes, 20 January 1931, NPA.
4. Statements of Albert Beach, 9 and 10 January 1931, and John Oliver, 9 January 1931, NPA.
5. Statements of Robert Dunn Wilson, 9 January 1931, Mary Murray, 9 January 1931, and William Glendinning, 11 January 1931, NPA.
6. Statements Mary Murray, 9 January 1931, George Ashford, 11 January 1931, and Wilfred Ralph Leighton, 11 January 1931.

CHAPTER 22
1. Telephone message from Lancelot Robson, 8 January 1931, NPA.
2. Statements of John Anderson, 16 January 1931 and William Pringle, 16 January 1931, NPA.
3. Statement of Alastair Hamilton Maitland Bull, undated, NPA.
4. Statements of James Cairns, 14 January 1931, William Frederick Blackham, 12 January 1931, and John Geddes, 20 January 1931, NPA.
5. Statements of Robert Gibson Towns, undated, and Thirumalalai Iyengar, 10 and 13 January 1931, NPA.
6. Statements of Edward Stappard, 12 January 1931, Walter Hugh Tully, 12 January 1931, and Thomas Taylor, 18 January 1931, NPA. The fourth member of the party, William Birkett, did not make an official statement.
7. Jonathan Goodman, The Burning of Evelyn Foster, op. cit., pp131–2.
8. Statements of Alan Matthew Bell, 12 January 1931, and Matthew Wallace, 12 January 1931, NPA.
9. Statement of William Johnstone, undated, NPA.
10. Statements of Albert Beach, 9 and 10 January 1931, and John Oliver, 9 January 1931, NPA.

CHAPTER 23
1. Statements of William Kirsopp-Reed, 12 and 13 January 1931, and Margaret Kirsopp-Reed, 15 January 1931, NPA.
2. Dr Joseph Goodall (1876–1936) lived at Mirlaw House, where he had been in general practice since 1900, Morpeth Herald, 28 February 1936.

REFERENCES

3. Statements of Annie Brown, 20 January 1931, and William Thompson, 12 January 1931, NPA.

4. Statement of Walter Brydon, 13 January 1931, NPA.

5. Statement of John Telfer, 20 January 1931, NPA.

6. Statements of John Robson, undated, and Oswald Young, 13 January 1931, NPA.

7. Fullarton James was not personally acquainted with William Kirsopp-Reed, as a memo enquiring about him on 18 January 1931 makes clear. NPA.

8. Statements of William Kirsopp-Reed, 12 and 13 January 1931, and Margaret Kirsopp-Reed, 15 January 1931, NPA.

9. Statements of Cecil Johnstone, undated, 14 and 20 January 1931, and Thomas Rutherford, 12 January 1931, NPA.

10. Statement of Albert Ernest Robson, 13 January 1931, NPA.

11. Annotated Statement of William Kirsopp-Reed,13 January, NPA.

12. Statements Robert Edwin Harrison, 10 and 13 January 1931, NPA.

13. Statement of Eva Morrison, 14 January 1931, NPA.

14. Undated memos of Fullarton James and statements of Alfred Thompson, 8 and 16 January 1931, NPA.

15. Statement of Bessie McDonnell, 10 January 1931, NPA.

16. Statement of Alice Ord, 13 January 1931, NPA.

17. Statements of John Joseph Foster, 10 January 1931 and William Jennings, undated, NPA.

18. Statement of John Charlton Stott, 12 January 1931, NPA.

19. Statement of Sydney Henderson, undated, NPA.

20. Statements of John Robert Coulsdon, 7 January 1931, John Telfer, 20 January 1931, Sidney Renwick, 15 January 1931, Annie Armstrong, undated, and Robert Hall, 13 January 1931, NPA. The sixth witness, Hilda Luke, did not make a separate statement.

21. Statement of Walter Smith Beattie, 8 January 1931, NPA.

22. Statement of Robert Beattie, 17 January 1931, NPA.

23. Statements of Robert Edwin Harrison, undated, and Cecil Johnstone, undated, NPA.

CHAPTER 24

1. In June 2012, Terence Armer was convicted of the murder of Stacey Mackie. Details of the case are derived from contemporary newspaper reports and the TV programme Countdown to Murder, first shown on Channel Five, August 2014.

2. In the early hours of 6 November 1930, Alfred Arthur Rouse set fire to his car, incinerating both the vehicle and the body of an unknown man within it. Rouse was attempting to fake his own death and thereby defraud an insurance company, but he was spotted leaving the scene, and at the time of the fire at Wolf's Nick was still awaiting trial. He was found guilty and executed in 1931. The man in the car has never been identified.

3. Statements of Robert William Welton, 8 January 1931, Annie Jackson,

undated, Sarah Thornton Reid, undated, and John Baxter, 8 January 1931, NPA.

4. Statement of George Jackson, 7 January 1931, NPA.

5. Telephone message from Hexham Police Station to the chief constable, 7 January 1931, NPA.

CHAPTER 25

1. Letter from Fullarton James, 11 February 1931, NPA.

2. Memo from Fullarton James, 8 February 1931, NPA.

3. Joseph Foster's remarks to this effect were widely reproduced in the newspapers.

4. Memos indicating that Fullarton James was assembling notes of precisely who had done what and when start to appear in the files from 11 February 1931. NPA.

5. Memo from Fullarton James, 12 February 1931, NPA.

6. Memo from Fullarton James, 16 February 1931, NPA.

7. Colonel Douglas Clifton Brown (1879–1958) served as MP for the Hexham constituency from 1918–23 and 1924–51, was one-time speaker of the House of Commons and a member of the Privy Council from 1941. He was eventually elevated to the peerage, taking the title, Viscount Ruffside of Hexham.

8. Evening World, 11 February 1931.

9. The text of the letter appeared in almost every major daily newspaper.

10. Police forces were organised on a regional basis and the chief constable was answerable to the local watch committee. For some reason the Home Secretary used the term standing committee; other reports and records in this particular case used both terms interchangeably.

11. Letter from Fullarton James, 5 March 1931, NPA.

12. Letter from Fullarton James, 8 March 1931, NPA.

13. Letter from the Home Office, 8 March 1931, NPA.

14. Undated copy letter from Fullarton James. A date in March 1931 can be inferred. NPA.

15. Letter from Fullarton James, 8 March 1931, NPA.

16. Letter from the Home Office, 30 March 1931, NPA.

17. The findings of the standing committee were forwarded by letter to Joseph Foster, who passed them on to the press. They were reproduced in numerous daily newspapers.

CHAPTER 26

1. Evening Chronicle, 9 February 1931.

2. Evening Chronicle, 12 February 1931.

3. Evening Chronicle, 12 and 19 February 1931.

4. Jonathan Goodman, The Burning of Evelyn Foster, op. cit., pp131–5.

5. The information regarding Charlotte Clark and Troughend which appears in this chapter is derived from census returns for England and Wales, monumental inscriptions at Elsdon parish church, a family history compiled

by John Myles (great-nephew of Charlotte Clark) and The Northumbrian Magazine, Issue 126, 2012.

6. Information regarding the dispute between the Clarks and the Fosters derives from report of Thomas Shell, 17 March 1931. Among working-class families in the north of England, it was customary for neighbours to call on a bereaved family. This was less of an expectation among the middle classes, who wrote, attended the funeral or sent a wreath. It may be that Mrs Clark had caused offence by inadvertent omission, rather than deliberately staying away.

7. The account of the Charlotte Clark affair given here relies on report of Thomas Shell, 17 March 1931, statement of Alfred Norman Johnstone, 16 March 1931, and annotated letters from Margaret Foster, dated 2, 9 and 10 March 1931, NPA.

8. When Jonathan Goodman was researching the case in the early 1970s, Mrs Dorothy Groves, daughter of schoolmaster William Blackham, told him that her father and others had been convinced of Mrs Clark's involvement. Jonathan Goodman, The Burning of Evelyn Foster, op. cit., p134.

9. Report of Thomas Shell, 17 March 1931, NPA.

10. Typical of these were the accusations levied against a Mr Taylor of Gosforth, who was having an affair with a relative of the informant, and against a married female car owner, with an allegedly interesting sexual history, who had lived in Hexham, but was found on investigation to have moved to South Africa in 1930.

11. Report of Thomas Shell, 17 March 1931, NPA.

12. Ditto.

13. Report of John Eckford, 13 January 1932, NPA.

CHAPTER 27

1. Message from Cumberland and Westmorland Police, 10 January 1931, and memo from Newcastle Police, undated, NPA.

2. Alfred Rouse had been attempting to fake his own death by staging 'an accident' and had presumably lured someone into his car, then killed him, before setting fire to the vehicle.

3. Details of the Morton murder in this chapter are derived from ASSI 45/93/14, HO 144/19499, The National Archives and Yorkshire Post, September 1933 – January 1934.

4. Jonathan Goodman, The Burning of Evelyn Foster, op. cit., p144.

5. A number of papers reported that Dorothy Morton was hissed and booed as she left court on the third and fourth days of the trial, including Empire News, 17 December 1933.

6. Typical photographs appear in Yorkshire Evening Post, 9 September 1933 and 17 October 1933, and Daily Express, 14 December 1933.

7. At his appeal, Brown wore the same brown suit and canary yellow pullover that he had worn at his trial, Daily Express, 16 January 1934.

REFERENCES

CHAPTER 28

1. Report from Kirkcudbright Constabulary, 28 January 1932, NPA.

2. Report from Supt Cunningham, 1 and 6 February 1932, NPA.

3. Report from Supt Cunningham, 6 February 1932, NPA.

4. Letter from Kirkcudbright Constabulary, 13 April 1932, NPA.

5. Though Northumberland police made no attempt to establish whether Kirkpatrick was a physical fit for the description provided by Evelyn Foster, prison records establish that he was 5ft 8in tall, HH21/49/14, National Archives of Scotland.

6. Report from Dumfriesshire Constabulary, 25 April 1932, NPA.

7. Relationships and various addresses of the Kirkpatrick family have been established with reference to census returns for Scotland and Birth, Marriage and Death registrations.

8. Details of the 1919 offence can be found in AD15/19/127, National Archives of Scotland. The file giving details of the 1932 offence remain closed.

CHAPTER 29

1. Among the cars traced who had travelled past Elishaw that day, more than half were going as far as Newcastle.

AFTERWORD

1. When presiding over inquests into the deaths of members of the Sidney family in 1929, Dr Henry Jackson, coroner for Croydon, refused to bow to police pressure and, in so doing, may have saved an innocent person from the gallows. See Diane Janes, Poisonous Lies: The Croydon Arsenic Mystery, op. cit.

Index

INDEX

INDEX

INDEX

INDEX

Acknowledgements

This book would not have been possible without the generous co-operation afforded to the author by Northumberland Police, and in particular by Hayley Morrison, their disclosure manager, who by coincidence grew up in Otterburn. Resources found in Northumberland County Archives, The National Archives, The National Archives of Scotland and the British Library have proved invaluable, as have those made available by Dumfries and Galloway Libraries and Devon Libraries.

Thanks are due to Jo Sollis, Paula Scott, Mel Sambells and Julie Adams at Mirror Books, Charlotte Cole, Val Wilson, Cathy Gibb, Joe and Jane Walton, Les Pringle, Peter Hyland, Jane Conway-Gordon and the various friends and family who have listened to endless reconstructions of an 80-year-old car journey. The 'A' Team – Erica and Peter Woolley and my husband Bill – deserve, as ever, the biggest thank you of all.

Also by Mirror Books
Published April 2017

The Boy in 7 Billion
Callie Blackwell and Karen Hockney

If you had a chance to save your dying son… wouldn't you take it?

Deryn Blackwell is a walking, talking miracle. At the age of 10, he was diagnosed with Leukaemia. Then 18 months later he developed another rare form of cancer called Langerhan's cell sarcoma. Only five other people in the world have it. He is the youngest of them all and the only person in the world known to be fighting it alongside another cancer, making him one in seven billion.
Told there was no hope of survival, after four years of intensive treatment, exhausted by the fight and with just days to live, Deryn planned his own funeral.

But on the point of death – his condition suddenly and dramatically changed. His medical team had deemed this an impossibility, his recovery was nothing short of a miracle. Inexplicable. However, Deryn's desperate mother, Callie, was hiding a secret…

Callie has finally found the strength and courage to reveal the truth about Deryn's battle. The result is a book that everyone should read.
It truly is a matter of life and death.

Also by Mirror Books

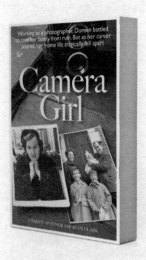

Camera Girl
Doreen Spooner with Alan Clark

The true story of a woman coping with a tragic end to the love of her life, alongside a daily fight to establish herself and support her children.

A moving and inspiring memoir of Doreen Spooner –
a woman ahead of her time. Struggling to hold her head high through the disintegration of the family she loves through alcoholism, she began a career as Fleet Street's first female photographer.

While the passionate affair and family life she'd always dreamed of fell apart, Doreen walked into the frantic world of a national newspaper. Determined to save her family from crippling debt, her work captured the Swinging Sixties through political scandals, glamorous stars and cultural icons, while her homelife spiralled further out of control.

The two sides of this book take you through a touching and emotional love story, coupled with a hugely enjoyable portrait of post-war Britain.

Also by Mirror Books

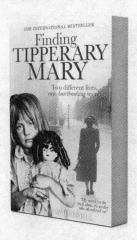

Finding Tipperary Mary
Phyllis Whitsell

The astonishing real story of a daughter's search for her own past
and the desperate mother who gave her up for adoption.

Phyllis Whitsell began looking for her birth mother as a young woman and
although it was many years before she finally met her, their lives had crossed on
the journey without their knowledge.
When they both eventually sat together in the same room,
the circumstances were extraordinary, moving and
ultimately life-changing.

This is a daughter's personal account of the remarkable
relationship that grew from abandonment into love,
understanding and selfless care.

Also by Mirror Books

1963 - A Slice of Bread and Jam
Tommy Rhattigan

Tommy lives at the heart of a large Irish family in derelict Hulme in Manchester, ruled by an abusive, alcoholic father and a negligent mother. Alongside his siblings he begs (or steals) a few pennies to bring home to avoid a beating, while looking for a little adventure of his own along the way.

His foul-mouthed and chaotic family may be deeply flawed, but amongst the violence, grinding poverty and distinct lack of hygiene and morality lies a strong sense of loyalty and, above all, survival.

During this single year – before his family implodes and his world changes for ever – Tommy almost falls foul of the welfare officers, nuns, police – and Myra Hindley and Ian Brady.

An adventurous, fun, dark and moving true story of the only life young Tommy knew.